Praise for *Haunted by Slavery*

"What a refreshing book! Gwendolyn Midlo Hall's spunky, riveting chronicle of a life of political activism and groundbreaking historical scholarship reminds us of the left's crucial role in the Black struggle against white supremacy and of her own revolutionary use of digital technology in the remaking of American history." —NELL IRVIN PAINTER, author of *The History of White People* and *Southern History Across the Color Line*

"Gwen Midlo Hall is a people's historian in the best sense of that term. Her scholarship, informed by a deep commitment to the struggle for freedom, maps the lives and struggles of oppressed and enslaved people over time and place. In her newest work, she traces her own freedom journey and offers insight into the making of a white radical antiracist historian, whose life and work as a scholar, left-wing organizer, daughter, wife, and mother reveal the breadth of her humanity and remarkable accomplishments." —BARBARA RANSBY, author of *Ella Baker and the Black Freedom Movement*

"In *Haunted by Slavery*, renowned scholar and activist Gwendolyn Midlo Hall tells her remarkable life story with the same passion, conviction, depth, and beauty that have guided her work for decades. Drawing on her personal experiences and extensive knowledge of history and politics, Midlo Hall's memoir lays bare the intricacies of race, gender, class, and power." —KEISHA N. BLAIN, author of *Set the World on Fire: Black Nationalist Women and the Global Struggle for Freedom*

"*Haunted by Slavery* gives us a rare, up-close look at the Black freedom struggle across the twentieth century and the massive repression of Black and white radicals encountered by a white freedom fighter-scholar who throughout her life refused to be a 'good girl.'" —JEANNE THEOHARIS, distinguished professor of political science, Brooklyn College, author of *A More Beautiful and Terrible History*

"*Haunted by Slavery* is a magnificent account of the revolutionary life of a southern Jewish woman who fought racial inequalities during one of the most dreadful times in US history. When women's fate was to be confined to the domestic space, Gwen became a militant who challenged gender norms, escaped anti-Communist persecution, married a prominent African American activist, and raised her children across several states and countries. This memoir is an inspiring testament written by one of the most esteemed historians of slavery in the United States, who dedicated her entire life to fighting for social justice, a striving that persists today." —ANA LUCIA ARAUJO, professor of history, Howard University

D0174209

"In the overwhelmingly male-dominated, historically conservative field of southern history, Gwendolyn Midlo Hall has been a trailblazer. From an inspiration to countless women historians as well as scholar-activists, Midlo Hall's *Haunted by Slavery* is an intensely intimate—and at times disarmingly honest—memoir. It offers a glimpse into the life of a white Jewish woman in the Deep South, complicating our prejudices about both the region and its people. *Haunted by Slavery* is a must-read for anyone interested in questions of race, gender, class, and power in America. Midlo Hall is a national treasure."—KERI LEIGH MERRITT, author of *Masterless Men*

"Like Dr. Gwendolyn Midlo Hall, this book is bold and engaging. As this white woman from the South recounts her life, we learn how she shaped history as an unrelenting civil rights activist and rewrote history as a pathbreaking scholar of slavery in the Americas. All along, Dr. Midlo Hall urges us to fight for justice, seek education, and teach others. There can be no doubt that the world would be a better place if we followed her lead."—WALTER HAWTHORNE, professor of African history, Michigan State University

"Dr. Hall's memoir offers a thorough and necessary exploration of the misinformation, violence, and fear that create the circumstances for white southerners—white southern women and girls, in particular—to participate in segregation and enclosure even when it is against their own interests. Luckily, Hall also provides a recipe for fighting that: grit, truth, and the defiance to face down the family you are born into in order to form a more inclusive family of your own creation. Hall's book charts a path for understanding southern white identity, but also a reminder that the most toxic parts of that world can be excised and new lines of relation with Black, immigrant, poor, and other dispossessed people can by drawn—if you've the courage to try!"—JESSICA MARIE JOHNSON, author of *Wicked Flesh*

"*Haunted By Slavery* is a beautifully written memoir. Gwendolyn Midlo Hall offers an inspiring life story, detailing her lifelong commitment to upending racism and white supremacy, sexism, labor exploitation, and global oppression. Midlo Hall's fascinating and engrossing personal histories illuminate the makings of a "revolutionary internationalist," radical, intellectual, and activist-historian. It provides a firsthand and fresh perspective on some of the most important political and social justice movements of the mid- to late twentieth century. A wide-ranging political autobiography, this remarkable narrative is an intimate account of an activist's interior life."—LaSHAWN HARRIS, author of *Sex Workers, Psychics, and Numbers Running*

"In this gripping memoir of a radical American life, the pathbreaking historian Dr. Gwendolyn Midlo Hall draws on almost a century of living memory to tell a story that races from New Orleans to Paris, New York, Mexico, Detroit, North

Carolina, New Jersey, Mississippi, and more. It's all here: her presence at W. E. B. Du Bois's 'Behold the Land' speech in 1946; her arrest at an 'interracial' party in 1949; a frank account of her thirty-year marriage to the brilliant and troubled Black revolutionary Harry Haywood; her friendship with Mabel and Robert Williams; her struggle to survive and grow as a professional historian in a bluntly sexist society; her years-long harassment by the FBI; her painstaking archival and pioneering database work to restore the historical identities of enslaved Africans and Black Americans. It's not a story you've heard before, and it's one you won't forget." —NED SUBLETTE, coauthor of *The American Slave Coast*

"Dr. Midlo Hall's memoir tells an intriguing story of survival. It is a love story about heartbreak, courage, and scholarship. As an awarded professor with over seventy years of study in courthouses and archives, Dr. Midlo Hall has helped countless students and scholars understand the history of Africans in Louisiana through her slave database. For the first time, readers will learn the secrets behind the life of this scholar, who as a teenager started her work as a civil rights activist and freedom fighter while working in her father's law office in New Orleans." —KATHE HAMBRICK, founder, River Road African American Museum and director of interpretation, West Baton Rouge Museum

"The 'Allées Gwendolyn Midlo Hall' is a memorial built at the Whitney Plantation Museum of Slavery near New Orleans and dedicated to remembering and honoring all the people who were enslaved in Louisiana. This book allows everybody to understand why the name of its author was chosen in the naming of the said memorial." —DR. IBRAHIMA SECK, director of research, Whitney Plantation Museum of Slavery

"Those who know historian Gwendolyn Midlo Hall from her pathbreaking research on the lives of enslaved Africans and their descendants might be surprised to learn of all the activist trailblazing she did as a young woman—building interracial coalitions against segregation in her hometown of New Orleans in the 1940s and organizing for workers' rights through the Communist Party, all the while struggling against the sexism that kept women from positions of leadership and careers of their own. But as her fascinating memoir *Haunted by Slavery* makes clear, the whole of her life's work, as an activist and a scholar, has been in the service of fighting injustice and broadcasting the stories of the oppressed, past and present." —MARY NIALL MITCHELL, Ethel & Herman L. Midlo Endowed Chair in New Orleans Studies, University of New Orleans

"This autobiography is an inspiring example of the convergence of political commitment and scholarly contribution. The author's life coincides in youth with the Civil Rights Movement and in the half-century that followed with the persistence of systematic racism in the United States. Daughter of an East

European immigrant who became a civil rights lawyer in segregated New Orleans, wife of a Black Communist militant, mother of an activist physician in Mexico, she describes her fight for social justice and racial equality throughout her life. In the last five decades at Rutgers and more recently at Michigan State University, not only has she written prize-winning books and articles reflecting the paradigm shift from slaves as silent victims to resilient and resourceful actors in history, but she has also led major projects in comparative and digital history. Recounting how all this has been achieved against constraints of gender convention, racial prejudice, and petty FBI harassment makes for fascinating reading about segregated New Orleans and Louisiana, the Communist Party in postwar America, and much else besides appreciation of the noteworthy persona who is the memoir's principal subject." —**PAUL LACHANCE**, professor of history, University of Ottawa

"Part feminist memoir, part labor philosophy, part Louisiana history, part civil rights chronicle, part the academic genealogy of an African diaspora historian: *Haunted by Slavery* is all that one might expect of the autobiography of one of the most distinguished scholars of several generations. And in its intricate and fearless writing, the book is even more." —**LAURA ROSANNE ADDERLEY**, associate professor of history, Tulane University

"Deeply moving and exceptionally current. Professor Hall has kindly opened a window and allowed us to peer through into her extraordinary life. A life full with both joys and sorrows, but more than anything, signalled by her unwavering commitment to make our world a better place." —**MANUEL BARCIA**, Chair of Global History, University of Leeds

"Part autobiography, part narrative of the lived experience of class conflict and antifascist solidarity against the deprivations and injustice of racial oppression, Gwendolyn Midlo Hall's *Haunted by Slavery* recounts the long and tumultuous history of twentieth-century America.

"Throughout this epoch, from the enduring legacy of slavery, refashioned under Jim Crow in 1930s New Orleans, to the hysteria of the Red Scare and FBI surveillance and harassment, to the historic engagements and tensions in the 1960s between the Communist Party, Civil Rights, and Black Nationalist movements, Hall—woman, spouse, mother, historian, and Red—is as much a protagonist as raconteur, interweaving her own story and these defining moments of American history.

"We are indebted to her principled stand and courage in the project of world-making to which *Haunted by Slavery* is yet another remarkable contribution."

—**EILEEN JULIEN**, founding director of the West African Research Center, Dakar, Senegal (1993–95) and author of *Travels with Mae: Scenes from a New Orleans Girlhood*

Haunted by Slavery

A Southern White Woman
in the Freedom Struggle

Gwendolyn Midlo Hall

Haymarket Books
Chicago, Illinois

Published in 2021 by
Haymarket Books
P.O. Box 180165
Chicago, IL 60618
773-583-7884
www.haymarketbooks.org
info@haymarketbooks.org

ISBN: 978-1-64259-274-0

Distributed to the trade in the US through Consortium Book Sales and Distribution (www.cbsd.com) and internationally through Ingram Publisher Services International (www.ingramcontent.com).

This book was published with the generous support of Lannan Foundation and Wallace Action Fund.

Special discounts are available for bulk purchases by organizations and institutions. Please call 773-583-7884 or email info@haymarketbooks.org for more information.

Cover design by Rachel Cohen.

Printed in Canada by union labor.

Library of Congress Cataloging-in-Publication data is available.

10 9 8 7 6 5 4 3 2 1

Contents

Guanajuato, Mexico, July 2018

FOREWORD

Pero Gaglo Dagbovie

I was horrified by the society I grew up in and have spent my entire life doing all I can to make it better. It has not been easy, but looking back on the last eighty years, I did accomplish quite a bit. I learned from experience that I was at least twenty years ahead of my time. I didn't really know why. Now, I have begun to understand that I helped create the best of my times. That's what this book is about.
                                                —Gwendolyn Midlo Hall, 2019

I am delighted and honored to have been asked to offer some reflections on the author of this expansive, fascinating, and at times sobering memoir authored by a remarkable woman who has lived a full and extraordinary life. The prologue that I offer here for Dr. Gwendolyn Midlo Hall's *Haunted by Slavery: A Memoir of a Southern White Woman in the Freedom Struggle* is largely based upon a paper entitled "Gwendolyn Midlo Hall, the Civil Rights-Black Power Movement, and the Struggle to Defend Robert Franklin Williams" that I presented for a celebratory panel devoted to exploring the many years of rigorous scholarship and steadfast activism of Dr. Hall and the tradition of armed self-defense during the southern Civil Rights Movement, at the 127th Annual Meeting of the American Historical Association in New Orleans, LA in early January 2013. Throughout this foreword, I refer to the author interchangeably as Dr. and Professor Hall and simply Hall and Gwen based upon the various contexts in which I know her and in line with conventional historical writing.

In the process of writing this paper nearly a decade ago, I recall how amazed I was to discover the wide-reaching scope of Hall's life as a scholar-activist. After reading *Haunted by Slavery*, it has become even more clear to me that she explicitly embodies what longtime executive editor of *Ebony* magazine and popular historian Lerone Bennett Jr. often called "living history" in reference to those freedom fighters in Black history who shared their life stories and varied experiences with upcoming generations. Hall is a quintessential witness-participant of close to a century of American life and history.

Born in New Orleans, Louisiana, in 1929, Hall became conscious of the world that she was existing in at an early age. "I never saw anything like justice in the world I grew up in," she remembers, "all I saw was inequality and tyranny." She became committed "full-time to radical politics" and developed into what she calls a "revolutionary in the deep South" and a "revolutionary internationalist" in 1946, at the young age of sixteen, when she joined the Communist Party of Louisiana. Among other organizations that she, early on in her life, participated in—in both leadership roles and behind-the-scenes efforts—include the New Orleans Youth Conference (as a result of her participation in this organization, Hall remarked, "I integrated myself into the Black community"), the Southern Negro Youth Congress, the Southern Conference for Human Welfare, the Civil Rights Congress, and the Provisional Organizing Committee to Reestablish the Communist Party. As a result of her radical politics that was unambiguously expressed through her actions and writings, she, like many of her contemporaries, was surveilled by the FBI. After gaining access to her FBI files, she wondered: "I couldn't understand why I was such a focus of their attention in 1965 and 1966 when they surely had more dangerous people to worry about . . . I don't know whether they considered me particularly dangerous, or took vengeance on me, or both."

In *Haunted by Slavery*, Hall muses on her experiences in the aforementioned organizations and scores of other social justice movements, while candidly reminiscing on her family history and growing pains; her relationship with African American Communist and Black liberation theoretician Harry Haywood (1898–1985), whom she married a decade before *Loving v. Virginia*, which ruled that states' bans against interracial marriages were violations of the Equal Protection Clause; her life as a

mother of three; her interactions with countless African American freedom fighters and white radicals; her world travels from Paris to Mexico
to Africa to elsewhere; her relentless struggles against patriarchy, sexism, archaic gender norms, racism, and classism; her various educational experiences; her academic and teaching careers, namely at Elizabeth
City State College, the University of Michigan, Rutgers University, and
Michigan State University; and her impactful scholarship.

Hall, who earned her PhD in history from the University of Michigan in 1970 and was supported by John Henrik Clarke early in her career, situates her dynamic life within the contexts of major turning points
in US history, such as the Great Depression, World War II, the Cold
War era, the modern Civil Rights Movement, and the Black Power era.
For those interested in more of the details of Hall's captivating life, the
Gwendolyn Midlo Hall Papers, covering the period of 1939 until 1998
and consisting of five and a half linear feet, are housed in the Bentley
Historical Library at the University of Michigan, Ann Arbor. There is
also a collection at the Amistad Research Center at Tulane University. It
is worth noting that she is among the small group of women historians
to have a paper collection chronicling her life and research.

I first met Dr. Hall in the summer of 2010 after she joined the Department of History at Michigan State University (MSU). I applaud our
then chairperson, Dr. Walter Hawthorne, for actively recruiting Dr. Hall
to MSU to work with him and several colleagues on an Atlantic slave
database (after all, this was an excellent opportunity for collaboration
because Dr. Hall had a wealth of experience in this realm dating back to
the mid-1980s). Although retired, during her brief yet productive stay at
MSU, she continued to be active as a scholar. While in East Lansing, she
completed *A Black Communist in the Freedom Struggle: The Life of Harry
Haywood* (2012) and worked on the memoir that you are now embark-
ing upon, parts of which she generously shared with me about a decade
ago. Always eager to share her knowledge with her new colleagues, she
quickly contributed to our department's intellectual growth and reputation, especially with her work on *Slave Biographies: The Atlantic Database
Network*. The specific occasion when I first encountered Dr. Hall was
special. I did, of course, know who she was. As a graduate student, I had
read her classic, pathbreaking, and multi-award-winning 1992 *Africans
in Colonial Louisiana* and more than a decade later I had assigned her

provocative 2005 study *Slavery and African Ethnicities in the Americas: Restoring the Links* for a graduate seminar on the African Diaspora that I taught for MSU's then African American and African Studies PhD Program.

In the summer of 2010, Hall arrived in East Lansing, Michigan, with her good long time friend Mabel Robinson Williams. Given my interest in African American women's history as well as the Civil Rights Movement and Black Power era, I anxiously arranged a meeting with them in hopes of scheduling interviews with Mrs. Williams so that I could write an article on her. That piece was published several years later, in 2013, in *The Black Scholar* ("'God Has Spared Me to Tell My Story': Mabel Robinson Williams and the Civil Rights-Black Power Movement"). Generally speaking, Mrs. Williams (1931–2014) is probably most widely remembered as being the wife of Civil Rights-Black Power Movement activist Robert Franklin Williams (1925–1996), who advocated for armed self-defense or "armed self-reliance" when many major Civil Rights Movement leaders embraced nonviolent direct action as a strategy for mass civil disobedience and a direct challenge to segregation in the South. In 1957, WW II veteran Robert F. Williams became head of the Monroe, North Carolina, NAACP chapter; he singlehandedly revitalized the organization, and spearheaded many local civil rights campaigns against segregation that had national and international consequences. In August 1961, when Freedom Riders ventured to Monroe, Williams was charged by the FBI of kidnapping a white family that he was actually protecting from a large group of justifiably frustrated Black protesters. Fleeing the FBI, Williams and his family escaped to New York, then Canada, and then fled to Cuba and traveled abroad as self-appointed ambassadors for the Black Freedom Struggle.

Though largely ignored in the historiography of the Civil Rights Movement, Mabel Williams made enormous sacrifices for a dangerous cause that her husband embraced. For five decades, she was not only Robert's devoted "helpmate" and "co-warrior" (as she has often described her role), but she also developed into an activist in her own right. In this sense, Hall and Williams were kindred sisters. They both married, collaborated with, and completely supported, through all of the ups and downs, iron-willed men who committed their lives to the Black Freedom Struggle. Just like their husbands, Hall and Williams made enormous sacrifices and took monumental risks for their beliefs and principles and the causes they embraced. Mabel Williams, like her beloved friend and former housemate Professor Hall still does, also embodied "living history." Their memories and personal histories serve as valuable windows into the not-so-distant past and as inspiration for those seeking to challenge injustices.

In the process of interviewing and researching the contributions of Mrs. Williams, Professor Hall was a constant source of historical information, insight, and encouragement. Oftentimes as I interviewed Mrs. Williams in their East Lansing apartment, Professor Hall—sitting in an adjacent room overhearing our conversations—would inject her recollection, interpretations, and analyses. She routinely helped historicize our discussions about the turbulent 1950s and 1960s. For someone who was born during the middle of the Black Power era, these first-hand accounts were especially revealing, more powerful than most of what I have read in traditional monographs on the subject. Professor Hall and Mrs. Williams were close friends for more than four decades. In the early 1960s, Hall was aware of, and sympathetic with, Robert F. Williams's activities and she corresponded with the Williams family. While in Mexico during the early 1960s, she helped, in a behind-the-scenes manner characteristic of many women activists of her generation, organize support for the Williams family with the CP in Mexico that supported the family's escape to Cuba. Hall first briefly met the Williamses when Robert F. Williams, flanked by Republic of New Africa members, returned to the US in September 1969. She first spoke extensively with Williams at a meeting that she attended with him and former State Department official Allen S. Whiting in Ann Arbor, Michigan, in about 1970 when Williams was granted a Ford Foundation–sponsored position at the Center for Chinese Studies at the University of Michigan. In her 1996 essay "A Tribute to RFW: A Towering Figure in the CRM," Dr. Hall reflected: "Rob spent the year briefing the Chinese experts at the State Department about how to approach the Chinese and the pitfalls to avoid."

While the main purpose of this particular meeting was to advise the Nixon administration to develop diplomatic strategies to interact with the Chinese government, Professor Hall and Williams also spoke at length about the enduring struggle for Black liberation. Williams was later tried in Monroe, North Carolina, in December 1975, and Dr. Hall chaired his Defense Committee and helped mobilize widespread support to get the trumped-up charges dismissed. As a result of the efforts of many, the state of North Carolina dropped all charges against him by 1976. Hall and the Williams family soon developed a deeper relationship. They spent time in each other's homes, and Hall enjoyed attending several of their family reunions in Monroe, North Carolina.

The more I listened to Hall's stories while meeting with her and Mabel and the more I engaged with Hall's early writings, the more I realized how much of a dynamic historian-activist with a broad range of experiences she was. She belongs to a multi-generational tradition of historians of the African American past who believe that scholarship is not simply an academic endeavor. For Professor Hall, history must not only correct and revise previous interpretations in search of the "truth," but should also be focused on contributing to progressive social change. In the September 25, 2000, issue of *People*, there is an article entitled "Unlocking the Past" on Professor Hall's research on "Databases for the Study of Afro-Louisiana History and Genealogy, 1699–1860" that she created by carefully combing through archives in Louisiana parish courthouses. With this research, she provided descriptions of more than one hundred thousand enslaved African descendants. One leading genealogist noted: "This is a revolutionary breakthrough in African American genealogy . . . It's the most significant publication of its kind since *Roots* in 1976."

Professor Hall's research had practical implications, offering many African Americans opportunities to discover their African heritage decades before Henry Louis Gates, Jr.'s well-known "African American Lives, Genealogy & Genetics Curriculum Project." As those of us who know her can testify, Gwen does not hesitate to share her unreserved and candid opinions about the past, present, and future. She shared in laymen's terms with *People* her vision of history's function. In explaining why she decided to earn a PhD in history and teach the history of African-descended people, she noted: "I thought history could explain why this mess exists, and maybe I can find some way to change it." In justifying her work on African American genealogy despite the fact that it may expose some sensitive facts—such as a former Louisiana governor's direct ties to slavery—she declared: "Colleagues kept telling me not to record all of the names . . . But these people were real, alive. I'm a historian and I teach the truth."

In the remainder of these introductory remarks, I touch upon examples of Dr. Hall's life as a scholar-activist during the long Black freedom struggle and the conventional Civil Rights-Black Power Movement. I draw largely upon selections from earlier drafts of *Haunted by Slavery* that she shared with me about a decade ago as well as her iconoclastic writings from approximately 1967 until 1972 in the *Negro Digest* [renamed *Black World*].

Gwendolyn Midlo Hall was inspired to be an activist at an early age. In particular, her father, who began practicing law in Louisiana in 1930, shaped her early notions of social justice. He took on a host of controversial cases, namely those involving police brutality. He also accepted vulnerable African American clients who, in defiance of de facto segregation, were often invited into the Midlo home. Hall recounts: "My father, Herman Lazard Midlo, influenced me much more than anyone else in my life. He won the admiration of so many people because he stuck his neck out for justice, and he taught me to follow that example." As a child and adolescent belonging to, in Hall's words, "a marginalized family within the marginalized world of New Orleans Jews," she witnessed the harsh brutalities of the Jim Crow South. "Black workers on sugar plantations," she recalled, "were treated, quite literally, worse than livestock."

As previously mentioned, Hall embraced a radical sense of politics at an early age, joining the CP of Louisiana and embracing Marxism-Leninism when she was a teenager. During the 1940s, she helped organize the interracial New Orleans Youth Council; challenged racial segregation laws; participated in African American voter registration drives; and was elected to the executive board of the Southern Negro Youth Congress. In an essay for *Blackpast.org* on the Southern Negro Youth Congress, Dr. Hall underscored: "I write as a historian whose life and work was inspired by the movements for racial equality in the South during the 1940s." She was active in the Civil Rights Congress and the Southern Conference for Human Welfare. By the 1960s, Hall, as she has put it, "came to understand that the best way for me to make a better world was to become a good historian." Still and all, her notion of the historian's craft was intertwined with social activism and consciousness raising.

In the mid-1960s, Hall engaged in civil rights activism in a manner that she later took great pride in. "When I was asked what was the one thing I had done in my life of which I was most proud," she shared with me, "my answer was teaching and encouraging my students to defend themselves with arms against the Ku Klux Klan." In 1965, she began teaching at Elizabeth City State College, a Black college in a lumber town in northeast North Carolina that during that time became home to an active group of students who confronted white supremacy, in turn, prompting the FBI to establish an office in Elizabeth City.

Hall was truly in the trenches: most of her students came from tobacco sharecropping families; "the students' average reading level was sixth grade;" and the students had been taught to memorize instead of to think critically. Reflecting on her brief stint there, Hall described the college town as "an isolated, ingrown community." She remained there for only eight months because she was "blacklisted" by the college and the FBI. When she began teaching at Elizabeth City, she passed as an Afro-Creole since the college's Board of Directors assumed that whites who applied to work there were communists. As a mother of two Black children, Hall faced certain challenges in North Carolina. "My kids and I were nearly assaulted for trying to buy a take-out pizza from a white restaurant," she recalls. Because the Klan was active in the area, she instructed her son "to keep away from white people, especially people with confederate plates on their cars." In *Haunted by Slavery*, she offers a riveting account about her experiences teaching social activism within the context of armed self-defense in the tradition of Robert Franklin Williams, Malcolm X, Medgar Evers, the Deacons for Defense, and the activists showcased in Akinyele Umoja's and others' scholarship. She writes: "I watched the Klan demonstrations getting bolder and bolder. The last day of my class in American history, I explained that there were two points of view about how to deal with the Klan. There was the passive resistance of Martin Luther King and the armed self-defense of Robert Williams, who was from further south in North Carolina, near Charlotte. Harry [Haywood] and I had strongly supported Rob since he started loudly advocating armed self-defense." Hall continues, "I wrote the name of his book on the blackboard: Robert F. Williams, *Negroes with Guns*. My students didn't have to see it or read it. They got the message from the title. They went home for about a week. When they returned, lots of them signed up for my summer course. The first day of class, they said, 'Robert Williams's way works.' They gave me no details, and I didn't ask."

Hall's radical writings in the *Negro Digest* during the Black Power era dovetailed with her early activism, echoing the sentiments of nationalist Black historians of her generation and younger. Clearly influenced by the Black radical, rhetorical tradition of the Black Power era, between 1967 and 1972 she wrote about a half dozen essays in this important magazine. *Negro Digest*—published from 1942 until 1950 and from 1962 until 1969 and then from 1970 until 1976 as *Black World*—served as an important outlet for African American historians and activists. The magazine's motto reflected pragmatism and commitment to "the cause": "Knowledge Is the Key to a Better Tomorrow." The roll call of leading Black activists and scholars who published in this magazine during the Black Power era is impressive, to say the least, from CLR James to John Henrik Clarke to Harold Cruse to Amiri Baraka to John Hope Franklin to Reverend Albert Cleage Jr. to Abbey Lincoln to Stokely Carmichael to Benjamin Quarles. Hall was one of the few women and white people to regularly publish in this magazine during the Black Power era. In my estimation, her essays belong to two major genres: straight forward historical essays about topics like the Haitian Revolution and slavery, and opinionated essays on the state of the Black community vis-à-vis white society. Several essays, both from 1969, stand out to me.

In February 1969, she published an essay entitled "Africans in the Americas" and shared her Carter G. Woodson–like vision of practical, activist-oriented historical scholarship. Advocating for self-determination and African American studies as an autonomous and corrective institution, she pronounced:

> If you look for the Afro-American past in history textbooks, you won't find it. Why? Because history is written by people. Mostly by people who don't know much about the real world. Their success depends upon the opinions of their colleagues, who are also naïve, sheltered, comfortable people who can't understand what happened in the past, because they have no idea what is going on around them right now. It takes a lot of time, money, and freedom to concentrate in making a historian—even to make a bad historian. This means that historians come mostly from wealthy, comfortable backgrounds where the world is nothing but a bowl of cherries. People who know better haven't produced many historians. And that is the main thing wrong with the historical profession . . . I hope that those of us who have some compe-

tence in Black Studies will congregate at an institution where we can develop a doctoral program strictly under our control . . . I look at the children of the ghetto—the kids who do so badly on white tests—and think of what they could become if educators would confine themselves to giving them breadth, scope, and self-confidence, instead of destroying their creativity . . . When it comes to Afro-American history, we should not be bound by scholarly tradition. Much of this tradition is irrelevant.

In 1969, she published a two part essay entitled "Mechanisms for Exploiting the Black Community" that in no uncertain terms critiqued institutional racism and the various devices used to oppress Black people in the inner cities, including manipulative credit systems; faulty drug rehab programs; the prison industrial complex; inferior housing; and poor schools. Though based upon scholarly inquiry, a significant part of her analysis was based upon her intimate, first-hand experiences living in Black communities in Brooklyn, Watts, and Detroit. According to Hall, most whites were plagued by a "perception gap," an inability to understand the plight of Black Americans in part caused by residential segregation throughout the nation. She asserted:

> The problem is, whites, even scholars—experts on the race crisis—cannot themselves admit to themselves a simple fact which every poor Black knows—has to know from daily, if not hourly experience. Blacks are pushed to the wall because the Black community is ruthlessly exploited by parasitic elements in the white community through legal, semi-legal, and illegal means. And these parasitic elements are bolstered and protected by the inſtitutions of our society.

In the end, during the Black Power era Hall called for what she deemed a "redistribution of wealth and power in favor of the Black community at the expense of the parasitic elements in the white community."

Gwendolyn Midlo Hall has been for more than half a century wholeheartedly committed to the cause of Black social justice, and her pioneering research continues to shape the course of African American and Afro-Diasporic history. I feel blessed to have had the opportunity to get to know Dr. Hall, to have listened to her stories, to have helped her with various household chores when she was living in a condominium kitty-corner from the MSU Department of History. Two of my sons now live in this building, and I routinely think about Gwen whenever I infrequently drop in on them. Gwen's departure from MSU was abrupt. To my knowledge, she did not leave because she did not enjoy her experiences at MSU, for she routinely reminded me how she was mistreated at Rutgers University and how the diverse MSU department of history community was a welcoming space. I became aware of her decision to move to Mexico, where she lived from more than a few years during the Civil Rights Movement, when, one day, she sent me an e-mail filling me in on how she had returned to her second home. At that point in her life, I assume that she felt that it was necessary for personal and health reasons to return to a place that had special meaning to her, not to mention the fact that she could live with her son Haywood, who could provide her with the care she needed. And she deserved such care. After all, she spent most of her life caring and sacrificing for others.

While in East Lansing, Gwen was like a surrogate grandmother to me. She reminds me much of my maternal grandmother, who was killed by a drunk driver when I was a freshman in high school. Though my grandmother was her senior, they both belonged to the so-called "Silent Generation" (although neither of them were silent), they were both profoundly shaped by the Great Depression and the era of World War II, they were both committed to their husbands and family, and they both shared with me profound bits of knowledge that influenced my worldview. *Haunted by Slavery* provides an illuminating narrative and window into Gwendolyn Midlo Hall's life journey, a life that has been filled with opportunities, challenges and obstacles, relationships, and accomplishments and joy. It is only fitting to end my commentary with Gwen's own words from *Haunted by Slavery*, words that my grandmother could have uttered. "I always knew my life had meaning—I had no conflict about that. So I was always highly motivated. The more obstacles I faced, the more determined I was to overcome them. I usually succeeded, but not always."

PREFACE

I pledge allegiance to the flag of the United States of America and to the Republic for which it stands, one nation, indivisible, with liberty and justice for all.

These were the words we all had to say at Wilson Elementary School as we assembled each morning, with hand on heart, to watch the hoisting of the Stars and Stripes. I didn't know what the words meant. They confused me because I was born and grew up in New Orleans during the 1930s, where "justice" was at best a bad word, and there was no equality for African Americans or women or poor whites. Even "one nation, indivisible" didn't make much sense given the racist adoration of Confederate generals, depicted on horseback in huge statues throughout the city in public spaces.

I took my first history class when I was nine years old. Our teacher and our textbook told us that liberty and equality had been won through the brilliance, daring, and sacrifice of our Founding Fathers. These men gave us a government to protect us from tyranny, and we didn't have to worry about it anymore. But I never saw anything like justice or equality in the world I grew up in. All I saw was inequality and tyranny.

I raised my hand and asked, "Teacher, what is liberty?"

She laughed and said, "You'll find out after you grow up."

I sure did. I spent my next eighty years trying to figure out not just what liberty meant but how to help make it happen. And I did find ways. I have written this book to try to explain how I did it, for myself as much as my readers, and to help us understand that even one person can make a difference. This guided me in everything I did throughout my complicated life.

I battled for liberty and freedom on many levels, starting in my childhood and youth. My first battles were for gender equality: a painful, never-ending struggle, often against the people I loved most. Women of my generation were supposed to be wives and mothers. There were no opportunities for us to do anything else. Higher education? That was to find a husband. My father said I could become a nurse or a teacher in case I couldn't get a husband. Instead, I became a temporary legal secretary during the Red Scare of the 1950s and 1960s. Temp work had one main advantage: by the time the FBI arrived to get me fired, I had already left for my next job.

All southern whites were taught to believe that African Americans were dangerous racial inferiors. But I never believed this, even as a small child. In this and many other ways, my father was a profound influence on me. Shaped by the internationalism of his Jewish ancestors and relatives, he was one of the few lawyers in New Orleans who accepted labor, civil rights, immigration, and police brutality cases. I witnessed his battles throughout my childhood. He showed me photographs and documents from his cases and brought his clients home to tell us about their fights for justice.

I was twelve years old in 1941, when the United States entered World War II. But well before that, I had learned about the rise of the Nazis in Germany by watching my father and his siblings as they listened in horror to shortwave radio broadcasts of Adolf Hitler's anti-Jewish tirades. They were so stunned they couldn't speak. The war remained at the center of my consciousness and inspired my dedicated support. But I also recognized that we were being taught white supremacy in the South, in the middle of a war against the Nazis, who got many of their racist ideas and laws from the United States.

During the war, the US government sponsored the publication of a pamphlet titled *The Races of Mankind* by the great anthropologist Ruth Benedict. I was thrilled to read it because it argued against racism and racist beliefs; it made the case that race is a social construction and not based in biology. I was also excited because it was written by a great woman scholar. Could I become one? It took me more than twenty years before I believed I could.

Before that, I led the life of a political activist. After the war, I helped organize the New Orleans Youth Council (NOYC), the only interracial youth movement in the Deep South. This led me into the Communist Party (CP) and the organizations it sponsored, such as the Civil Rights

Congress. I got my introduction to the struggles of the working class on the docks of New Orleans, where the Communists had a strong presence among Black sailors and longshoremen.

After leaving New Orleans, I eventually ended up in Manhattan, where I began to work with Harry Haywood, one of the main Black leaders of the CP and later a well-known figure in the New Left of the 1960s and 1970s. He had been recruited into the CP in the early 1920s and was sent to study in Moscow, where he helped develop the theory that African Americans were an oppressed nation in the United States with the right of self-determination. We started living together in Brooklyn in 1955 and were married in April 1956, several months before our son, Haywood, was born. Our daughter, Rebecca, was born in Mexico in January 1963. Our marriage lasted for thirty years until Harry died in January 1985.

During the first decade of our marriage, I devoted almost all my time and energy to supporting Harry and his work, with no recognition—especially from him—of the value of my contribution. I started helping him write in 1953, and we produced an influential pamphlet titled *For a Revolutionary Position on the Negro Question* in 1956. Thanks to such writings and our organizing, we helped almost all the Black Reds find their way out of the CP and into the Civil Rights and Black Power movements of the 1960s. This little-known story is told here, including the relationship of former CP members to some of these movements' most outstanding leaders.

While living in Mexico, we wrote another manuscript that had great influence on the African American liberation movement. In 1965, it began appearing in serialized form in *Soulbook* magazine, which was published by one of the first movements in the Bay Area to call themselves Black Panthers. Ernie Allen was editor, and Bobby Seale later of the Black Panther Party for Self-Defense was distribution manager. In the late 1960s, Harry lived in Detroit in the home of John and Edna Watson, who were busy organizing Black autoworkers into the Dodge Revolutionary Union Movement (DRUM), which quickly spread throughout Detroit in all the auto plants, universities, and even high schools. In the 1970s, Harry became a major figure in the international New Communist Movement, which was supported and backed by Maoist China.

I couldn't follow him there. I had chosen an independent path for myself: becoming a historian, which is how I would create a powerful weapon against racism. This was a long, extremely difficult path, because women from my generation were not supposed to be historians and scholars. And I was not just a woman but a mother and a Red. During the last twenty years of my marriage to Harry, I cared for three children alone while studying for my PhD at the University of Michigan and then teaching at Rutgers University in New Jersey. During the Red Scare, Leo, my son from an earlier marriage, was taken away from me by a judge on the New York State Supreme Court. But Leo sought me out during his adolescence, when he was already suffering from a serious mental illness. I looked after him for more than fifty years through extreme difficulties. But near the end of his life, I was helpless to aid him, although I knew he was in deep trouble. He died of smoke inhalation in June 2020, when he was sixty-nine years old.

I drew on my years in Mexico to save me as I faced these challenges. Harry and I lived there between early 1959 and early 1964, and I resumed my undergraduate studies after a decade-long interruption and continued on to graduate work. Thanks to Mexico's policy of welcoming refugees, I studied with some of the greatest scholars in the world, including survivors of the Spanish Civil War. They were decisive in encouraging me and my work as a historian, as well as instrumental in protecting me from the FBI.

I was able to have my own independent effect on the Black freedom struggle, publishing numerous essays in African American intellectual magazines during the late 1960s and early 1970s. Later, I had an enduring impact with my historical scholarship, which rests largely on three books that draw heavily on archival research into original manuscript documents. The first, a formative work in Caribbean studies, is a comparative history of slavery in St. Domingue and Cuba. The second, the winner of nine book prizes, is about the creation of Afro-Creole culture in Louisiana. It changed the way scholars and the wider public view American culture by drawing attention to the interaction of its diverse, formative strands. The third is a pioneering study in African-Atlantic history that traces historical and social developments across African regions and most of the Americas.

Probably my greatest scholarly contribution, though, is the groundbreaking work I did in digital history. I was one of the first historians to work with computer databases, beginning with one that documented Louisiana enslaved people from 1719 through 1820. Its more than 104,000 records, with varying amounts of detail, give information on just about every enslaved person in the state during that time period, as well as how they were bought and sold and by whom. After that work gained international media attention in 2000, further inspiring digital humanists, interdisciplinary scholars, and genealogists throughout the world, I began working with other researchers on a platform to connect the growing number of databases of enslaved people. This monumental, collaborative work will continue for the foreseeable future.

The important characteristic of this scholarship is that it tells the story of the oppressed, wherever they are from, not only as victims but as people in a constant state of struggle and creation.

In a toast for my ninetieth birthday celebration, the great historian Steven Mintz wrote: "To someone who has utterly transformed our understanding and restored the voices, lives, and agency of those who made our world." That thread runs through my whole life, back to my childhood and youth in New Orleans—where I became a revolutionary in the Deep South at a time when few white people dared to oppose racism, and those who did most uncompromisingly were almost all Communists.

Gwendolyn Midlo Hall
Guanajuato, Mexico, 2021

With my son, Dr. Haywood Hall, Kathe Hambrick in the background, celebrating my ninetieth birthday in Guanajuato, Mexico.

Me at three months old.

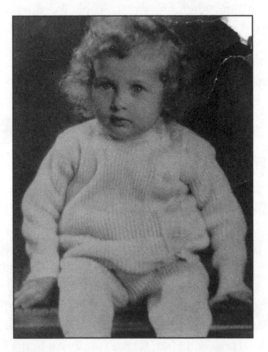

1931. Two years old. A skeptic already.

PART ONE

GROWING UP IN NEW ORLEANS

I was born in New Orleans on June 27, 1929, and was blessed with a calm, happy temperament. Like many other creative people from New Orleans, I am also a skeptic. We learn to be free-thinking rebels: musicians, writers, graphic artists, independent-minded scholars, political activists.

Why? Because it's hard for us to believe in a stable world. Nature never lets us forget who is boss. Our lives revolve around tropical downpours, hurricanes, winds, floods, and sometimes even tidal waves. Heavy rains turn our streets into rivers. We never know where the land begins and the water ends. Native and migrating waterfowl embrace us with color and song. Woodpeckers hammer away at our tall longleaf pines. Spanish moss hugs our huge oak trees. Tropical gardens, lush with flowers, explode from the rich topsoil washed ashore by the mighty Mississippi River long before we "tamed" her. Now, the levee system for flood control stops the silt from building up along her banks and drops it uselessly into the Gulf of Mexico. Oil refineries and pipelines erode the shoreline, destroying our already weak protection from hurricanes and floods. Our engineering feats have greatly increased the instability of our world.

When I was growing up in New Orleans, the long, five-month summer crushed us with extreme heat and humidity. Air conditioning? Unheard of. Window fans were a new luxury, and attic fans were high tech. Only rich people had refrigerators. The rest of us were lucky if we had iceboxes.

1

Big trucks delivered the blocks of ice, and their drivers also made snow-balls of various flavors. We would hop up on the ice trucks, watch them scrape the ice, and pick out our syrup flavors.

Despite the heat, there was an active street life. Vendors walked around singing their messages: "Blackberries! Five cents a carton. Get your fresh blackberries!" Farmers rode around the streets in mule-drawn carts, selling great piles of fresh fruits and vegetables. At every major intersection, Mexicans sold delicious hot tamales out of hand-pushed wooden carts, adding their voices to the street cries: "Hot tamales! Get your hot tamales! Fresh-cooked!"

To get us to fall asleep despite the heat, my parents would drive us around the city with the car windows wide open. We stopped at Brown's Velvet Dairy ice cream shop on Carrollton Avenue and at a watermelon stand next to it when melons were in season. After we fell asleep, my parents drove home and carried us upstairs to our beds. I still tend to fall asleep in moving vehicles.

New Orleans is a port city, and that has made our culture unique. During the nineteenth century and well into the twentieth, it was the second-biggest port in the country, thanks mainly to the maritime slave and international cotton trades. It is still an oil refining and shipping center. The port has declined, but New Orleans is still the most cosmopolitan city of the Deep South. Our culture—with its powerful Chitimacha, Choctaw, and Senegalese foundation and its tangled French, Canadian, German, Spanish, Cadjun, Haitian, Mexican, Cuban, Canary Island, Yankee, Irish, Sicilian, Jewish, Chinese, Central American, and Vietnamese roots—is a gumbo of richly blended ethnic and religious diversity. New Orleans never loses her powerful grip on her children, wherever we live. Our city is an embodiment of our diverse, creolized regional cultures—our nation's true greatness.

My Social Democratic Yiddish Family

My father was a first-generation immigrant from a large Yiddish-speaking Jewish family from Sosnowiec in Upper Silesia, now Poland. When the family lived there, it was part of the Russian Empire under the czar. My mother was a third-generation immigrant from a family with roots in Slonim, Belarus. My family identified with Yiddish culture but was not religious. They viewed the world from the perspective of the internationalist, wandering, persecuted Jews who identified with the poor and oppressed wherever they lived.

My father was born in 1902 in Sosnowiec. As far as I know, his family members were all tailors. But the word *mydlo* means "soap" in Slavic languages, so the Midlos probably were soap makers at the time Jews were given the honor of having surnames, usually based on the kind of work they did. My paternal grandmother's maiden name was Granitman, so her family probably worked in the granite quarries of Upper Silesia. Both soapmaking and quarry labor were hard, dangerous work.

Sosnowiec was no little rural shtetl like Anatevka in *Fiddler on the Roof*. The region of Upper Silesia is rich in coal, iron, and other important industrial minerals. By 1859, a branch line of the Warsaw–Vienna Railway stopped in Sosnowiec, making it a cosmopolitan communications and industrial hub. There was a Jewish workers' movement in Sosnowiec, which started its first major strike in 1894.

Poor Jews like my family all worked hard but starved. All the Midlos were short, no doubt from malnutrition. My father was the fourteenth of the sixteen children of Gittel and Shapsa Midlo. Only six of them survived childhood. The family lived in cramped quarters with their sons-in-law, a few grandchildren, and apprentices who were also their boarders—and, for some of them, eventually their sons-in-law. The family kept chickens under the table. When a chicken laid an egg, it was boiled and divided into four pieces that were given to those family members lucky enough to get a piece.

As a small child, I remember how proud my father and his siblings were of their oldest brother, Joseph Wolf Midlo, who as a teenager was active in the 1905 Revolution to overthrow the Russian czar. A family story was passed down that revolutionary literature was hidden in my father's diapers and crib. He was born with rickets, a condition caused by vitamin D deficiency: a mark of starvation among the Eastern European Jewish working class. He couldn't walk until he was four years old. His mother gave up on him. She saved the little food they had for her other children, who had a better chance of surviving. His sister, my aunt Mena, told me she saved him by sneaking him some of her food. He limped badly all his life, could hardly walk without a cane, and was likely in constant agony. Although he never complained, he sometimes had fits of rage, no doubt from his pain.

By 1907, the anti-czarist revolution had been crushed, and intense oppression roiled the entire empire. The whole Midlo family moved to Offenbach, Germany, near Frankfurt, where there was a large, influential Jewish community, including wealthy Jews like the Rothschilds. My father went to elementary school and became literate in German. His older brother, my uncle Charles, fared even better. Although still a young child, Charles showed great aptitude for medicine. When the Midlos were about to emigrate to America in 1913, his teacher begged them to leave Charles behind, promising to provide for him, educate him, and treat him like his brother. The family refused, which probably saved his life.

Uncle Charles went to Johns Hopkins Medical School, where he did cutting-edge research on inherited body markings such as fingerprints. In 1943, he coauthored the book *Finger Prints, Palms and Soles,* which is still a standard work in the field. He taught neuroanatomy at both Louisiana State University and Tulane Medical School. Aspiring Jewish doctors, excluded from medical schools in the Northeast by the Jewish quotas enforced at the time, enrolled at the southern schools. Charles was a devoted and inspiring professor who taught some of the most renowned physicians to emerge after World War II. When I consulted a physician anywhere in the United States, I was often asked in awe if I was related to Dr. Charles Midlo. When my first book was published by his alma mater, Johns Hopkins University Press, Uncle Charles asked me to use my maiden name, Midlo. I have used it ever since.

The Midlos' life in Offenbach came to an end in 1913, when World War I was about to begin and the German government started checking immigration papers. The family had none, of course. This bad luck saved the entire family from the Holocaust. The Midlos were among the more than two million Yiddish-speaking Ashkenazi Jews who emigrated to the United States before 1924, when a new immigration law tightened the quotas for Eastern European Jews. The entire family left for America in December 1913, in three separate steamship voyages on the Hamburg America Line. Almost all Ashkenazi Jews landed at Ellis Island, and most remained in the New York metropolitan area. Some moved to the industrial Midwest. In Chicago, they created a large and influential Jewish working-class trade union enclave where my mother, Ethel Samuelson (née Glassovitzki), was born.

Meyer Mendelvitz, Joseph Midlo, and Reuben Gaethe, circa 1910

The Midlos did not believe that the United States was the promised land. Joseph Wolf Midlo and his son-in-law Reuben Gaethe had already gone to New York City in 1910 to pave the way for the rest of the family, and when they returned, they reported that life in the New York garment district was so awful that they should aim to move elsewhere. As a result, the Midlos were among the few Yiddish-speaking Jews who landed and lived in the Deep South, where they were forced to respond to its virulent anti-Black Jim Crow apartheid.

The Midlos arrived in New Orleans in January 1914—just in time to avoid the outbreak of World War I in Europe, but not a good time for Jews in the Deep South. In Atlanta, the Jewish businessman Leo Frank had just been wrongfully convicted of the murder of a thirteen-year-old girl and was sentenced to death by hanging. Frank spent two years appealing his case from prison. After his death sentence was commuted by the governor, a mob instigated by some of Georgia's leading politicians and jurists led an invasion of the state prison in 1915. These prestigious gentlemen and other members of the community kidnapped Frank from prison and lynched him. About half the Jews living in Georgia moved out.

The Midlos likely lost their enthusiasm for the Deep South because of the Leo Frank lynching. They moved to Chicago, where for several years the entire family—men, women, and children—worked in the miserable conditions of the Chicago garment district for five dollars a week. But during the early 1920s they returned to New Orleans and opened Universal Tailors in the 500 block of South Rampart Street.

The Midlo family identified with the Yiddish community and belonged to Chevra Thilum Synagogue on Lafayette Street, but they were not observant Jews. My father never made a bar mitzvah. He wore a yarmulke and a prayer shawl when he went to synagogue, but I have no memory of his praying at home. We only attended services on the high holidays, mainly to show off our new clothes. Nobody in my family kept kosher. We all loved New Orleans' spicy seafood: boiled, stuffed, and soft-shell crabs; shrimp; oysters; seafood po'boys.

My relationship with the Jewish community has been strained all my life because I have never been a Zionist. I am clearly not a conformist, and my distrust of groupthink and all institutions, especially religious ones, is profound. I went to one Zionist meeting at Tulane University when the state of Israel was born. All I heard there was contempt for the Palestinians. That was the last Zionist meeting I ever attended. But I always identified myself as a Jew, and my sense of Jewish identity, like Albert Einstein's, increased with the Holocaust. Above all else, I am an internationalist, which is rooted in fellow feeling with the persecuted and oppressed—something that hypernationalist, xenophobic Zionism can never destroy.

I only recently learned that my profound attachment to socialist internationalism stems from the Jewish Labor Bund of Poland's influence on my father and his family. When I was a child, I heard my aunt Mena speak reverently of "the Bund." Nobody told me what it was, and I didn't ask. In fact, the General Jewish Labor Bund, founded in Vilnius, Lithuania, in 1897, campaigned for a "socialist revolution that would link the struggles of Russian Jews with the general struggles of workers throughout Russia," according to the YIVO Institute for Jewish Research.[1] Its outlook was internationalist, socialist, secular (in fact, anti-religious), and anti-Zionist. It defended Jewish cultural autonomy, with Yiddish as the national language. The Bund played a prominent role in the 1905 and 1917 revolutions to overthrow the czar. The new Soviet government outlawed all forms of discrimination against Jews and made antisemitism a crime.

Jewish Labor Bund Self-Defense Group with three dead members in Odessa, 1905

In Poland before World War II, the Bund organized much of the Jewish community, teaching and practicing socialist ideals, not individualistic capitalist greed. Before the Holocaust, Jews were 10 percent of Poland's population and one-third of the population of Warsaw. They voted as a bloc, sometimes with the Polish Socialists. The Bund's well-organized communities maintained kitchens that provided food to those in need, health centers, women's groups, youth groups emphasizing sports, and armed self-defense units that fought czarist pogroms but rejected political terror. While the Zionists supported immigration to Palestine, the Bund encouraged its members to stay where they lived in Central and Eastern Europe, maintain Jewish strength and voting power, and fight for their rights and equality.

The Bund was the first to organize the Warsaw ghetto population to fight the Nazi extermination squads. It published underground newspapers, created widespread community organizations to smuggle food and other goods from outside the ghetto walls, and organized discussion groups, cultural events, and military units. Allied with several military forces from other Jewish organizations, Bundists led the 1943 Warsaw Ghetto Uprising. The Bundist Marek Edelman was one of its main leaders and one of the few survivors. He wrote about his experiences in great detail shortly after World War II ended.[2]

Now I understand why my Midlo aunts, one by one, took me aside during the height of the cold war Red Scare hysteria and told me I was carrying on the family tradition. The Bund had many female members and even some female leaders. There were many fighting women members of its armed self-defense groups and in Jewish partisan bands fighting the Nazis during World War II. What I admire most about my father and his family is based on the ideology of the Jewish Labor Bund of Poland, which, unlike its Russian branch, opposed Soviet violation of human rights and fought for freedom of thought.

How My Father Taught Me to Be a Revolutionary

My father, Herman Lazard Midlo, influenced me much more than anyone else in my life. He won the admiration of so many people because he stuck his neck out for justice, and he taught me to follow that example.

My father, Herman Lazard Midlo, cerca 1930

When the family returned to New Orleans from Chicago, he insisted on continuing his education before he agreed to take responsibility for the new family tailoring business. He went to night school at John McDonogh Senior High School and earned his high school diploma. One of his teachers found out he was a good debater and encouraged him to go to law school. He attended Loyola University Law School at night while continuing to work days as a tailor. That way he could help Uncle Charles with his medical education and provide for his own new family after he married my mother in 1926 and my sister Razele was born in 1927.

He inspired trust and confidence in everyone who met him and was scrupulously honest and courageous. That's what made him a successful lawyer in the Louisiana of the 1930s and 1940s despite his CIO, African American, Communist, immigrant, and pacifist clients.

I was born four months before the Wall Street stock market crash of 1929. One of my first memories is talk about ruined stock market speculators jumping to their deaths from Wall Street skyscrapers. I grew up surrounded by the misery of the Great Depression but also by the hope of the new industrial labor movement. Mass unemployment, homelessness, hunger, desperation, racist and antilabor violence, Jim Crow segregation, police brutality—I was exposed to it all as a small child and was amazed that so few others recognized what a violent, corrupt system we lived in.

We lived in a racially mixed neighborhood in uptown New Orleans on the corner of Penniston and South Robertson Streets. Parents of some of the kids in our neighborhood put them in orphanages so they would not starve to death. A parade of hungry people stopped by our house, offering to work for a little food. A Black woman stopped me on the sidewalk in front of our house and asked me if we had any shoes to give her. I gave her a brand-new pair of my father's shoes. That seemed reasonable to me because he could buy himself another pair. My mother didn't see it that way. She was afraid I had already learned my father's generous and ascetic ways. She was right. I was a social critic from a very young age.

To make a living, my father practiced real estate law, checking titles and preparing mortgages and title transfers. He represented mainly Jewish owners of small retail businesses. More important, he organized a group of Jewish lenders who sold mortgages on homes and churches to African Americans when banks, homestead associations, and mortgage companies would lend only to white people. Right after World War II, my mother bought temporary housing (hutments) left over from the war and erected them on lots in the Ninth Ward in New Orleans, where they were bought mainly by returning African American veterans. But my father's greatest achievement was winning the respect and approbation of an increasingly influential sector of the legal community in New Orleans. Many of his fellow lawyers hated the violent, deeply corrupt system they functioned in but dared not challenge it. My father led the way by fighting fearlessly for justice.

His body was a constant burden that he dragged around all his life. Although I never thought of him as crippled, when I was a teenager I overheard a fellow passenger in a ferry boat crossing the Mississippi River describing him that way and admiring his spirit and courage. That was the first time I realized he was so physically handicapped. His determination was all I saw. He woke up every morning at four o'clock. After he dressed, he made sure everyone else in the house was up and dressed, too. No one was ever allowed to sleep late—he said he needed our company. I am still an early riser.

My father became known as the best lawyer in the state for getting the wrongfully imprisoned out of jail. With great determination he taught me about what he did, bombarding me with the gory details about the downside of American democracy.

When I was ten years old, my father showed me photos of sheriff's deputies shooting down women shrimp-packers on strike in Violet, a town in St. Bernard Parish. One of them, Angela Treadway, died three days after being shot in the stomach. She, her sister, and several other eyewitnesses knew the shooter and identified him on sight and by name. But Leander Perez, the district attorney and political boss of oil-rich St. Bernard and Plaquemines parishes, immediately downriver from New Orleans, refused to arrest or prosecute the shooter.

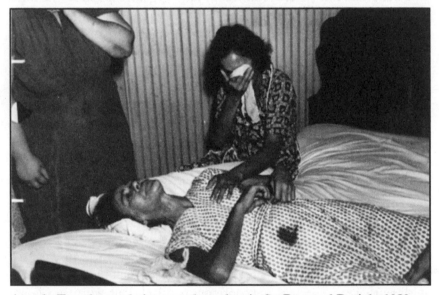

Angela Treadway, shrimp packer, shot in St. Bernard Parish, 1939.

Thugs walking away from the shooting. Photos from Herman L. Midlo Collection, Earl K. Long Library, Special Collections, University of New Orleans.

After Angela Treadway's death, some residents of St. Bernard and Plaquemines parishes, represented by my father and his office mate, A. P. Schiro III, signed a petition to investigate Perez's obstruction and to have him removed from office. Some of his henchmen visited my mother and asked her what her husband wanted, but she didn't understand that they were trying to bribe her. They knew very well that they dared not try to bribe my father. Perez sued to stop the investigation. Midlo and Schiro won in the lower court and then in the Louisiana State Supreme Court. Then some people were successfully pressured into removing their names from the petition. Others disappeared. The case against Perez was dropped.

Historian Adam Fairclough described Perez as "the most powerful ultra-segregationist in Louisiana." He certainly was. But his influence was felt across the entire South. He was a leading founder of the White Citizens' Council, a slightly more respectable version of the Ku Klux Klan with much larger numbers and enormous political clout, which was largely responsible for the massive resistance to desegregation. At the height of the Civil Rights Movement twenty-five years later, Perez was still in power, showing off the concentration camps he built in the swamps for civil rights demonstrators, protected by his gunslingers, electric fences, bloodhounds, snakes and alligators, and the Mississippi River. From the 1930s until a decade after Perez's death in 1969, Perez and his two sons siphoned off oil and mineral wealth and revenue belonging to the citizens of St. Bernard and Plaquemines.

During the mid-1930s, the Congress of Industrial Organizations (CIO) began to organize in New Orleans and surrounding areas. They paid my father a $100-a-month retainer to get their organizers out of jail, where the police brutalized and tortured them. On weekends, we drove the organizers to Mississippi, where they were safer than in New Orleans. My sister Razele and I listened to their stories and were inspired by their courage and their dedication to the exciting new labor movement, which taught white southern workers to reject racism and create integrated industrial unions. The CIO converted many southern white workers to interracial solidarity, especially in and near New Orleans.

In the Louisiana I grew up in, no independent thought, belief, action, or ethical conduct went unpunished. Freedom of religion was not tolerated. The Jehovah's Witnesses found this out when their members were persecuted and jailed for proselytizing in several parishes over a period of years. Some of them, arrested in Alexandria, Louisiana, were released after posting bail but were never charged with any crime. The Jehovah's Witnesses' national office retained my father to get their bail money back. We turned his trip to Alexandria into a family outing to the country. The small farm where we stayed belonged to a family of Jehovah's Witnesses. Judge Gus A. Voltz was indignant that the Jehovah's Witnesses refused to salute the American flag and were pacifists who refused to fight for their country. My father defended their right to practice their beliefs. He went to court in Alexandria, surrendered the prisoners, got the bail money back, and presented Judge Voltz a writ of habeas corpus to force him either to charge the prisoners or release them.[3]

Circulars Hostile to State Charged

NEW ORLEANS, Sept. 20.—(By A. P.)—Herman L. Midlo, attorney for Henry W. Hermes and John Antolovich, arrested a month ago and charged with distributing circulars "intended to excite and promote hostilities and opposition to the government of the State of Louisiana," filed an application for a bill of particulars in criminal district court today.

The Town Talk, September 20, 1937, page 7

When my father did not return from court, my mother went to town on a mule cart to find out what became of him. Here's what happened: the judge was outraged that this big-city lawyer came into his court with a writ he had never heard of before. As my father was getting into his car, the judge sent the police to bring him back. Judge Voltz grabbed him by the lapels, punched him in the face until he was nearly unconscious, and jailed him for contempt of court. My father sued the judge for assault and battery and false arrest. When my mother, my sister, and I attended the trial, my mother concealed in her purse a string of coins attached to a long belt that she could swing as a weapon. Luckily, she didn't need it. My father won $1,500 in damages, a very big piece of change then, which he contributed to the Jehovah's Witnesses defense fund.[4]

JUDGE VOLTZ SUED FOR $5,000

(CONTINUED FROM PAGE ONE)

Bible and Tract Society," and two other companions, Harry Slipakoff and Neil A. Armstrong, Jr., before he entered the grand jury room, calling to him in the corridor as follows:

"You ——— ——— ———, I'll take care of you when you get through testifying before the grand jury."

Midlo accused the judge of attacking him when he left the grand jury room, stating he ignored Judge Voltz when he called out, "Come here, I want to talk to you," but that the judge allegedly grabbed him by the collar and "punched" him in the face repeatedly until he was "almost knocked unconscious" and the affray was halted by two men.

Midlo's petition said the difficulty with the judge arose out of the attorney's efforts on behalf of Robert Graham, who had been jailed June 15 charged with distributing "religious liaterature known as 'Watch Tower Bible and Tract Society pamphlets' of the 'Witnesses of Jehovah.'

Accompanied by Blackwell, whom he stated had engaged him to defend Graham, Midlo said he appeared at Judge Voltz' office several days following Graham's arrest and sought to obtain his release. He alleged in the suit Judge Voltz told him there would be a "mobbing" in Alexandria if Gra-

ham didn't leave town, whereupon Midlo inquired whom would make up the mob and asked Judge Voltz why he didn't take steps as an officer to prevent such a mob if he knew of it.

This made Judge Voltz "very angry," Midlo's petition stated, whereupon the judge allegedly threatened to fight Blackwell if the latter would enter his office. Midlo stated he and Blackwell then went to the courthouse and obtained from District Attorney A. V. Hundley a promise that Graham's bond would be fixed at $250 for his release.

Jailed by Police

Shortly afterward, Midlo stated, he was arrested by a policeman named Jacobs as he entered his automobile, carried to the city jail and told he was charged with contempt of court and that his bond had been fixed at $250. Midlo alleged jail authorities refused him use of the telephone to arrange bond. He said he later obtained release "through a city detective" whose name was unknown, after spending two and a half hours in jail.

Midlo charged in his suit that his arrest and incarceration were "malicious and for the purpose of intimidating" him into leaving town and not protecting or defending his client. He alleged he was never "formally charged or brought to trial" for contempt.

———————————————

Only 1 per cent of the accidents on dry roads involve skidding; on wet roads, the percentage is 27, while on snowy-icy roads, the percentage leaps to 50 per cent.

The Town Talk, Thursday, June 19, 1941, page 16

My father's defiance of Jim Crow shocked many of his contemporaries. A. P. Tureaud, the attorney for the NAACP in New Orleans, was one of only three African American lawyers in the entire state of Louisiana. He filed anti-discrimination suits that slowly opened some white institutions of higher education to African Americans. He and my father were contemporaries and friends. For years, Tureaud had been denied a notarial commission, so my father helped him get one. Meanwhile, before Tureaud's office closed every evening, all his clients with documents needing to be notarized came to my father's office. My father invited Tureaud to accompany him to services at his synagogue, creating a long-reverberating scandal. Tureaud came to dinner at our home several times. One of my father's closest friends left our home in shock when he found an African American man sitting with us at our dining room table.

Sadly, there was an ugly side to my relationship with my father. He was socialized into the Eastern European Yiddish tradition of extreme misogyny, including violence against women. Women were revered for their role as supportive wives, mothers, and homemakers, but those who refused to accept their assigned roles were rejected as dangerous subversives.

When I was barely sixteen years old until I was eighteen, I had a wild romance and then a marriage with my second cousin, Maurie Samuelson. I had loved him for as long as I could remember because he treated me like an equal, even though I was a girl and five years younger. My parents were determined to break us up. They appealed to Nick Karno, another cousin, who owned some retail variety stores. Nick suggested he have Maurie beaten up. But that was too much for my parents. Maurie was married, and his marriage was breaking apart amid rumors of gambling, drinking, womanizing, and physical abuse. Nick got his private detectives to follow Maurie around to get the goods on him.

After Maurie went to get a divorce in Reno so we could get married, my father started to beat me severely every day. He was furious about how much I loved Maurie and that I had given up my all-important virginity. Under my clothes I had bruises all over my body. My mother would sometimes protest, and she caught a few blows herself trying to protect me. She told me my father was trying to kill something in himself. After weeks and weeks of being brutally beaten, I threw a stool across the living room. I didn't throw it hard, but my aim was good, and it hit my father on the nose. He cried out, "Ethel, she hit me, she hit me!"

My mother had trouble concealing her glee. He never hit me again.

Aside from his violence against me, for which I never could forgive him, we had a complicated relationship. He had no sons. He loved my sister Razele the most, partially because she was more obedient and accepting of her assigned gender role. But he chose me as his disciple, even though I was a girl and younger than my sister. My father saw something special in me, as his most intelligent, courageous child and the one who best embraced and carried on his teachings.

When he was dying, in 1978, I was teaching history at Rutgers University and living in Brooklyn. I visited him as often as I could. Sometimes he told me some of what he remembered about his early life. On one visit, we made plans to tape more of what he wanted to tell me, but I had to leave that day. He was terribly disappointed, and so was I. I never saw him again. He died shortly after I left.

I never got over the beatings from my father. In spite of his extreme backwardness about women, though, he was the most influential person in my life, whom I admired deeply and revered. I owe a great deal to my father. Throughout my childhood, he taught me to defy the violent, racist, corrupt society we lived in. I was so moved by what he taught me that I have struggled for equality and justice all my life.

My Mother

My mother was born in Chicago in 1909. Her maiden name was originally Glassivitsky, which means glazier or glass tile maker. When her grandparents Julius and Deborah arrived from Slonim, Belarus, at Ellis Island in 1885, the immigration officer didn't know how to write their name, so he renamed them Samuelson, because Julius's father was Samuel (Shmuel in Yiddish). My mother's parents, Samuel Jacob Samuelson and Beatrice Babetch, met and married in Chicago. Partnering with Grandpa Sam's oldest sister, Becky Samuelson Wolfson, they moved to Donaldsonville, in the Louisiana sugar country, to open a tailor shop when my mother was three years old.

Above: The tailor shop in Donaldsonville, 1910. Below: The same building still standing in 2007.

My parents met when my father was traveling in sugar country, peddling suits to small farmers and sugar plantation workers. They married in 1926, when she was sixteen years old and he was twenty-three. She had to drop out of high school. No girl or woman who had sexual relations, whether student or teacher, could attend or teach school back then because it was thought they would contaminate the virgin girls.

Years later, she went back and finished high school with teenagers as her fellow students.

My parents' wedding, 1926.

My parents married before my father passed his bar exam. My mother read to him aloud from his law books while he cut out suits in his tailor shop on South Rampart Street and as he drove their car to the countryside on weekends to peddle suits. Admitted to the Louisiana bar in 1927, my father continued to work as a tailor until he got enough paying clients. It wasn't easy. He opened his first law office in 1930, when almost everybody was dead broke. Few of his clients could pay. He never cared about money, but my mother did. She took in boarders and complained about my father's generosity.

My mother told me she married him to escape from Donaldsonville, where there weren't many Jewish men to court her, and move to New Orleans. But she quickly came to love my father. Her love for him was fueled first by compassion and then respect for his courage and integrity. He was several inches shorter than she was, and she called him "Little Man" with fondness, not contempt.

My mother circa 1935

She was beautiful, intelligent, talented, and ambitious. She came of age during the 1920s and considered herself a flapper. Flapper women defied their place in society by smoking, drinking, driving cars, and flirting. Not exactly revolutionary feminism, but my mother never believed in male superiority. She tried to teach me to adjust to it but failed miserably.

My mother had a strong aesthetic sense, mainly for poetry and nature. She taught me to love poetry, too, by reading some of the world's greatest poems to me. One of her favorite poems was "Yet I Do Marvel" by Countee Cullen, the African American poet of the Harlem Renaissance of the 1920s. It was his reproach to God:

> I doubt not God is good, well-meaning, kind
> And did He stoop to quibble could tell why
> The little buried mole continues blind,
> Why flesh that mirrors Him must someday die,
> Make plain the reason tortured Tantalus
> Is baited by the fickle fruit, declare
> If merely brute caprice dooms Sisyphus
> To struggle up a never-ending stair.
> Inscrutable His ways are, and immune
> To catechism by a mind too strewn
> With petty cares to slightly understand
> What awful brain compels His awful hand.
> Yet do I marvel at this curious thing:
> To make a poet Black, and bid him sing.

I think she identified with this poem because her own talents were ignored, and she was squeezed into a role she deeply resented and could never escape.

My father didn't love nature and poetry the way my mother and I did. His aesthetic taste focused mostly on music: the light classics. He taught himself how to play the violin and bought 78 rpm phonograph records. I still remember hearing Stephen Foster songs and recognizing that they were obviously stolen from slave songs. For example, "Old Folks at Home" begins, "Way down upon the Swanee River," and is assumed to be about enslaved people missing their old beloved former masters. But the song is about self-liberated enslaved people living in the intractable runaway slave communities located in the swamps along that river. My mother, for her part, bought scratchy Bessie Smith records. We listened to them without understanding their sexual meanings. We didn't know what "You've Got to Give Me Some" and "I'm Wild About That Thing" meant, but we enjoyed the songs anyway.

So we grew up with African American music. And we became emotionally creolized by Native American culture, too. Razele used to say our mother hardly raised us, and it was Suzie who "grewed us up." Suzie worked in our home: an Afro-Creole who may have also been Native American. She wore her thick hair in two long braids down her back. An excellent cook and pastry chef, she enlisted our help when she baked cakes and let us lick the pots, spoons, and bowls. She cleaned the house, washed and ironed, dressed us, played with us, and told us fascinating stories about spirits lurking in the trees.

Although I never was obedient, I was still my mother's favorite child. She used to say about me, "The tongue always goes to the aching tooth." That image of me did not begin to fade from her mind until shortly before she died, when I at last got serious recognition for my creative work.

My father adored my mother. He couldn't believe he was lucky enough to marry such a beautiful, desirable woman. He defended her no matter what she did, even though there was a deep cruel streak in her. Her keen perception of emotions guided her vicious, biting tongue. Sometimes she could be exceptionally compassionate, empathetic, kind, supportive, and comforting. But not to her children or her sister, our little aunt Dotsey, who was a year younger than my sister Razele and like a sister to us. My mother only comforted men, maybe because she thought they were the weaker sex.

She was always extremely acquisitive: the exact opposite of my father, who gave away everything he owned. He never wanted to accumulate money or buy consumer goods. She reviewed all his checking accounts and never let him carry money on him because he would give it all away. Long after I was grown, he had to ask me for a nickel to buy a newspaper. But my mother insisted on investing in real estate. His ultimate excuse for her was that she'd had a hard life. It was true. She was the oldest child, female, and responsible for her eight younger siblings, only three of whom survived childhood. Unlike my father, who was too young to remember his dead siblings, all of my mother's remained vivid in her memory. I remember one of them well: her sister Ester Ada. She used to visit us regularly, and we were excited every time she came because she read *Grimm's Fairy Tales* to us and told us stories she had made up herself. She died suddenly when she was only thirteen, and no one could figure out why. There were so many funerals in my mother's family that she cried when she saw cut flowers. She became overprotective of her own children. We were not allowed to leave the house without her or cross a driveway, much less a street, by ourselves. Children who wanted to play with us had to come to our house and stay in our fenced yard.

My parents could not understand or appreciate each other's best qualities. I used to think they were so different that they killed the best in each other. But they controlled the worst in each other, too. My father had fits of rage that would sometimes turn violent. He was in his worst state when he came home from work. My mother took care of that. One night, he deliberately broke a plate on the dining room table. My mother told us, "Kids, go down in the basement." Then she proceeded to break every dish and glass in the dining room, yelling at him, "You think you can break plates? I can break plates, too!" That was the last time I ever saw him deliberately break anything.

She supported and participated in his dangerous fights for justice. But she wanted more attention from him and control over his time. Men-only weekend fishing trips were intolerable to her. She put a stop to that by buying several lots at Henderson Point near the St. Louis Bay Bridge, east of New Orleans in Mississippi, and building a house that overlooked the bay. We caught crabs in nets hanging off the pier in front of the house, and she boiled them in hot Louisiana sauce. My father stored his skiff and outboard motor on the pier and went fishing out in the Gulf of Mexico. He took me with him for the first time when I was about ten years old. The first fish I ever caught was a hammerhead shark: the typical story of my life.

This was one of the places we went in the summers, when everyone who could do so relocated to a cooler place. When I was seven years old, we stayed for a few weeks at Aunt Becky Samuelson Wolfson's summer house in Covington in St. Tammany Parish on the north shore of Lake Pontchartrain. Later, my parents bought four acres along the Bogue Falaya River near Covington and built a house near the river bluff.

My parents on our beach at the Bogue Falaya River, about 1937

Until then I had been sick often throughout my young life. My mother told me she could only afford to eat bread and onions when she was pregnant with me, and that's probably why I was fragile, undernourished, and often so nauseated I could hardly keep food down. When we stayed in Covington, I started getting better. The gurgling sulfur waters of the Bogue Falaya and its clean, sandy beaches, the sound and smell of the pines, the gorgeous singing birds, the scurrying wild critters, the red clay bluffs, and the sprawling oak trees hung with Spanish moss were all enchanting. We children sang "Go Down Moses," "Swing Low, Sweet Chariot," and other African-American spirituals with obvious revolutionary messages while swinging on oak tree branches.

The forest was magic. It took me into another world. I didn't put on shoes or comb my hair all summer, and I walked barefoot in the woods, carrying a stick to ward off the poisonous snakes. I was proud that my feet got so tough I could walk barefoot on oyster-shell roads without pain. My mother's brother, my uncle Hymie, was the closest thing I had to a brother. He was a civil engineering student at Louisiana State University. Uncle Hymie had dammed the river to make a swimming hole. At night he built outdoor fires for us to sit around and sing, tell stories, and watch the stars. He taught us the constellations and the myths behind them. I fell in love with the pine forest, its rivers, creeks, and gullies, and the critters who made their homes there. The forest saved my life and health. Except for osteoarthritis, I've been strong and healthy during most of the rest of my long life. Why? Because I have always tried to escape from smoky, polluted cities to spend as much time as I could in the forests. I also credit swimming.

Sadly, my mother sold our paradise in the pine forest for money to invest in real estate in New Orleans.

~

When I was eight years old, my parents left me to watch my three-year-old sister, Lita, while they were building our house along the Bogue Falaya. We saw a dog in the distance. Lita got frightened and wanted to run away. I told her not to run and that the dog would not hurt her. It ran up to me, stood up against me, and licked my hands. Then it ran up to Lita and stood up against her, but she was tiny and was knocked down. She ended up facedown on the ground. I thought the dog was licking her face. I called for help, and the dog ran away. Lita's face and eye were scratched—I thought it was because she hit something on the ground when she fell, but everyone else thought the dog attacked her. We rushed her to Charity Hospital in New Orleans. Her wounds were treated and bandaged, and she was discharged and sent home. Over several weeks, I was taken to the hospital to get a series of anti-rabies shots in my stomach.

On my way home from school, I bought little presents for her every day from a little corner grocery store. But she was only home for a little before she went back in the hospital. One day, I bought her some wax lips. I went to the hospital to see her and give her the present, but my mother chased me away. A few days later, all the adults went out without telling any of us children where they were going or why. My sister Razele later told us that Lita was dead, and the adults had gone to her funeral. I left the wax lips on the marble top of my little antique chest of drawers for months.

No one ever talked to us about Lita's death. I tried to bring it up once to my aunt Mena, but she said disapprovingly, "We don't talk about that." Was it a Yiddish fear of drawing the evil eye if we talked about the dead? Or was that how death was dealt with in those days? I was overcome by guilt because I was supposed to be taking care of her. She wanted to run away from the dog, and I told her not to.

I was told that Lita died of rabies and the vaccine had not worked. Many years later, my mother finally told me what really happened. We children had been cared for by Dr. Maude Loeber. My mother was fascinated by medicine and preoccupied with the health of her children because of the deaths of her siblings. Dr. Loeber diagnosed us with all kinds of illnesses we probably never had. She insisted that we both get rabies shots—even though the dog had never been found, there was no proof the dog was rabid, and I kept trying to tell everyone the dog had licked my hands and not attacked me or, so I believed, my sister. No one paid any attention to me. Years later, my mother told me that another doctor had argued that we should not be given the vaccine; it was too potent and dangerous, especially for a three-year-old. Dr. Loeber and the other doctor had a tremendous argument in front of my mother. She had to choose, and she made the wrong choice. She knew it but could not admit it to herself or to me at the time.

Above: Me in the middle holding up my little sister Lita, Aunt Dotsey on the left, sister Razele on the right. Left: Lita with our pregnant mother, 1937. Below: Lita and Dad in Dugas-LeBlanc cane field, 1937, happier days.

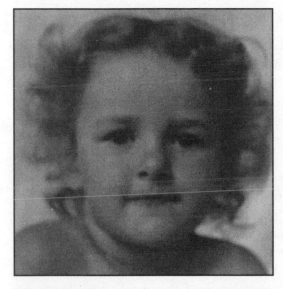

My sister Lita

My family's emotional equilibrium was shattered by Lita's death. My father was mute for several weeks. My mother became emotionally detached and lost most of the qualities I admired, like her love of nature, song, and poetry. Her fourth child, their first boy, was born dead shortly before Lita died. This stillbirth, followed by Lita's death, was more than she could bear.

Over the years, my parents' relationship evolved into undying devotion. She dominated him and enjoyed her prestige and power as his wife. They were proud of their financial success. I think it was their compassion for each other that brought them together the most. They shared in the love of their children and my sister's children, though not mine, as I was to learn later.

My parents in 1975

Growing Up as a Woman in a Patriarchal Society

Women and girls were treated with undisguised contempt in the Jewish community, including the little girls by little boys. To this day, I have no taste for ritual, perhaps because women and girls were not allowed to participate when I was growing up. We were hidden behind a curtain upstairs and could only sneak peeks at what the men performed below. I did always enjoy the music, with its pitches that wandered in, out, and around the whole tones.

At social gatherings, women were expected to converse among themselves and dared not participate in the important male conversations, which my mother called "man talk." She sometimes shocked the family by participating in this "man talk." What she said was always much more insightful than what any of the men said. Intelligent, ambitious, and independent-minded, she longed for a life of her own. Although she was fascinated by science and medicine, my father would not allow her to break out of her purely domestic role even to take a single course.

In her way, my mother taught me a lot about feminism, or at least feminist attitudes. She never believed in the myths of male superiority. When repairmen came to fix things in the house, she watched what they did and learned how to do plumbing, carpentry, and appliance repair. She got so good that my father began to believe she could fix anything. She became a self-taught contractor and learned how to build houses. When my parents built their home in the woods, my mother was the contractor, and she told the workers where to put the nails.

Although Yiddish culture was officially patriarchal, power relationships were not so clear in my family. My monolingual, Yiddish-speaking great-grandma, Ida Babetch, was the matriarch of my mother's family. The women, not the men, made the decisions. She worked all her life as a masseuse in a Yiddish sweat bath (*schvitz bud*) in Chicago, supporting her sick husband until he died young, and then single-handedly raising their children. She earned the money, controlled the family finances, and ruled her family with an iron hand, even from a distance—or at least she tried to. I remember her still working in the sweat bath when she was quite old. The family believed she had the gift of prophecy. When she predicted something bad would happen to someone, everyone winced. Every time she went back to Chicago after she visited us, she wept inconsolably and said—in Yiddish, of course—that we would never see each other again. About that she was no prophetess.

Four generations of my family in 1929. My great-grandmother, grandmother, mother (pregnant with me), and my sister, Razele.

Aunt Becky was the matriarch of the Samuelson family. The oldest sibling, she had the most money by far. She lived in New Orleans in one of the biggest, best-furnished, and most extravagant of the several homes she owned. With money she made in real estate, she financed her brothers' businesses and bossed them around shamelessly. Maybe she knew more about business than they did, but I think she was just tougher and they were more soft-hearted.

My mother passed on to me the wisdom about sex she received from my paternal grandmother, who supposedly told her, "If I had a basket under my bed, I could have anything I want." What she meant was that by withholding sex, she could force her husband to give her anything she wanted. I rejected this advice, along with all the other so-called wisdom I received about the role of women.

In this little world in which I grew up, women existed to serve men in every way. Men could play around; women had to be chaste or they were "ruined." Violence against women, especially husbands beating wives, was common. It was whispered about, but nobody talked about it openly or ever did anything about it. I could never accept that. When I was sixteen, a pregnant older cousin told me her husband was beating her severely because he believed the child wasn't his. I told her she shouldn't tolerate it, no matter how crazy he was or how sorry she felt for him. She divorced him and then married another man. I met her daughter from her first marriage many years later at a family reunion. She told me that her mother had mentioned the good advice I had given.

My experience with men was different. All the important men in my life were unstable in some way, but no man ever laid a hand on me, except for my father. I finally learned that men were attracted to me in part because I calmed them down. I was attracted to them because they had big problems but were basically good and talented people with a lot to offer the world. If I could live my life over, I would choose more stable men and put myself first, because I have a lot to offer the world, too. That's an important side of life I sometimes regret giving up.

My parents had no aspirations for me except that I should become the wife of a Jewish professional, at best, or at least the wife of a small businessman. My father said it might be a good idea for me to become a teacher or a librarian in case I didn't manage to get a husband. My mother's attitude was deeply influenced by her experience of growing up in the South. She had more than a little bit of southern belle in her. Girls were supposed to dazzle. The more suitors they had, the better. Sex was a weapon that women used to control men. A girl was supposed to be seductive but never have sex—even with her husband, except to get what she wanted from him.

My mother's most chilling advice was "Never let the boy know you are smarter than he is." I could not imagine being subjected to the personal whims and tyranny of a husband upon whom I was financially dependent, while trying to conceal my intelligence to avoid offending him. Becoming the wife of a Jewish professional or businessman was unthinkable to me. I wanted to be self-supporting so I would not have to depend on a husband or on my father. This meant taking economic responsibility for myself, although I was well aware that professional opportunities for women were almost nonexistent.

I turned fifteen in June 1944. We were staying at my parents' vacation home in Henderson Point, on the Mississippi Gulf Coast. My aunt Dotsey and my sister Razele would go to Gulfport to see popular movies. I refused to go with them. I was spending all my time practicing classical piano, reading Tolstoy's *War and Peace* (which took me all summer), and teaching myself Latin grammar, just for fun. Not a good girl, certainly not marriageable—I wasn't going to play dumb.

After we returned to New Orleans in the fall, my alarmed mother took me to the Child Guidance Center. The psychologist there was the first and last mental health professional I ever consulted with—the Freudian views of women, which prevailed for decades, horrified me. But this particular therapist helped me a lot. I was finally able to talk to someone about my sister Lita's death. He told me it was not my fault, and he treated my mind with respect.

When he told me he had done all he could for me, his parting words were "Always remember: you can achieve whatever you set out to do in life." I did always remember what he said, though I didn't believe him. But it turned out he was right.

Life on Rampart Street and the World around Us

Jazz and rhythm and blues were born, flourished, and evolved in New Orleans, on South Rampart Street, where the Jewish tailors lived. It was the shopping center for African Americans in New Orleans and beyond. The latest jazz, rhythm and blues, and Cuban music blared from loudspeakers into the street from all the stores. Everyone walking down the street rocked to the same rhythm.

Yiddish and Afro-Creole music shared a lack of attachment to the classic pentatonic scale, instead moving freely within the whole tones. But the greatest influence of Yiddish music and culture on early jazz came through Louis Armstrong. In his final memoir, written shortly before he died, he wrote that the Yiddish Karnofsky family employed him when he was a young child and helped him get his first horn. Armstrong always wore a Star of David around his neck to honor his Jewish family. He spoke fluent Yiddish and kept a mezuzah on his door.[5] He learned "Russian Lullaby" from the Karnofsky family and made it one of his earliest featured songs. The moving final verse is:

> Rock-a-bye my baby
> Somewhere there may be
> A land that's free for you and me
> And a Russian lullaby

Irving Berlin copyrighted Armstrong's version in 1927 and claimed it as his own. Ella Fitzgerald and other stars sang it over the years. My mother sang it to us, too.

In the Jim Crow South, Black people were not allowed to shop in stores where white people bought clothes: *What if some [n-word] tried the clothes on first?* Indeed, few whites were willing to touch African American men to measure them for suits. The Jewish tailors did not share this prejudice. South Rampart Street became the main place where African American men shopped for clothes, and they had expensive taste.

Jewish tailors, including both my father's and my mother's extended families, carved out a niche of semiautonomous existence by catering mainly to appreciative Black customers. In the 500 block of Rampart Street, every tailor shop belonged to a different member of my paternal or maternal family. Samuelson tailor shops and clothing stores spread to Beaumont, Houston, Austin, and Waco in Texas, and to Little Rock, Arkansas, and Jacksonville, Florida.

Most of the first-generation Jewish immigrants were, like my father and his siblings, refugees from ghettoes, pogroms, poverty, and hunger. They treated their Black customers with respect, took pride in their work, didn't cheat, and resisted anti-Black racism. They had carved out enough economic autonomy to resist pressure to make them conform entirely. They owned their businesses and the buildings where they lived and worked, and they did their own work so they didn't have to meet a payroll. Jews looked out for each other and didn't need to borrow money from outsiders.

Aunt Mena and her husband, Uncle Meyer Mendelvitz, lived modestly above their store. In the back they had a typical New Orleans tropical brick patio with bamboo, plantain trees, elephant ears, tropical flowers, fig trees, and pomegranate bushes. For Passover, Aunt Mena cooked and served sumptuous meals with much ritual. I enjoyed the rich food and sweet wine. Most of all, I loved the stories about Moses leading the children of Israel out of slavery in Egypt to the promised land, a story that had helped inspire the powerful African American culture of resistance around us, in spirituals such as "Go Down Moses." Louis Armstrong's version stresses how Moses led the Jews to the promised land with much miraculous help from the Lord.

My father's family firmly resisted racism, but this was less true of some of my mother's family. Grandpa Sam and his brother Mitchell owned National Tailors on South Rampart Street. They hired both Black and white workers to sew the suits, but Uncle Mitchell boasted to me that he segregated the workers in the shop. I saw their salesmen humiliating their customers into buying suits and bragging about how they cheated them.

But I was involved in one incident that showed the depth of fellow feeling among these southern Jews. A young Black man came running into National Tailors with the police in hot pursuit. The salesmen hid him in the dressing room until they decided it was not safe enough, so they led him into a courtyard and placed a ladder against the wall so he could climb into a vacant apartment on the second floor. The police came running in, looked around the dressing room, then left. A salesman gave me an empty suit box to take to the young man. He trembled all over when he saw me. I slowly handed him the suit box, and he understood that I had brought it to help him. He waited a little while, then went downstairs and walked calmly down South Rampart Street, carrying the suit box. No one knew what this young man had done, if anything. But we all knew he would have been beaten to a pulp if the police caught him. All of us helped him, no questions asked.

Still, this fellow feeling had its limits. The majority of southern Jews, with the exception of some recent immigrants, feared rocking the boat. They believed that if it weren't for Black oppression, white racist rage would be directed against them. This led many New Orleans Jews to accept racist beliefs, act in openly racist ways, and put strong pressure on other Jews to conform, or at least keep their mouths shut. They absorbed the prevailing ideology, and some of them profited from anti-Black exploitation and repression.

So was my family unique among Jews in opposing the racist oppression of Blacks in the Deep South? No, indeed. But many of those who did were Communists or members of the Jewish Workmen's Circle, which helped fund Black liberation and Communist organizers throughout the South during the early 1930s. Even my maternal Grandpa Sam was proud of me for helping African Americans vote in New Orleans. Both my parents and maternal grandparents sat in the front row of an integrated "Henry Wallace for President" meeting in New Orleans in 1948.

Mutual support among Jews and southern Blacks remains part of the silenced history of the long Civil Rights Movement. Parallels between the situation of African Americans in the United States and Jews in Eastern Europe have long been embedded in the language: the terms ghetto, pogrom, diaspora, and Sanhedrin, for example, are shared in both cultures.

~

On weekends, we visited Assumption Parish, in the heart of sugar country. It was a world unto itself. Before World War II, not many people there spoke English. Those who did had such thick accents that we could hardly understand them. It was a sliding scale of Afro-Creole and Cadjun, with a little bit of English thrown in.

To get there, we rode in our open Model A Ford over a dirt road along the west bank of the Mississippi River, with its huge old plantation homes. We were covered with mud when it rained and with dust when it was dry. Along the way, there was a store in the town of Thibodaux where we always stopped for their delicious homemade ice cream. Decades later, I learned that unarmed striking sugar cane workers had been massacred there by union-busting gunmen in 1887. It was the second-most deadly strike massacre in the history of the United States. Few remember it now.

We went to Assumption Parish to visit Jamelia, who had been my mother's closest friend since they both were three years old in Donaldsonville. We called her Jim. She came from a large, poor, Syrian Catholic family. When she was fifteen, she married Charles Dugas, a rich sugar planter in his fifties, who divorced his wife to marry Jim. She was sure the old man was about to die of old age and sometimes expressed her impatience for this terminal event. Sadly for her, he lived for thirty more years, usually in a drunken stupor after downing several bottles of wine.

Me and my sister, Razele, in Dugas-LeBlanc sugar cane field, 1937

He owned the Dugas-LeBlanc sugar plantation in Paincourtville, which means "shortbread town." The work in the fields was done much as it had been a century before. Once the grinding season started, activities reached a frenzied pitch. They had to harvest and mill the entire crop before the first frost ruined it. The heavy, sticky cane stalks were cut by hand with machetes, piled on ox carts or private railroad cars, and transported to the sugar mill. After being weighed, the cane was hand-fed into huge, dangerous metal grinders to squeeze out the juice, which was then processed in sprawling, connected copper pans and vats. Walkways spiraled around inside the mill. The heat was unbearable.

Women cutting sugarcane in Baton Rouge, Louisiana

The large, overwhelmingly Black labor force lived on the Louisiana sugar plantations. The workers had to buy whatever they needed at the company store, using the plantation's script, which they received instead of wages. They were, of course, overcharged and forced deep into debt, and they couldn't move away until all their debts were paid—one of our country's several versions of forced labor. Black sugar workers were treated worse than livestock. Charles Dugas once explained to us why he refused to send for a doctor when an old Black man who had worked for him all his life became sick. "I'd send for a doctor for my mule," he said, "because he's still useful. But that old [n-word] will never work again."

Sugar country was a violent world. On our weekend trips, we would hear excited gossip about gambling, whoring, and the latest lynching. I remember a story about a white man who was hanged from a bridge, mutilated and castrated, for having sexual relations with a Black woman. Surely this act was not out of respect for the Black female body. My guess is that the woman was considered the property of the wrong, powerful white man.

The poor white people were mostly Cadjuns. By the time the women were thirty, they were already aged, wrinkled, and emaciated. When rural areas were deliberately flooded to save New Orleans during a hurricane in 1947, many rural poor whites took refuge in the city. They were so emaciated they looked like concentration camp victims.

My mother's friend Jim gave birth to one child, a boy named Felix, whose nickname was Cutsie. His every whim was immediately indulged. He was allowed to drive a car off-road around the plantation when he was six years old, and everybody had to scurry out of his way. He bossed everyone in sight, regardless of color, age, or gender. After he grew up, his willfulness led him to crime, and he was arrested for robbing a bank in the Midwest. When Cutsie's parents showed up to talk to the judge, he warned them not to try to bribe him, or he would file a complaint and their son's sentence would be more severe. The Dugases were amazed. They were used to dealing with judges they owned.

Cutsie spent several years in prison. In 1953, after he got out, he helped organize thousands of eager sugar workers, including those on his father's plantation, into the National Agricultural Workers Union of the American Federation of Labor (AFL)—and they struck. The strike failed after the bosses brought in scabs from Florida, Mississippi, and Alabama, cut off the strikers' water and electricity, evicted them from their company-owned homes, and engaged in the anti-labor violence and terror typical of Louisiana. During the strike, Cutsie came to see me in New York City. He knew I was a Communist, and by asking for my help, he was making an appeal to the Communist Party to help the strike. That was a bold action in 1953, but sadly, there was nothing I could do.[6]

Sugar Strike Spreads Wider

RESERVE, La. ⒨ — The three-day old strike by Louisiana sugar cane field workers, threatening to cripple the state's vast sugar industry, has spread to four new companies and now includes 1,600 workers.

Hank Hasiwar of Garyville, president of the National Agricultural Workers Union (AFL), said yesterday the new companies affected are:

Uncle Sam, Mt. Airy and Grammercy; Duga and LeBlanc, Paincourtville; Caldwell Sugars, Thibodaux; and Armelise Planting Co., Paincourtville.

Hasiwar said these companies, in addition to four others previously reported affected by the strike, own about 55 plantations.

Since the start of the strike, Hasiwar said, the strike-bound companies have served 4 notices of eviction on "key union personnel" living on various plantations. Hasiwar flatly denied reports by company officials that some of the strikers have returned to work. He sid the basis for this report was the importation of workers from Florida, Alabama and Mississippi by one of the companies.

The basic region for the strike, Hasiwar said, is that the companies failed to recognize the union and grant a union contract. He said the strikers are members of the 2,000-member Local 317 of the NAWU.

In Washington, Atty. Gen. Brownell has been asked to investigate alleged violations of civil liberties of striking workers in Assumption Parish.

H. L. Mitchell, president of the NAWU, told Brownell in a telegram he had information that "armed strike breakers and plantation foremen deputized by the sheriff of Assumption Parish were invading workers' homes and using force and violence in an effort to drive striking workers back to the sugar cane fields."

Mitchell said sugar corporation officials had shut off the water supply of workers, cut gas and electric linee and "used e v e r y method they can think of to drive their employes back to the fields."

Hasiwar said no negotiations are being held. He added that the union is' not engaged in picketing.

The Town Talk, October 15, 1953

Years later, as I studied documents about Africans who had been kidnapped, enchained, beaten, raped, starved, dehydrated, and shipped across the Atlantic, packed together like sardines, to be sold to work the sugar plantations of the Americas, I had a good idea of what their work was like. I heard the loud bell waking them up to go to work long before dawn and saw the white overseers riding their horses around the fields, waving long, vicious whips.

PART TWO

A REVOLUTIONARY
IN THE DEEP SOUTH

When I was an adolescent, I made frequent visits to the main branch of the New Orleans Public Library, at Lee Circle. I had to walk under a huge statue of Robert E. Lee on a sixty-foot-high pedestal. It was a potent symbol of the crude sexism, racism, and glorification of the Confederacy I was taught from elementary school through high school and Tulane University.

I was aware of the wide gap between the myths and the realities of the white supremacist world and how shallowly white people felt and how little they perceived. Black folks perceived much more and felt deeply. They had to know the reality and the truth or they would not survive.

White racist thought was more open, crude, and ridiculous then. Most southern whites were poor and oppressed, and racism hurt them badly by keeping all poor people down, divided, and terrorized. But that's what white people were taught in school, on the radio, at the movies, and in newspapers and magazines. If they challenged this bloody, exploitative, terroristic ideology, they were considered dangerous white agitators and driven out. They could never get hired or hold a job or get credit to buy furniture, a car, a business, or a home. They were threatened with violence, and some were murdered.

No one said "Black people" or "African Americans" then. The only polite words were "coloreds" or "negroes," written in lower case, but few white people used these polite words. The ["n-word"]s were considered mentally inferior and could not and should not be educated or trained, except to perform menial tasks. Supposedly they did not have the same sensitivity as white people, so—it was assumed—they were less affected by mistreatment. The alleged proof was that Black people did not resist being mistreated. *Really?*

The Robert E. Lee statue I had to live with growing up, finally coming down in 2017.

Denial was a powerful factor in maintaining white racism. White people did not want to know the depths of Black oppression enforced by terror. They didn't want to hear or talk about lynching, forced labor, and police brutality. But once racial segregation was ended, some of the same people who had once accepted the most absurd racist beliefs seemed to be relieved later on that they no longer had to believe what they were required to before. At least, that's what they told me.

I had this dangerous habit of thinking, and I never thought the way other people did. Besides the influence of my Yiddish, socialist, internationalist family, I was born with a powerful memory and a mind that never allowed me to adjust to the culture or subculture I found myself in. I still remember vividly perceiving, even as a tiny child, the vast gap between what people said and what they felt. I deeply resented the insincere, condescending way adults spoke to little children.

The first time I got into trouble for thinking in school was in seventh grade. My teacher was talking about the Spanish–American War: how terrible it was that Spain had an empire and how good it was of us to take it away. I spoke up in class and said that if it was wrong for Spain to have an empire, it was wrong for us to have one, too.

My teacher said, "Oh, Gwendolyn! And I always thought you were a good girl!"

I wasn't. I never was. My earliest memories were of rejecting my assigned gender role. I carried my feminism to extremes. I did not have dolls, nor would I accept them as presents, and I refused to play with them. I would not babysit for the children of my parents' visiting friends, protesting that I didn't know how. In elementary school, the girls studied domestic arts—how to wash dishes and sweep floors—while the boys went to shop class to learn skilled trades. I resented that. The only course I ever flunked was sewing, because I couldn't thread a needle, so I never finished the dress I was supposed to make.

As I got older, my perception of the unconscious feelings of others was diminished by socialization. But I was always driven to think my own thoughts and make my own decisions about what was true and what was right. I rarely believed something because I was supposed to believe it.

Racism was strongly reinforced in the schools at all levels. In my freshman year in high school, I found a map of the world in our history textbook. Western Europe and the United States were circled in white.

The rest of the world was shaded dark gray. The caption under the map said that the area in the white circle was the home of the "Great White Race," and this was the only race that had ever contributed anything to civilization. That's what we were being taught right in the middle of the war against the Nazis.

It wasn't just Louisiana and the South. Right after World War II, I was shocked to find busts of heads at the American Museum of Natural History in New York City that were arranged in a hierarchy of "superiority," with an ape at the lowest level, then a Black man, then an American Indian, an Asian, and a southern Mediterranean type, culminating at a white Greek Apollo.

Much teaching time in my schools was devoted to racist diatribes. They were usually directed against Black people, but sometimes against others, too. My sister's teacher once asked her to leave the classroom so the teacher could make antisemitic remarks. My teacher vilified Sicilians, who were a large immigrant group in New Orleans. She singled out a Sicilian boy in our class for persecution and praised the light-skinned, blue-eyed, Aryan northern Italians, who supposedly created the Roman Empire and other good things by themselves and were unrelated to the dark-skinned, dark-eyed, inferior Sicilians like Anthony.

Our textbook informed us that enslaved people at Pointe Coupée rose up in 1795 to seize and rape white women, so their heads were cut off and left on pikes along the Mississippi River to save the white race. After I became a historian, I researched and wrote about the Pointe Coupée Slave Conspiracy. It was very effectively organized by enslaved people of Louisiana of various origins: Africans of several ethnicities, Louisiana Creoles, Blacks, and mulattoes. The goal was to abolish slavery. White indentured servants, French soldiers and merchant seamen, teachers and tailors, and free people of color supported it. The enslaved conspirators were well informed about the Haitian Revolution of 1791, when enslaved Hatians rose up and abolished slavery—which was followed by the abolition of slavery in all French colonies by the revolutionary French National Assembly in 1794. The Pointe Coupée rebels thought they had been freed, too, and sent messengers to New Orleans to see if it was true. The conspiracy was nothing like what Louisiana historians wrote about it for generations and what my teachers and textbooks said about it.

Things only got worse for me when I started attending Eleanor McMain High School for White Girls. I had entered adolescence and stopped keeping my mouth shut. Our English teacher, Miss Breading, spent hours talking about how kind her slave master ancestors had been to their simple "darkies," who loved them and enjoyed slavery. Robert E. Lee was her greatest hero.

During one of her racist diatribes, I started staring at her in disgust. She stared back at me and got worse and worse. She finally came out with her key argument: "Yankees say [n-word]s are just as good as white people, but I always say, 'Would you want your daughter to marry one?'" I continued to stare at her in disgust. She looked straight at me and asked, "If there is anyone in this classroom who would marry one, please stand up." I stood up. That settled it. Gwendolyn was not a good girl!

We were taught to be narrow-minded and prudish as well as racist. Our English teacher asked each of us to bring a book to class so we could read at our desks and not bother her. I brought *You and Heredity* by Aram Scheinfeld, a Book of the Month Club selection in 1939. My teacher prowled down the aisle, grabbed the book away from me, and said, "Gwendolyn, let me have that!" She phoned my mother and told her to come in to see her because she had caught me reading obscene literature. When my mother came to the school, my teacher opened the book to a line drawing of a sperm cell fertilizing an egg cell. She asked my mother gleefully, "Now, why would a thirteen-year-old girl be interested in *that*?"

After a few more calls from a few more of my teachers for similar reasons, my mother decided I was in the wrong school. For my sophomore year of high school, my parents sent me to Isidore Newman School, the most elite private school in New Orleans. One thing I enjoyed there was singing—early English madrigals in the school choir and in the chorus of our production of Gilbert and Sullivan's *The Pirates of Penzance*. At least I learned something: English composition. Our biology teacher spent class time disparaging Black folks, but in a somewhat more polite, detached manner. And she actually spent some of her time teaching biology. My math teacher didn't just give us problems to solve but showed us how to use math principles to solve them. Although I thought I was bad in math, I liked his classes.

By the time I was fourteen, I was reading great literature, including Charles Dickens, Mark Twain, and translations of Russian novels: most of Dostoyevsky and much of Tolstoy. When I submitted a book report on Dostoyevsky's *Crime and Punishment*, my English teacher told me I should read *Little Women* instead. I was insulted, so I never read that book.

When I was fifteen, I applied for a two-year program at the University of Chicago, which offered college-level courses for talented high school students. I took the College Board standardized entrance exam along with eighteen-year-olds from all over the country. C. C. Henson, my school's principal, called me into his office and told me I got the third-highest grade in the country in reading comprehension. Then I researched and wrote a long unsolicited research paper about Black disenfranchisement in the South, which my teacher passed on to Henson. He returned it to me without saying a word, but with an admiring though apprehensive smile. I think he had decided I had extraordinary ability but was unable to convey this to me or to anyone else. The University of Chicago did not admit me, probably because I was a girl. Even if they had, my mother would not have let me go. Because of my outstanding scores on the College Board exams, the administration at Newman School decided my academic program was too thin. So they sent me to the YWCA every afternoon to learn cooking and hat making. I never learned how to cook or make hats.

I was socially maladjusted—a great crime in those days. I refused to wear sneakers and bobby socks or the other volunteer uniforms of adolescent girls of the times. I wore my clothes in disarray so I wouldn't attract attention from boys and have to deal with them. At Newman High School, there was a gentile sorority, a gentile fraternity, a Jewish sorority, and a Jewish fraternity. I was the only student who didn't belong to any of them. In fact, I hardly remember having a conversation with any of my fellow students.

The Coming of World War II

My generation lived through World War II, the most globalized, mechanized, destructive war in history, with widespread genocide motivated by racism. Those of us lucky enough to live in the United States were spared these horrors. But the world we grew up in and lived through was still terrifying.

When World War II broke out in Europe with the Nazi invasion of Poland on September 1, 1939, I was barely ten years old and only vaguely aware of world affairs. I did start to learn some world geography from paying attention to current events through radio and the movies. In our house and car, we listened to comedy shows like *The Jack Benny Program*, *The Burns and Allen Show*, and *Amos 'n' Andy*. We kids went to the movies every Friday night and watched cowboy films featuring Roy Rogers and the Lone Ranger, cartoons like Bugs Bunny, and kids' shows like *The Little Rascals*. Movietone News projected brief images of current events with little or no analysis or comment while we eagerly waited for the latest cowboy movie to start. Most radio commentators talked a lot about sex scandals among female Hollywood stars. I wasn't interested in that.

I was twelve years old when the Japanese bombed Pearl Harbor, on December 7, 1941. By then I knew a lot more. I had already read my father's copy of William L. Shirer's *Berlin Diary*, an informed and well-analyzed eyewitness account by one of our greatest foreign correspondents of the Nazis' rise in Germany, their horrible beliefs and barbaric practices. I took it with me wherever I went, including to elementary school.

After we entered World War II, radio broadcasts and news footage at the movies got a lot more interpretive but not very objective. Most of them glamorized warfare and glossed over the intense suffering and high casualty rate of our frontline troops. These films did not mention the Nazis' horrendous mass murder of the population on the Eastern Front, including Jews, Slavs, Roma (known as "Gypsies"), Soviet prisoners of war, and other "racial inferiors" (*Untermenschen*). Racial segregation in the US military, if mentioned at all, was presented as normal and proper. Sometimes US war films descended into crude, racist propaganda. The "Japs" were depicted as "little yellow men" who were sadistic, fanatical, and evil.

The US government did publish a pamphlet by the esteemed anthropologist Ruth Benedict, *The Races of Mankind*, intended for US troops, that specifically argued against racist ideas. But during the war the Nazis were largely given a pass on their mass murder of millions of innocent civilians and the deliberate genocide of the Jews of Germany, Poland, the Soviet Union, and all the many other countries the Nazis occupied.

I knew about the Nazi persecution of Jews but had no idea of the depths of depravity to which they sank. The Nazi drive for world conquest and domination was based on mass murder, massive theft, and ruthless exploitation of their remaining victims, who were worked to death while they starved. Not just Jews but millions of other innocent civilians were deliberately murdered by the Schutzstaffel (SS) and the Wehrmacht. The SS, a paramilitary unit, was initially in charge of shooting thousands of Jews and burying them in mass graves. But the psychological impact of carrying out these horrible deeds was too much for German troops. So Heinrich Himmler, the leader of the SS and overseer of the "Final Solution" to eliminate Europe's Jews and "undesirables," oversaw the creation of mechanized death camps to avoid demoralization in the armed forces and to quickly dispose of the bodies of those they killed. The Nazis murdered many millions of Jews, Communists, Soviet officials, dissidents and intellectuals, homosexuals, mentally ill and other sick and disabled people, Roma, Poles, Russians, Soviet prisoners of war, Polish and Jewish partisan fighters, and anyone who helped them. Winston Churchill and Franklin Delano Roosevelt knew all about it, but they neither said nor did anything. They even refused to bomb the death camp ovens or the trains leaving for Auschwitz.

I don't remember hearing from US news media about these Nazi atrocities during the war. The first news I had of the Holocaust was from the *USSR Information Bulletin*, published by the Soviet Embassy, which I received by mail as a member of the American-Soviet Friendship Committee. There was an article by Ilya Ehrenburg about the Nazi massacre at Babi Yar on the outskirts of Kiev. In September 1941, the Nazis and their Ukrainian allies forced 33,771 Jews into a deep gully and shot them to death. The few survivors of the shooting were buried alive along with the dead. That was only the first huge massacre at Babi Yar. Between a hundred thousand and a hundred fifty thousand people were murdered there during the Nazi occupation.[1] When I tried to talk about it, no one believed me because it wasn't reported in the US media.

Only one person in this photo of our family in Slonim survived the Holocaust.

Although I wasn't yet in my teens when the United States entered the war, I followed the news fanatically, especially of the war in Europe. The Nazis were clearly a bastion of racism, and I had no doubt that right was on our side. I listened to the radio and read the newspapers and magazines.

Shortly after we entered the war, in the US media, the Soviet Union was transformed from the Red Menace to Our Glorious Ally. Communists were considered brave, good people. Stalin was chosen Man of the Year by *TIME* magazine in both 1939 and 1942. After the Nazis invaded the Soviet Union in June 1941, they quickly conquered Belarus, Estonia, Latvia, Lithuania, all of Poland, the Ukraine, and the western part of the Soviet Union, coming within a few miles of Moscow. Mussolini's forces in Italy occupied Ethiopia, Trieste, Albania, Greece, and Yugoslavia, but Italian ground troops had little enthusiasm to kill or be killed and were considered unreliable. The Nazis, in contrast, had highly mechanized, seemingly unbeatable armed forces. Hungary, Romania, and Finland joined the Nazis and invaded the Soviet Union; Finland blockaded Leningrad (now St. Petersburg) from the north and helped starve to death about a million Soviet civilians. Before the Soviet Red

Army stopped them, it looked like the Nazis would win the war.

We who paid attention to the battles—and most of us did because we had close family members fighting overseas—knew that the Soviet Union did its best to avoid the war, then won it with great courage and determination but at a terrible cost. My generation remembers, and those still alive often have more positive views of communists, communism, and the Soviet Union than most radical leftists today.

The war in the Pacific was less clear to me. I did not know or care as much about Japanese conquests in Asia. The racist character of our anti-Japanese propaganda turned me off. Their reported atrocities were not as shocking to me as the atrocities I knew about in the Deep South, which few whites noticed, much less talked about. I was never convinced we had more right to own the Philippines than Spain or Japan did. Of course, the Philippines didn't want to be owned by anyone.

I later learned more about the war in the Pacific, including the official exclusion of Blacks from Australia heartily endorsed by General Douglas McArthur, when I edited and published a book of the diaries of my uncle, Captain Hyman Samuelson, written while he was stationed in the Pacific.[2] Uncle Hyman was one of the southern white officers in an all-Black construction battalion that was among the first to arrive in Australia and then New Guinea. After a long voyage across the Pacific, the Black troops weren't allowed to get off their ship. They were quickly sent to remote places in Australia and New Guinea. The white officers on leave in New Guinea could go to Australia, but not the Black troops. Australian women welcomed the Black troops, which enraged the white troops. The Black troops rose up time and again to protect themselves, but news of their rebellions was thoroughly repressed. My uncle quickly overcame his prejudice against Black people as he got to know his men and the harsh discrimination they suffered.

Me and Uncle Hymie at book signing, New Orleans, 1995.

Back in New Orleans, we feared bombings and invasions and participated in blackouts and air raid drills. Nothing happened. We were well
protected by the vast oceans separating us from Europe and Asia. My
father volunteered to be an air raid warden but was turned down as a security risk, probably because he defended CIO organizers, Communists,
and the civil and constitutional rights of the terrorized poor of all colors.
He was deeply hurt and indignant. My mother volunteered in a hospital
and made bandages for our wounded troops. We were encouraged to
grow vegetables in our yards in "victory gardens" and collect scrap metal
to melt down for arms and ammunition. Unfortunately, we were urged
to bring in our old metal phonograph records to melt down for scrap,
with the result that much of the earliest recorded music of New Orleans
was lost forever. We received ration cards, which gave us the right to buy
essential food items and a little gasoline. But toward the end of the war
there was nothing to buy, so if you wanted butter, meat, or gasoline, you
had to pay high prices on the black market.

For Poland And America; Refugee Here Piles Up An Enviable Record

By Marjorie Roehl

Warsaw is bloody and desolate and unbeaten.

Sosnowic of Silesia resounds to clumping German boots.

A little Polish Jewish couple left Germany to find a homeland here in America in 1914.

So Mrs. Meyer Mendelvitz has sold $112,000 in war bonds single-handed in two months, has knitted seven sweaters in four weeks, is working with flying fingers on 500 pairs of hospital slippers, and plans to toss off 100 sponges in the next three weeks.

Her reasons for her one-woman victory campaign were phrased a little differently. "I will tackle anything for a good cause," Mrs. Mendelvitz said with fire, "and this is for both my old and my adopted country. Our boys give their lives and this is so little."

Relatives Still There

Both Mr. and Mrs. Mendelvitz were born in Poland, she in Sosnowic, he in Warsaw. His three sisters are still there—or were when the Germans took over the country. No one has heard from them since, nor from the number of uncles and cousins Mrs. Mendelvitz has left in Poland.

Mrs. Mendelvitz was educated in Germany where she met Meyer, then a young man working for her father, she smiled shyly. "It was unpleasant for Jews in Germany even then," she sighed, "nothing like now, of course, but unpleasant. Meyer and I were married in London on the way to America in 1914. We wanted to come to Galveston, but we missed the boat. So we decided to take the next one and it came to New Orleans.

"We didn't know anyone but we both were willing to work and when he hadn't a job I got one." Now they own a neat little tailoring shop at 540 South Rampart street and live in an apartment above.

Mrs. Mendelvitz' first outstanding drive was made in 1939 when she turned over $250 in collections to the Red Cross. It was just before Christmas that she began to earn her reputation as the "bond marshal of Rampart street."

Brought $1000 Cash

"I started with relatives and the people next door," she said modestly, "and worked up to strangers." In the Carnival bond drive, she distributed 250 kits to stores for the American Women's Voluntary Services, of which she is

MRS. MEYER MENDELVITZ

also a super-active member.

"That woman walked on Carondelet and Baronne and Rampart, from Canal to Howard street," Mr. Mendelvitz beamed, with pride spilling over his smile. "And she says it was nothing. People come in now to bring her money. She has them trained."

There was the man who brought Mrs. Mendelvitz $1000 in cash one day for war bonds. The couple sat up all night watching their safe and resolved afterward that the

ly to headquarters. There was Mrs. Mendelvitz's butcher who brought in to the store $400 in one dollar bills and meekly asked that it be counted. There is the delicatessen store man and the one who deals in the nickel machines. There are the poor who bring her $2 a week for war stamps and the prosperous ones who bring in $750 weekly on bonds.

Husband Helps

There are the people to whom no one else has been able to . . . bonds. Mrs. Mende . . .

My aunt Mena
Midlo Mendelvitz

During the war, New Orleans became a major shipbuilding and repairing port. Higgins Shipyards, manufacturer of the Higgins boats used as landing crafts during D-Day, became one of the biggest industrial enterprises in the world, with upward of eighty thousand workers and government contracts worth nearly $350 million. Grain was shipped down the Mississippi River from the Midwest to help feed our soldiers and allied countries. The Port of New Orleans was the main source of gasoline and refined oil. Nazi submarines hovered in the Gulf of Mexico, their resident spies in New Orleans seeking information about when ships left and where they were going. Many of our tankers were torpedoed and sunk, especially during the early stages of the battle to control the Atlantic Ocean. Almost all the merchant seamen aboard were either burned to death or drowned. A famous World War II poster read "Loose Lips Sink Ships." Indeed they did.

As the young men departed for war and the port and its shipbuilding and repair industries boomed, we went quickly from massive unemployment to acute labor shortages. They got so severe in New Orleans that African American women were hired to drive streetcars and serve meals behind lunch counters in drugstores, places they were not otherwise permitted. However, racial discrimination persisted in the hiring for factories and skilled trades. White women were hired to work in factories; many did so only reluctantly and with the understanding that when the men came home from the war they would get their jobs back. Some whites were even brought in from rural areas to work in the factories, whereas African American workers, including highly skilled building tradesmen, had to move to California to get jobs in the aircraft and armaments industries.

The turning point in the war in Europe took place on the Eastern Front. Every day from August to December 1942, the press reported that Stalingrad had fallen to the Nazis or predicted it would fall that day. But it never fell. Red Army bunkers were attacked by Nazi artillery and planes, captured, then taken back by the Red Army. I didn't know until very recently that the Soviet Union defeated the Nazi invaders with a seemingly endless supply of superior tanks, artillery, aircraft, and handheld automatic rifles produced beyond the Ural Mountains in cities in Siberia, outside the range of Nazi aircraft. Certainly I didn't learn that from reading the newspapers and listening to the radio at the time. After Stalingrad was reduced to a pile of rubble, the Red Army encircled and smashed several *Wehrmacht* armies. It took two more years of bitter fighting to drive the Nazis out of Russia and Ukraine, pursue them across Eastern Europe, and finally capture Berlin.

Red Army troops raise the Red Flag over the Reichstag in Berlin, May 1945. Original photograph by Yevgeny Khaldei.

Despite Hannah Arendt's baseless claims that they didn't, millions of Jews fought the Nazis. My cousin Danny Samuelson volunteered for the US Air Force. A tail gunner on flimsy B-17 bombers stationed in Britain, he miraculously survived thirty-five bombing missions over Germany and German-occupied countries in Western Europe. Danny recently told me he volunteered so he could take revenge against the Germans for what they did to the Jews. These were his thoughts and feelings every time his missions dropped their bombs over Germany.

Meeting the Communist Party

My first political activities were inspired by gratitude to the Soviet Union for stopping the Nazi invasion at Stalingrad. It was like waking up from a nightmare. I joined the American-Soviet Friendship Committee chapter in New Orleans. We agitated for the United States to open the second front in France. When Soviet ships docked in New Orleans, we entertained their officers and crew. I was deeply impressed upon meeting a Soviet woman ship captain when, at the time, it was inconceivable for a woman to hold such an authoritative job in the United States.

Ilya Ehrenburg's writings had an enormous impact on me. He and Vasily Grossman were great Jewish-Soviet writers who traveled with the Red Army as war correspondents. Grossman lost his beloved mother when the Nazis murdered all the Jews of Berdichev, where he was born. His novels are now esteemed throughout the world. Ehrenburg was an extraordinarily open-minded, courageous, prolific writer who deserves a lot more appreciation than he gets now. In his first novel, published in 1929, he predicted the Holocaust in great detail. He mentored good but controversial writers in the Soviet Union and was awarded a Stalin prize for his novel *The Fall of Paris*, published shortly after the Nazi invasion of the Soviet Union. Ehrenburg was admired and protected by Stalin, who considered his writings as a war correspondent worth several army divisions.

Both Grossman and Ehrenburg collected documents and interviewed survivors of the Holocaust, which they jointly edited into a book that they expected to publish in the USSR. But when the war ended, the Soviet Union chose to deny the specifically antisemitic crimes of the Holocaust, in part to avoid publicizing atrocities committed by Ukrainians, Lithuanians, Latvians, Poles, Romanians, Hungarians, or other citizens of the new Eastern Bloc nations allied with the USSR. Parts of the documentary account of the Holocaust were published in the United States and elsewhere shortly after the war, but the famous *Black Book of Soviet Jewry* went unpublished in Russia until 1980.[3]

I didn't learn much about the Soviet Union, socialism, or Marxism from my early political activities. What I learned, ironically enough, was to love my own country. There had been nothing in my childhood to make me patriotic. All I saw was blatant hypocrisy regarding our supposed freedom and democracy. I longed for a government to protect equality for all. Franklin Roosevelt was the only president I remembered, and he died when I was almost sixteen years old. It was his wife, Eleanor, who fought for racial equality. FDR's hands were tied by the political clout of the racist southern Democrats.

My new political life took me out of the social milieu of my age-group peers. I entered happily into a world of older, more intellectually sophisticated people. We met in various people's apartments, mainly in the French Quarter, to talk about politics, literature, and psychiatry, and to listen to records, including post-Baroque classical, jazz, blues, and folk. Josh White, Leadbelly, Woody Guthrie, Sonny Terry, Burl Ives, Richard Dyer-Bennet, and Paul Robeson were some of the artists I heard. My sister Razele and I became enthusiastic fans of left-wing folk singers. Woody Guthrie taught me to love the courageous, dauntless struggles of our working class. I learned more about US labor history from his songs than anywhere else. Paul Robeson taught me to love the international working class. Leadbelly taught me to love Black folk culture.

I started sitting alone on a bench in Jackson Square and talking to strangers, something I was forbidden to do. But I learned a lot about how other people lived and thought by punching my way out of the bubble of my protected middle-class world of left-wing intellectuals.

Most of my new friends were students at Tulane Medical School, which had lots of Jewish students, mostly from Brooklyn. Other medical schools had tiny quotas for Jews, but there was no quota at Tulane. Arthur Maisel and Stanley Orloff were studying neuroanatomy with my uncle, Dr. Charles Midlo. They were both nephews of Herbert Aptheker, the Communist historian. They spoke often and with great pride and respect about their Uncle Herbie. They were both aspiring psychiatrists enthusiastic about Freud. I borrowed their books about psychiatry and avidly read them. I still cringe at the thought of much of the content about women. The impact on my already shaky self-confidence and self-image was shattering. I came to fear a destructive, inferior, irrational female lurking deeply in my unconscious mind. When I finally became aware of my unconscious mind twenty years later, I was delighted to find that it was much more constructive and ethical than my conscious mind—and a lot more perceptive, smarter, better organized, and more creative.

From my friends I heard the latest line from the Communist Political Association, established in 1944 when the Communist Party was officially dissolved. The gist was that everything would be fine after the war, and social justice and democracy would triumph throughout the world without the need for class struggle. This problematic assumption that Communists would become integrated into mainstream political life after the war was the rationale for the party's dissolution into an association. One result was that the Communists abandoned their insistence that all organizations be interracial, as they explained, to avoid offending the sensibilities of white southerners. As I recall, the American-Soviet Friendship Committee in New Orleans was entirely white.

The New Orleans Youth Council

Early in the fall of 1945, shortly after World War II ended, I read an announcement in a New Orleans newspaper that an international youth delegation was returning from the founding conference of the United Nations in San Francisco. They were stopping in cities across the United States to organize a new international youth movement to promote the UN's aims, and I decided to go.

When I arrived at the meeting in New Orleans, everybody there was white. The organizers announced that they had met first with Black youth and then called this separate meeting for white youth. The Black youth then walked into the meeting in a group, sat down, and announced there would be no racially segregated youth movement in New Orleans, since that would be against the aims of the United Nations. I spoke up and, parroting the argument I had heard from promoters of the Communist Political Association, said that an interracial organization would be ineffective in the climate of the Deep South. Alvin B. Jones Jr., a handsome young African American man, looked at me and smiled warmly but with a gentle look of disbelief. I was delighted and shut up.

That was how the New Orleans Youth Council (NOYC) was born, which seems to have been the only interracial youth movement in the South. Alvin Jones and I became lifelong friends. At the time we met, he was organizing workers at Higgins Shipyard, dodging goon squads hired by the company to beat up labor organizers. We talked a lot. He told me about conditions in our racially segregated Black public schools: wood stoves for heat; leaking roofs; a few torn-up, leftover textbooks from the white schools. African Americans couldn't use any branch of the New Orleans Public Library except for the designated "Negro" branch, which hardly had any books.

To visit Alvin at his home I would walk through an uptown Black neighborhood. Alvin's father was a mailman—one of the highest-level jobs a Black man could aspire to at the time. He could not accept the idea that his son should have aspirations higher than his own and was abusive toward Alvin for not being satisfied with his lot. He had no idea about his son's amazing abilities. When Louisiana was forced to open a law school for African American students at Southern University in Baton Rouge, Alvin enrolled in its first class—five students, who met in a library. That was Louisiana's version of separate but equal. Alvin got his law degree, passed the bar, and opened a law office in the International Longshoremen's Association building in the 500 block of South Rampart Street.

The NOYC quickly became a large, active interracial movement, functioning as the youth arm of the CP. It functioned under various names for the next four years. We met as equals and actively fought racial discrimination, disenfranchisement, and segregation. We did not march or stage sit-ins. Enthusiastic and bold, we got on streetcars together, talking, joking, and laughing, all of us standing although there were lots of vacant seats. We picketed the downtown department stores with signs demanding that they let African Americans shop there. This led to the eventual ruin of the South Rampart and Dryades Streets clothing stores after the downtown stores relented. The NAACP Youth Council wanted to picket with us, but its parent organization would not allow it.

From the *Louisiana Weekly*, September 20, 1946.

New Orleans Youth Council Scores Fascism, Race Hate

By LUCIUS JONES

NEW ORLEANS—In one of the frankest, sincerest and most courageous "liberal and progressive" mass movements by white and colored youth ever initiated in the Deep South, the New Orleans Youth Council, Sunday afternoon, in its closing meeting of an enthusiastic three-day session in which democracy and brotherhood were not only preached, but also lived—denounced war mongers and race hate peddlers like Bilbo and Rankin and Talmadge; announced its firm stand and positive action for permanent fair employment, anti-lynching and anti-poll tax laws and all other progressive legislation, and strongly endorsed The Pittsburgh Courier's campaign to "unseat" Bilbo as a member of the United States Senate.

The Council also expressed sentiment for abolition of the County Unit vote electoral system in Georgia and bitterly denounced the Monroe, Ga., quadruple lynchings; the Minden, La., atrocity; the permanent blinding of Private Woodard, war veteran; the Elko, S. C., lynching, and all the other instances of mob violence since the end of the war, in which, by the oddest of circumstances, returning veterans have been the victims.

ALERT ON PROGRESSIVE ISSUES

Strong resolutions, calling for immediate positive action, were brought from two-hour panel sessions on the problems of minority groups, jobs and security; education, recreation and health; political action, civil rights. Veterans' problems, lasting peace and NOYC building—all of which firmly condemned racial discrimination and segregation everywhere—in all its vicious forms.

The Council urged the elimination of jim-crow seating, segregated accommodations and jim-crow signs in all public places and on all public carriers—locally, sectionally and nationally. It appealed for true world brotherhood, democracy and unity.

Summarizing the conclusions of the three-day conference, Bill Sorum, upper classman at Tulane University and vice chairman of the Council, asserted that "the work of this conference is not a climax; it is a beginning. It will put words into action, and action to that. It will be a mass progressive movement of all liberal people regardless of race or color. We must recognize our personal responsibilities for, seeing that this is done."

RISING TENSIONS CAUSED FORMATION OF COUNCIL

"The need for such an organization arose," Sorum continued. "We arose to the need—to wage a battle for the people's rights. We have been educating for death. Now is the time for us to educate for democracy. We have been keeping down Negro standards, but in doing so, we have also been keeping down white standards. Action is needed, not words. We must be efficient as well as enthusiastic. Enthusiasm cuts no ice —we must have money—we must reach more people. We must enlarge, because — large, we are strong; small, we are weak and easily crushed."

ADVANCE GUARD OF CRUSADING LIBERALS

Delivering the main speech of the closing session Sunday, James E. Jackson, executive director of the Southern Negro Youth Congress, with headquarters in Birmingham, Ala., said, "Youth of New Orleans, you have set a flame in the ominous, dark and cloudy heavens anew, a bright and shining star.

"Storm clouds of reaction cast their shadows over daily lives and our future. But your action can contribute to generating new winds of freedom to beat back the gathering storm clouds of reaction over our land."

POSITIVE ACTION FROM PANELS

Presenting resolutions from the panels of the conference was Miss Monica Fusiliere, co-ed at Newcombe College. The program of action was presented by Samuel Green; the financial report was given by Samuel Elson; the constitution after adopted was read by Mrs. Gwendolyn Samuelson and presiding over the closing session was Joseph W. Davis. Officers of the Council are:

Alvin Jones, president; Mr. Sorum and Miss Pearl Ringerman, co-ed at Newcomb College, vice chairman; Miss Beatrice Johnson, secretary, and Mr. Samuelson, treasurer.

Filling key spots in other sessions of the conference were Ernest J. Wright, CIO labor leader and director of the People's Defense League; Moses Turner Jr.,

From the *Pittsburgh Courier*

We had about five hundred dues-paying as well as fringe members, including students from all the universities in New Orleans, high school students, musicians, merchant seamen, factory workers, homemakers, dressmakers, domestic workers, and business owners. Many of our members lived in the Black public housing projects. Some were recently returned veterans of World War II eager to end racial segregation and discrimination. They also had their own group, the Louisiana Veterans' Organization. LVO worked closely with us and we attended each other's parties and dances in our offices and homes. One of our favorite restaurants was Portia's Chicken Shack on Louisiana Avenue, which served interracial groups. We went together to African American music clubs, bars, and restaurants all over town. Dew Drop Inn played the latest bebop music.

I integrated myself into the Black community, learned to sing "Lift Every Voice and Sing," known as the Black national anthem, and soon learned who Ida B. Wells, Mary McLeod Bethune, Carter G. Woodson, James Weldon Johnson, and W. E. B. Du Bois were. NOYC members went to Shakespeare Park to hear the street-corner speakers holding forth to the Black community. The Negro YWCA supported us and so did Ernest Wright, leader of the People's Defense League, an unusual merger of the labor and civil rights movements. Our convention met at the PDL headquarters.

In New Orleans, housing was not segregated by race nearly as much as in northern cities like New York and Chicago. New Orleans was not even segregated by class. Rich people and poor people of all colors often lived in the same block. We white members would canvass door to door in the Irish Channel, a poor uptown neighborhood along the Mississippi River docks where Black and white people were typically next-door neighbors. Some white people started out conversations with racist remarks, almost as a ritual greeting to a stranger. But as soon as I changed the subject to class, they became quite animated and seemed happy to forget about race.

One of the biggest lies of the South is the idea that race hatred comes mainly from poor white workers. It has always come from the ruling class to promote its super-violent exploitation and political terror. Poor whites have no love for the system that exploits them ruthlessly and then murders them when they try to organize to protect themselves. Many are smart enough to know that it is not Black folks who exploit and murder them. That is why both racist ideology and violence against labor have always been so extreme in the South, and why historians who tell the truth are so important.

I wrote almost all our leaflets. First, I typed the messages onto stencils using a heavy manual typewriter. Then, illustrations were scratched onto the stencils. I cranked out the copies on mimeograph machines—big, heavy cylinders with large tubes of ink inside. The stencils were wrapped around the cylinders, and blank pages were cranked around those, producing one page per crank. We were lucky if we didn't get the ink all over us.

That was how we got our message out, long before personal computers, cell phones, or the internet. We communicated to the public with leaflets and newspapers. I also wrote and cranked out a magazine for the NOYC. My FBI files indicate that they had a copy at one time. Radio stations informed the community of the time and place of our meetings and events. Some of us sold (or gave away) newspapers, mainly the *Daily Worker* or the *Southern Worker*, both Communist Party newspapers. Sometimes we used trucks with loudspeakers to broadcast our message to people walking down the streets.

But our main means of communication was distributing leaflets all over town and putting them in mailboxes or at building entrances. One of the most memorable leaflet distributions took place at the longshoremen's shape-up at 6 a.m. on the docks. At a shape-up, crew bosses pointed to each man they wanted to hire that day, yelling, "You!" We brought hundreds of leaflets. The longshoremen grabbed them, read them, folded them up, and put them in their pockets. Not one was left on the ground. Our leaflets called for full equality for all, stressed the right to vote, encouraged people to register and vote, and protested racial segregation, lynching, and police brutality. We invited the longshoremen to join the NOYC and attend our meetings and parties.

Most of our leaflets and our one magazine were mimeographed at the office of the Communist Party of Louisiana in the Godchaux Building on Canal Street. The building was about two blocks from the ferry landing to cross the Mississippi River. This was long before the twin-span Crescent City Connection Bridge was built. At the time, the ferry was the only way to cross the river downtown.

Maurie and Gwen, 1946

First Love Never Dies

These years right after World War II were also the time of my romance and marriage to Maurie Samuelson. Shortly before the United States entered the war, he had lied about his age to get into the paratroopers,

Special Agent KLINE WEATHERFORD that a Mr. McGEE, who also resides at
1619 South Carrollton Avenue, in Apartment A, had observed several
Negroes in the apartment of Mr. and Mrs. MORRIS SAMUELSON who lived
in Apartment D, 1619 South Carrollton Avenue. According to [____]
McGEE said that the Negroes appeared to be holding some kind of a
meeting. [____] continued that on the night of November 4, 1946, he had
observed a Negro standing in the living-room of Apartment D, apparently
leading some type of discussion. He said he also observed another Negro
on the floor and one sitting in the chair. He said that MRS. SAMUELSON
was present at the meeting.

[____] explained that Mr. and Mrs. T. W. CRUMP, of Apartment C,
had informed him that there is a group that meets regularly on Saturday
and Sunday nights in Apartment D and Mr. CRUMP said he had observed
some type of books which appeared to represent some type of youth organization. The informant said that the New Orleans Police Department
had been called about six weeks ago at the request of MRS. McGEE. He
said that the police talked to SAMUELSON concerning the Negroes and he
said that he would have "whoever he damned pleased" in his house.

[____] stated that SAMUELSON and his wife are approximately
twenty to twenty-one years of age. He said that the father of MRS.
SAMUELSON is HERMAN MIDLO, an attorney-at-law, who also owns the apartment house at 1619 South Carrollton Avenue.

For the information of the Bureau, HERMAN MIDLO is generally
regarded as the attorney for the Communist Party in New Orleans. He is
the subject of a closed investigation in this office and is generally
represented as the attorney of record for the Louisiana League for the
Preservation of Constitutional Rights.

partly because he loved adventure but even more because he and his
younger brother Danny wanted to fight against the Nazis. Maurie was
at Pearl Harbor on December 7, 1941, when the Japanese attacked. But
he was soon discharged for being underage and asthmatic. Soon after he
returned home, he got married, and then his daughter Judith was born.
But his marriage quickly broke up. When we began to get serious about
each other, I was very young. Girls marrying young was normal in my
family. All the female ancestors I knew about had married when they
were sixteen. My parents opposed the relationship less because of my
youth than because of Maurie's pariah reputation.

We got married right after his divorce. I was sixteen, and he was
twenty-one. Maurie worked long hours as a salesman in his father's busy
tailor shop, National Tailors, on South Rampart Street, selling suits to
returning World War II veterans. He supported us and always paid child
support for his little daughter, Judy. The first few months of our marriage
we lived on South Rampart Street, where we heard all the latest music
blaring from loudspeakers. We used to go to the Coliseum Arena, an

indoor sports stadium, and sit in the balcony for whites to hear the music and watch the sensational dancers. These were not concerts but public jitterbug contests. Everyone took part except for us.

Maurie joined me in my political activities with great skill and enthusiasm and became a leader of the NOYC. He published a column in African American newspaper the *Pittsburgh Courier* about the activities of our organization. I dropped out of high school to devote myself full time to radical politics. We both joined the Communist Party of Louisiana in early 1946. Even back then the FBI was monitoring me and other members of the youth council. They used wiretaps on our telephone lines and hid microphones in our offices and homes. They often listened in on us from the rooms next door.

In September 1946, the New Orleans Youth Council held a conference to discuss how to end racial segregation and disenfranchisement. The *Louisiana Weekly*, the venerable African American newspaper owned by the Afro-Creole elite Dejoie family, published articles and photographs about our conference. Two other Black newspapers, the *Pittsburgh Courier* and *Baltimore Afro-American*, covered our activities, too. The *Pittsburgh Courier* estimated that about five hundred people attended our conference. When Theodore Bilbo, the notoriously racist senator from Mississippi, came to New Orleans, the *Pittsburgh Courier* led a demonstration against him. We participated by sending a sound truck all over town, blaring messages from loudspeakers that demanded he leave New Orleans. People walking down the street were so startled they jumped.

The NOYC gained a lot of credibility among white people as well as Black people in immediate post–World War II New Orleans. But those happy, inspiring times did not last. The democratic, antiracist tradition died a rapid, terrible death, throughout the country but especially in the South, with the coming of the Cold War, with its anticommunist propaganda and hysteria.

My idyllic life came to an end, too. It was partly my fault, because I was too young to know how important we were to each other. Maurie started catching flak from the Communist Party about his political activities. He and some other NOYC leaders organized a large, public, interracial ball, and the Dooky Chase restaurant supplied the orchestra. The

Pittsburgh Courier announced it on November 9, 1946, just two days after a public CP meeting was violently broken up in the French Quarter.[4]

New Orleans Communist Meeting Ends in a Fight

Youth Council Sponsors Prom

NEW ORLEANS—A gala "Swing-Sweet" dance will be presented by the New Orleans Youth Council under the leadership of Jugurtha Butler, social committee chairman, and Morris Samuelson, treasurer, in Laborers Union Hall, 201 Bienville Street, Friday night, Nov. 15, at 8 o'clock. Dooky Chase's orchestra will perform.

Other officers of the NOYC are Bill Sorum, chairman; Joe Davis, vice chairman; Alvin B. Jones, organizational secretary; Valerie Ferdinand, sergeant-at-arms and Monica Fusiliere, secretary.

ADOPTS FEPC

At the recent all-city conference the NOYC adopted a broad program. It approved the creation of a social condition that will give all citizens their proper constitutional rights, regardless of race, color or creed; the elimination of anti-Semitism and jim crowism; and backing of all progressive legislation, particularly that for cancer and tuburculosis control, a permanent Fair Employment Practices Committee, and minimum wages.

The Communist Party leadership criticized him both for the idea of the interracial dance and for his undisciplined decision-making: the party, not the NOYC leadership, was supposed to make decisions. The CP started to criticize him on "the woman question"— whether he was committed to equality between women and men—because he didn't help me with housekeeping. The truth is, I really did need help. I was the world's worst housekeeper. People who drank my coffee choked. I hadn't figured out that I was supposed to wash the pot.

Looking back on it, I'm amazed Maurie never complained. He worked long hours while I did whatever I pleased, mostly politics.

Of course, since I had all this free time, my political work ballooned. Worse, the party leadership appreciated my grasp of Marxist-Leninist theory more than his.

Maurie announced to me that he was moving to Texas to open his own tailor shop. I could go with him or not. I loved him deeply and did not want to lose him. So I went with him, first to Fort Worth, where I hid all my Lenin readings under the bed in the boardinghouse where we stayed. I was so miserable that he suggested we move to Austin, where his brother Danny and my uncle Hymie were partners in a men's clothing store. Austin was better than Fort Worth. But being the wife of a Jewish small-businessman in Texas for the rest of my life was not an option for me. And Austin was too white. Where was the music, the Afro-Creole culture, the beautiful old architecture? Where were the tropical downpours, the lush vegetation, the flowers, the critters? Where was the labor movement? Where were the ships coming in and out from all over the world? Above all, where was the radical antiracist political movement, the only place I ever felt at least partially at home?

I left Maurie in Austin. I loved him for the rest of my life. But as an early feminist I could not accept my relatives' advice that I should stay if I loved him. I don't regret that I left. It was my first trip in an airplane. I cried all the way. I moved back into my parents' home, and they had the marriage annulled. Years later, my mother told me both she and my father regretted their role in breaking up our marriage because Maurie had been the only man in my life who behaved entirely responsibly and lovingly toward me.

It was only after my mother died, in 1997, that I learned that Maurie knew exactly why I left him and never reproached me for it in his heart. Among her papers I found a letter he had written and mailed to me the day I left. My mother had opened it and kept it but never showed it to me. I first saw it several years after Maurie died, fifty years after he sent it.

He wrote:

Dear Gwen,
I suppose this letter will arrive in New Orleans before you do. At any rate, you'll find it waiting for you.

I'm not sure a note of this nature is appropriate under the circumstances, but I do feel that an expression of some sort is forthcoming since my own feelings are feelings of appreciation and gratitude. I felt that once more I must reiterate what I said to you Friday: that you are a truly good person who deserves only the best and that I am really sincere when I wish that you know only happiness and a full life always. I for one can truly appreciate the high ideals which motivate so many of your actions. These goals which you've set for yourself are high, but so is your caliber; therefore these goals are not unattainable since their remoteness and apparent distance will act, for one such as you, as spurs. I admire your courage and spirit in the face of obstacles.

Again, thank you!

Yours truly, Moe

Communists in the Deep South

A few months after the NOYC was founded, William B. "Bill" Sorum showed up at a meeting. He was a tall, heavy-set, talkative medical student at Tulane. He had a black eye that I thought he got in a barroom brawl but was from football practice. Bill was dating a student at Newcomb College, Tulane's female division, an intelligent, beautiful, sociable young woman from an old Louisiana family and one of the best jitterbuggers in town. From conversations I overheard between them, I learned that both she and Bill were members of the Communist Party. They were reluctant to recruit me because, at the time, I was only sixteen. I insisted that they let me join despite my age.

The Communists were denounced as the most uncompromising fighters for racial equality in the South, and it was for that reason I joined. The cold war caricature of Communism and Communists was far from my experience. The Communist Party had just been reconstituted after having been dissolved during World War II. Led by William Z. Foster, one of the greatest union organizers in US history, the party was recommitted to an uncompromising struggle for workers' rights and fighting racism. There would be no more justifications for Jim Crow racial segregation as had taken place during the era of the Communist Political Association. The CP once again supported self-determination for the oppressed African American nation in the Black Belt South. The CP headquarters in New York paid a lot of attention to New Orleans and to recruiting new members throughout the South. New Orleans was then by far the biggest port in the Gulf South, and there was a bitter struggle over controlling the maritime unions.

Although I admired and was grateful to the Soviet Union for defeating the Nazis, my joining the CP had nothing to do with the Soviet Union or a belief in Marxism-Leninism, which I knew nothing about when I joined. But after joining I became attracted to the CP intellectually. We were expected to master complex economic, political, and social theories. Before I knew much about history, the grand Communist scheme explaining all of the past, present, and future was a great thrill. Our belief in human progress could not be questioned. Our intense political activities were to prevent costly delays. This was heady stuff for the ignorant kid I was.

I always had a hard time reading Karl Marx, partially because of his long Germanic sentences and abstract style. The only thing I clearly and quickly understood was the *Communist Manifesto*. But I read everything I could get my hands on by V. I. Lenin. I liked his *State and Revolution* best. After rereading it recently, though, I found it more naive than ruthless. The state is not just a tool of the capitalist class. State power is often more violent, dangerous, exploitative, and destructive than any other institution except for religion. The Soviet Union, founded by Lenin, was no exception, although it achieved near miracles during its first few decades and saved the world from fascism.

My experience in the CP of Louisiana was overwhelmingly positive. I was an enthusiastic, devoted teenager who had found the first and only society I felt comfortable in. I loved the asceticism of the Communists. Greed, consumerism, and careerism were intolerable to me anyway. That's what my father taught me, and I have never changed. I liked the CP's opposition to group terrorism as undemocratic because a handful of people are trying to impose their will on everyone else by force and violence. We revered Stalin, but none of us tried to justify his massive torture, execution, and imprisonment of millions of Soviet citizens with no rule of law. We simply didn't believe it, and we were not alone. Some of the most prestigious, well-informed experts on the Soviet Union didn't believe it either. It turned out to be much worse than anyone could imagine during his lifetime, though it was wildly exaggerated by prestigious Cold War scholars after his death.[5]

Most Communist leaders and organizers with long experience in the South were decent, courageous, and impressive human beings. They had to be ready to sacrifice their lives for the downtrodden masses in order to to defeat racism and fascism. CP bureaucracy was no worse than in other institutions I have experienced, and it was substantially more efficient.

I was deeply impressed by the organizing skills of the Communists. Raymond Tillman helped me organize our NOYC Conference on Racial Equality and against fascism with stunning skill. He and his wife, Grace, a social worker at the Negro YWCA, were members of the Southern Negro Youth Congress, which fought against lynching and Jim Crow segregation and for the right to vote. They organized a chapter in New Orleans during the early 1940s and were active in the Double V campaign—victory against fascism abroad and against racism at home—during the war. After he served in World War II, Ray returned to New Orleans and helped organize and lead the Transport Workers Union, which my father represented.

Nat Ross was my mentor. He was a New York Jew who spent most of his life as a Communist organizer in the Deep South, where he learned to love and respect the southern working class. He married the sister of Don West, the great Appalachian poet and cofounder of the Highlander Folk School. Nat was southern regional director of the CP throughout most of the 1930s and 1940s, when it was most active and effective. I learned respectful behavior toward southern white workers from Nat, and it saved me more than once.

Shortly after I joined the CP in New Orleans, Leon Weiner, stationed at Keesler Air Force Base in Biloxi, Mississippi, was discharged from the US Air Force and became the district organizer. I went with him to meet a CP club in Pointe Coupée Parish, site of the famous slave conspiracy in 1795. The club was a remnant of the Alabama Sharecroppers' Union, which had moved its headquarters to New Orleans and adopted the name Louisiana Farmers' Union.

Leon put a pistol in the glove compartment of the car before we left. It was raining hard when we arrived, and we had to wade through mud to get into the hut where the meeting was being held. The walls were lined with cardboard and newspapers in a vain effort to keep out water. There were ten or twelve members, all sharecroppers, men and women. We discussed their upcoming contract negotiations. The leader of the club, a distinguished-looking man named Sergeant, rode up on his horse. When the Congress for Racial Equality (CORE) began to organize in Pointe Coupée Parish twenty years later, during the 1960s, Sergeant's daughter was an active member. They proudly served us stewed chicken from their farms, freshly slaughtered. They showed us the school they were building for their children with the money they raised and with volunteer labor. (The parish school was only for white kids, although everyone paid taxes to support it.) They were excited about the literature we brought them. I was deeply impressed by their intelligence, dignity, irrepressible activism, and faith that the future belonged to them.

In New Orleans, we met in several clubs: the Youth Club, the Professional Club, and the Trade Union Club. There were some refined white southern ladies in the Professional Club. Lucille Owen was a retired schoolteacher who had helped organize the teachers' union during the 1930s. Her father had been a Mississippi riverboat gambler. Mary Lee Johnson was married to Oakley Johnson, an English professor at Dillard University. Oakley led the Civil Rights Congress in Louisiana, a courageous organization that fought against racist terror, taking cases that the NAACP would not touch. Back in the 1920s, William L. Patterson gave up a lucrative legal practice to direct the International Labor Defense, which promoted and supported the Scottsboro Boys case, among others. After the ILD morphed into the Civil Rights Congress, Patterson prepared and presented the petition "We Charge Genocide" to the United Nations, on behalf of African Americans of the United States, in 1951.

> Confidential Informant Birmingham T-1 reported that GWENDOLYN SAMUELSON had been named as a member of the Executive Board of the Southern Negro Youth Congress on a list furnished to him by LOUIS E. BURNHAM on July 12, 1948. BURNHAM was then the Executive Secretary of the Southern Negro Youth Congress, which organization has been cited by the Attorney General in his list dated November 24, 1948 as an organization within the purview of the President's Executive Order 9835.

I worked with Oakley on the case of Roy Cyril Brooks. Brooks, a Black man, got onto a bus in Algiers, right across the river from New Orleans. The bus driver told a white woman she didn't have enough money to get on the bus; she needed another nickel, which she didn't have. Brooks put a nickel in the box for her. The bus driver was enraged at the idea of a Black man helping a white woman. He called a cop named Bladsacker—I remembered his name by thinking of "bloodsucker"—who shot Brooks in the back, killing him. The cop claimed self-defense, even though Brooks was unarmed. In fact, he had a bag of peanuts in his hand. After much agitation, we got an indictment against the cop, which was unheard of then. Oakley and I attended a service at a Black Baptist church in Algiers to tell the congregation about the case and asked them to look for eyewitnesses to testify against Bladsacker. At first, several witnesses were willing, but they all disappeared before the trial began. Bladsacker was acquitted right away.

The Southern Conference for Human Welfare (SCHW) moved its headquarters to New Orleans in 1946, under the leadership of James Dombrowski, cofounder of the Highlander Folk School in Tennessee. I attended a few meetings but was too busy with other organizations to be active. Dombrowski kept it going throughout the worst of McCarthyism, the Cold War, and segregationist Massive Resistance campaigns. SCHW was on the US Attorney General's list of subversive organizations. When a CP representative instructed him to dissolve it, Dombrowski refused. He changed the name of the group to its nonprofit name, the Southern Conference Educational Fund (SCEF), and continued to propagandize for racial equality, editing and publishing its influential magazine *Southern Patriot*. The SCEF played a major role in recruiting southern whites to support the Civil Rights Movement.[6]

I got to know the national leaders of the Southern Negro Youth Congress (SNYC) and became one of the few white members of that now almost forgotten but extremely influential organization. In October 1946, I attended its Southern Youth Legislature in Columbia, South Carolina. There were delegates from a broad range of African American organizations throughout the South. We came as an interracial delegation from New Orleans, driving in two cars. When we stopped to buy gasoline, Bea Johnson, a Black member, pretended to be my maid. We weren't allowed to use their bathrooms, so we had to relieve ourselves in the woods. At the conference, I was elected to the executive board of SNYC, something that I later found out the FBI had carefully noted.

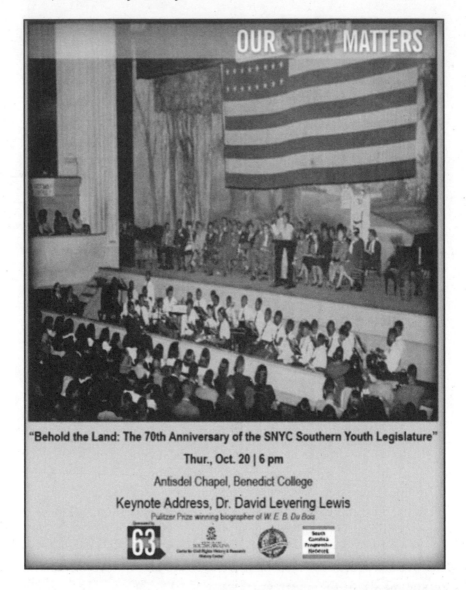

"Behold the Land: The 70th Anniversary of the SNYC Southern Youth Legislature"

Thur., Oct. 20 | 6 pm

Antisdel Chapel, Benedict College

Keynote Address, Dr. David Levering Lewis

Pulitzer Prize winning biographer of W. E. B. Du Bois

As W. E. B. Du Bois gave his influential speech "Behold the Land," I was sitting on the stage right behind him.[7] Du Bois implored this large audience of talented young people, representing a broad range of organized southern Black youth, not to abandon the South. He emphasized the international movement against colonialism and racism. Many subsequent activists in the Civil Rights and Black Power movements were in the audience, and they have mentioned the enormous influence this speech had on them. Herbert Aptheker, whom I always thought of as Uncle Herbie, also gave a speech about slave revolts in the history of the United States. I was deeply moved and inspired by both speeches. That's how I first learned the power of history.

In early 1947, I went to Washington, DC, as part of a SNYC delegation presenting a petition supporting a bill to make lynching a federal crime. We presented our petition to senator Glen Taylor of Idaho. Grace Tillman and I took a train from New Orleans to Washington, riding in separate, racially segregated coaches. In our nation's capital, the only restaurant where we could sit down together and eat was a lunch counter in the main bus station.

Southern Negro Youth Congress presenting an anti-lynching bill petition to Senator Glenn Taylor of Idaho, 1947. I am standing next to Louis E. Burnham as he shows our petition to Taylor.

~

I began to have serious misgivings about the leadership of the Communist Party when an order came down from the national headquarters in

New York to dissolve the NOYC and organize a branch of the Southern Negro Youth Congress in New Orleans instead. The CP had not founded the NOYC, and it knew nothing about why, how, and by whom it was founded because the CP had been dissolved at the time. The NOYC never got to discuss its fate; simply, no more meetings were called. I would run into people on the street, and they would ask me when we were going to meet again. I didn't know what to say. Grace Tillman was put in charge of SNYC in New Orleans and provided a rented office and a salary. I was the only white member. The interracial character of the NOYC had appealed to the young people. Nobody was interested in the Southern Negro Youth Congress by then.

I am not sure why the national office of the CPUSA decided to dissolve the NOYC. I suspected it was out of fear that we young people were too rambunctious and uncontrollable. But the action was part of a misguided shift of the SNYC national office to New Orleans from Birmingham, Alabama, where the situation was becoming impossible. Its leader, Louis Burnham, explained to us that the SNYC leaders were getting old. As he put it, he and his wife Dorothy were getting gray, and they had to move on and make room for us, the real youth. But Grace Tillman was no youth. Burnham was a responsible man and a friend. At this same meeting, he told us that when he was young, he was pressured by the party into leaving college to become a political organizer. He said it was a mistake he always regretted, and he advised us not to repeat it ourselves.

Other Communist leaders moved from Birmingham. James E. Jackson Jr., known as Jack, and his wife, Esther Cooper Jackson, were both founding members of the SNYC in 1937. Jack, who arrived to serve as district organizer of the CP of Louisiana, had been the major speaker at our NOYC conference in November 1946. Evidently the party thought it was a propaganda coup to have an African American introduced to the public as the man in charge of the Communist Party. Jack arrived first, probably to test the waters before moving his wife and kids. He worked out of our apartment at 1619 South Carrollton Avenue, spending a lot of time sending newspaper clippings and photographs of our activities to "New York," which meant CP national headquarters. Jack and I talked a lot and became good friends.

An openly publicized meeting was organized to introduce Jack to the community. It took place at the Mechanics Institute in the French Quarter and was brief. The New Orleans police lined the walls. A goon squad from the Seafarers International Union, an all-white AFL union, began attacking the speakers and the audience with metal folding chairs. The police, in obvious collusion with the SIU goon squad, waited until the attack ended before they arrested only the men among the speakers and the audience, not the aggressors. I went to night court to see what happened to the men. The judge asked the prisoners to choose a spokesman, and they selected an African American trade unionist. Shocked, the judge said, "You mean to say you white people are going to let a [n-word] speak for you?"

After everyone was released on bail, some members of the goon squad came looking for Jack. He locked himself in his apartment's bathroom and took off the top of the toilet tank to use to defend himself. The police arrived and arrested him—charging him with criminal mischief for breaking the toilet! As Jack left the courtroom, a mob was waiting outside. My father walked out of the courthouse with him and told the crowd, "I know every one of you, and you won't get away with it if you lay a hand on this man." The crowd allowed Jack to leave unharmed. My father never told me this story—years later, Jack told it to my husband Harry.

Jack left town shortly after. Our apartment on South Carrollton Avenue remained a safe haven for interracial meetings, though it attracted the ongoing attention of the other tenants, the police, and the FBI.

Over the years I had a few brief encounters with Jack. Once I ran into him at a Brooklyn subway station. He asked me where Maurie was, and expressed that he had fond memories of how Maurie stood by him during his worst days in New Orleans. Jack's wife, Esther, edited *Freedomways* magazine with John Henrik Clarke; it was an influential publication in the pre- and early Civil Rights and Black Power era that later published some of my essays.

Jack also emerged as the CP's new leading theoretician of the "Negro question." As a southerner and leader of the Southern Negro Youth Congress, Jack was devoted to the southern movement. When he heard me say at a meeting that the CP was afraid of the Black movement in the South, he was shattered and replied, "Really! Is that what this is all about?" But I recently read that the FBI's highest-level spy in the CP, Morris Childs, reported that, while both men were in Moscow, Jack had his arm twisted by a member of the Central Committee of the Communist Party of the Soviet Union to abandon the concept of an oppressed Black nation in the United States. I think Jack had his doubts about abandoning the CP's view that African Americans were an oppressed nation in the Deep South with the right of self-determination, a concept my future husband Harry Haywood had helped develop at the Sixth World Congress of the Communist International (Comintern) in 1928 and defended all his life.

The New Orleans Waterfront: Getting to Know the Working Class

I understand theory but do not trust it much. My mind thinks concretely, and that's why I am a historian, not a sociologist. I begin my writing with stories and go from there to generalizations but with great caution. I learned a lot of abstractions in the CP. The "Negro people" and the "working class" were what Communists talked about the most. I was well aware that I really didn't know much about either, and I wanted to know more. I lucked out: New Orleans during the last half of the 1940s was the best possible place and time to learn.

The CP was powerful in the Port of New Orleans. Its strength was in the left-wing CIO unions: the National Maritime Union (NMU), International Longshoremen's and Warehousemen's Union (ILWU), and the Transport Workers Union (TWU), which represented the truck drivers and workers who moved the ships' cargo to and from the docks and storage warehouses.

During the 1930s, the CIO unions, especially in the South, were built by courageous, dedicated organizers who would not tolerate racially segregated unions. Harry Bridges, leader of the ILWU in San Francisco, funded its organizers in New Orleans. The members and leaders of the left-led ILWU and the TWU in New Orleans were almost all African American. The all-white AFL union, the Seafarers International Union (SIU), was infamous for its union-busting goon squads and was most active in the Gulf ports. By contrast, although the NMU's members were mainly white, there were quite a few Black and Latino members, and some were prominent officials. Almost all of them had shipped out during World War II, and many had seen their fellows killed by Nazi submarine torpedoes and fascist planes. They were still inspired by hatred of fascism and racism.

Nobody was going to segregate members of the NMU, anywhere. When they landed in a port, if the stores, bars, hotels, or restaurants tried to exclude their Black members, NMU members trashed the place. These were not occasional events. It was an unwritten policy. Much of the union business was conducted in French Quarter bars. If the French Quarter gin mills wanted their business and NMU members were a big part of their clientele, they had to admit Black members when seamen showed up together. The owners provided us private rooms where we met in interracial groups, although we were violating laws against segregation in public places. I used to tag along to listen to these incredibly eloquent, cosmopolitan, talkative merchant seamen telling their stories from all over the globe.

Among them were the Communist war heroes who never stopped fighting against fascism even after they were discharged from the service. The most outstanding was Irving Goff, who became a major influence in my life. In 1947, the CP brought him in as our district organizer. I knew he was a war hero but only recently learned the details about the incredible things he did—and also, according to my declassified FBI files, how much he appreciated me and defended me.

Goff was born and raised in Brooklyn, where he worked as an acrobat and dancer at Coney Island. His parents were Jewish refugees from pogroms in Odessa. Goff volunteered to fight for the Loyalists against the fascists in Spain, where he was trained by the Red Army to parachute behind enemy lines and use pressure-sensitive explosives to blow up trains, bridges, railroad tracks, telephone and telegraph lines, and military installations. After some remarkable victories against great odds, he came home.

In 1941, Wild Bill Donovan, director of the Office of Secret Services (OSS), recruited Goff and other International Brigade veterans, including Spaniards, Yugoslavs, and Greeks, for underground activities, and the vets participated despite the strong objections of the Comintern. Donovan was a right-wing Republican, but he supported the best qualified and most courageous fighters against fascism, including Josip Broz Tito in Yugoslavia and Ho Chi Minh in Vietnam. Goff was first stationed in North Africa, where he was put in charge of training Spanish recruits to operate behind enemy lines. Donovan promoted him to second lieutenant. He was parachuted behind enemy lines in North Africa and then into Italy to help organize underground resistance to the Nazi occupiers, using his International Brigade contacts from Spain. When FBI Director J. Edgar Hoover warned Donovan that Goff was a Communist, Donovan said he knew—that's why he'd recruited him.

After the Allied invasion of Italy in 1943, the OSS Lincoln Brigade veterans were moved to Naples. Goff was appointed liaison officer to the Italian Communist Party. He trained Italian volunteers for guerrilla warfare behind the German lines in northern Italy. They parachuted thirty teams of radio operators into enemy-held areas and provided daily weather reports for the Allied air forces, with the help of Italian Communists. Goff later said, "We had guerrillas operating on every highway, every railroad, every German convoy. We had identifications, the material in every car on every highway, reported through the network of radios." The US Army awarded Goff the Legion of Merit.

Goff was the no-nonsense, tough guy we needed for our battles on the waterfront. That's where I got my real education. I used to go to the CP office in the historic Godchaux Building, where Goff worked. He let me listen in on reports coming in from sailors in just about every nook and cranny in the world as I was cranking out my leaflets on the mimeograph machine. I heard firsthand accounts from merchant seamen who were smuggling Czechoslovak arms to Israel during its war against Britain's colonial control of Palestine. Communist merchant seamen spread the news about the wave of anticolonialist wars escalating after World War II. I am sure Goff applied his underground skills to promote international anti-imperialist warfare, using merchant seamen as messengers to carry propaganda, arms, and money.

I was deeply impressed by the Communist merchant seamen. At sea, they couldn't go out after they were finished with work, so they read, studied, wrote stories and books, and created works of art. Some of their wonderful books were printed by International Publishers. The seamen were cosmopolitan, highly political, and eloquent. They had their own language, which I quickly learned to speak. I don't remember much of it anymore, only a few phrases: a bar was a *gin mill*; *getting dumped* meant being hit and knocked down; *setting the ship down* was a wildcat strike. A friend once overheard a long conversation between me and a merchant seaman on a street corner in New Orleans; he said he hadn't understood a word we said. I wasn't surprised that many merchant seamen feared the ocean, but I was surprised that few of them could swim. They told me knowing how to swim would not help in freezing cold waves or shark-infested warm waters.

African American Communists were officials in the NMU, ILWU, and TWU. Many rank-and-file members of the NMU were also members of the CP. Al Lanon directed the waterfront section of the CP. He was an impressive, highly competent, and courageous man with no patience for pretentiousness. He and Goff were the generals in the hidden warfare in the Gulf ports during the late 1940s.

The Taft-Hartley Act forced union officials to sign loyalty oaths or lose their jobs. The Catch-22 was that if they lied or quit the CP so they could swear they weren't members, they would go to jail for perjury. If they refused to sign, they couldn't be union officials. And their unions were being raided by rival unions, which meant the risk of losing accreditation with the National Labor Relations Board. When the Cold War started, Mike Quill, president of the TWU in New York City, disassociated himself from the left. Joseph Curran did likewise in the NMU. Raymond Tillman was voted out of office at the TWU. Communists and "left-wingers" were squeezed out of union leadership.

As for the rank and file, there were so many Communists in the NMU that the goon squads had to murder at least a few. The militant Communist and left-wing merchant seamen were soon driven off the waterfront and screened off the ships by the US Coast Guard, which issued loyalty cards that seamen were required to have in order to ship out.

I closely followed the protracted, bitter, violent struggle in the NMU, seeking out CP members who were close to the maritime scene. Judy Modigliani, the daughter of a Greek seaman, became my friend and mentor. She and her mother, a warm, loving, Turkish woman, lived on Bourbon Street. Judy was five years older than me and was close to the trade union organizing struggles in New Orleans from back in the 1930s.

Joe and Inez Wright were poor white people from Texas with long experience on the waterfront. Although well into middle age, Joe was tall, strong, muscular, and absolutely devoted to the CP and its waterfront battles. The Wrights told me they had overcome their racial prejudices from their experiences in the labor movement and in the CP. Bill Sorum later testified to the Senate Internal Investigating Committee that Joe Wright was the top leader of the CP in New Orleans. I have no idea what became of the Wrights.

I used to visit the Wrights in their home, where I met other merchant seamen. Vernon Bowen was a veteran of the Lincoln Brigade of the Spanish Civil War and the Merchant Marine during World War II. During the 1950s, Vernon and several other white people were arrested and jailed in Louisville, Kentucky, for protecting with arms a Black family who had moved into a white neighborhood. Eddie Hampton, an African American merchant seaman, was a real friend to me, giving me moral support when I needed it most. He told me my Communist "friends" in New Orleans were wrong to criticize me for refusing to obey the police when they demanded we break up an interracial party in the French Quarter, where we were arrested. Joe Mouledous, a tall, handsome, sweet young man from a middle-class New Orleans family, was a great, enthusiastic cook on the ships and at parties sponsored by our interracial youth movement. We went to Atlanta together in 1948 to get the Progressive Party on the ballot in Georgia.

The merchant seaman I got to know best and from whom I learned the most was a white seaman nicknamed Smitty, whose full name was Otto von Schmidt. He was born in rural Texas and orphaned as a young child. A white sharecropper family took him in, but they overworked and neglected him, so he ran away at the age of twelve and had been on his own ever since. He told me stories about working conditions on the United Fruit Company banana boats running between New Orleans and Central America before they organized the NMU. When they shipped out, the merchant seamen had to sign articles renouncing all their civil rights. At sea, they were overworked and paid no wages, only given food—usually nothing but bananas and bread pudding. Years later, Smitty still got nauseated at the sight of bread pudding. His ships had been torpedoed several times during the war, including one hit of an oil tanker, where he was the only survivor. He told me about the struggles going on in the Gulf ports over control of the NMU. In Galveston, Texas, the police issued their own loyalty cards to non-Communist merchant seamen. Those found without these cards were beaten up by goon squads from the SIU. Then the police started selling the loyalty cards.

A little guy, Smitty was called a "scrapper" because he was a fearless street fighter. But he was always gentle with me. I learned a lot from Smitty, but I hurt him badly where he was most vulnerable. Like many other merchant seamen, the CP and the NMU were Smitty's only family. He proudly showed me photographs of his ship, which he felt was his home, and then he took me to the wharf to show it to me up close. We spent a lot of time together and became intimate. He was shy. I might have been the only woman he was ever with. I got pregnant, and he was bursting with pride, but I didn't want to marry him or give birth to his child. That ended our relationship. I would hear about him, mostly admiration for how scrappy he was. Finally, it was reported that he was swept overboard during a voyage and drowned. I don't believe it was an accident. Murdered by a goon squad? Suicide because I deserted him? Despair over losing the NMU? I will never know.

The left-wing waterfront unions, in spite of their thousands of devoted, competent, brave fighters for workers' rights and racial equality, collapsed as a result of systematic antiunion efforts. US ships were registered in foreign ports—Liberia and Panama were favorites—to avoid enforcement of union contracts guaranteeing minimum standards for wages, hours, and working conditions. Later, whenever I passed the building on Decatur Street in the French Quarter where the NMU hall was housed, I remembered the days when it was bustling, noisy, and crowded with sailors trying to get ships. It is now a restaurant.

Henry Wallace for President

In 1948, Henry A. Wallace, who was Franklin Roosevelt's vice president during World War II, began his presidential campaign. I am still proud of whatever contributions I made. FDR left a terrible legacy by replacing Wallace with Harry S. Truman as his vice-presidential pick in 1944 to ensure the support of the white racist Democratic political bosses in the South. If Wallace had replaced FDR upon his death, we would never have dropped atom bombs on Japan, a decision made by Truman. Subsequently, the United States bombed North Korea so ruthlessly and massively that the death toll from the Korean War was far higher than the toll from the atom bombs dropped on Japan.

All sides in the Cold War sank into tyranny. The Korean War raged during the last three years of Joseph Stalin's life while he was ill, impaired, and increasingly paranoid and antisemitic. The United States descended into McCarthyism and Cold War ideology, which seriously threatened our best traditions and still badly distorts scholarship and public consciousness.

China became increasingly xenophobic with the advent of Mao's Great Cultural Revolution, which unleashed a wave of repression that destroyed many of the most devoted and competent people, replacing them with young, ambitious ideologues and creating chaos across the society, economy, education system, and culture. The war in Vietnam was an enormous crime against humanity and tore our country apart. The many destabilizing proxy wars that slaughtered many millions of nonwhite people in Asia, Africa, Latin America, and the Middle East—the "hot wars" of the Cold War—could have been avoided with a good dose of humility, humanity, knowledge, and intelligence.

Henry Wallace was a peace candidate who opposed militarization and the Cold War and supported the use of resources for social needs instead of expansion of the military. He also fought against Jim Crow segregation and for racial equality. All of this seemed like common sense to me. But at Tulane University, where I was attending college, these ideas were radical. The more idealistic fringe of students at Tulane and its sister college, Newcomb, supported Wallace. Most were locals. After the Progressive Party was organized to support the Wallace campaign, Students for Wallace became a chapter of the Young Progressives.

The organizing thrust came from professor Mitchell Franklin of Tulane Law School. I met him in 1948 when he was a vigorous forty-six-year-old. He had an extraordinary career, from filing a brief in support of Sacco and Vanzetti, the Italian immigrant anarchists who were executed in Massachusetts in 1927 for a crime they didn't commit, to advising the United Nations about international human rights law during its first years and at the Nuremburg trials of major Nazi war criminals in 1945–46. Professor Franklin remained intellectually active well into his eighties until he died in 1986.

He was a brilliant scholar of the philosophy of international human rights law and a well-informed and uncompromising civil libertarian. It would be hard to overestimate his impact on the legal profession as his students began to practice law in New Orleans. Two of his students became cochairs of Students for Wallace: Benjamin Smith, who later became a famous civil rights lawyer, and Fred Heebe, who became a federal judge. After Professor Franklin retired from Tulane, he taught at the law school of the State University of New York at Buffalo. Tulane Law School finally inducted him into its hall of fame posthumously in

2014, and there is now a prestigious Mitchell Franklin professorship at the school.

I have very fond memories of Mitchell Franklin. He sought me out and treated me like an equal. He caught a lot of flak at Tulane because of his politics and maybe even more because of the international recognition he enjoyed.

The Wallace campaign was exciting. Louis Burnham of SNYC organized the campaign throughout the Jim Crow South. We consistently defied all segregation laws and held large, racially integrated meetings at the Coliseum Arena, the large indoor stadium in New Orleans. Paul Robeson gave a concert there to support the campaign. Robeson was a great stage actor and extraordinary orator, with a magnificent bass voice and an overwhelming physical presence. He sang and spoke for hours. I watched as the white policemen assigned to maintain "order" were totally mesmerized by Robeson. I was convinced if he could reach these New Orleans cops, he could reach anyone.

Robeson shared his enormous repertoire with us, including spirituals like "Go Down Moses" and labor songs like "Joe Hill," plus "Song of the Volga Boatmen," "The Peat Bog Soldiers," and "Song of the Warsaw Ghetto Uprising." He sang each in its original language. And he sang about the Mississippi River, including "Old Man River" from *Showboat* and "River, Stay Away from My Door." Between songs, he talked about the struggles of workers throughout the world.

Another singer came during the Wallace campaign. I had never heard of him. He sang to a much smaller audience at the Wallace campaign headquarters. I watched his huge Adam's apple jumping around while he sang, and his optimistic energy was infectious. His name was Pete Seeger. He must have been about twenty-nine years old at the time.

The CP in New Orleans, led by Irving Goff, put great energy into the Wallace campaign. What pleased me most was that our citywide interracial youth organization was revived. We resumed our social events among students from all the campuses in New Orleans, not in public places but in private homes. We went back to the same neighborhoods where we had helped African American voters register when we were the NOYC and, working entirely with local volunteers, collected thousands of signatures of registered voters on a petition to put the Progressive Party on the ballot. Those already registered signed our petitions, and we helped register new voters, who also signed. My father was an elector for Wallace and was proud that he got considerably more votes than any other Wallace elector. My mother chaired Women for Wallace, which had little success because we young women refused to play the role of auxiliary to the male movement.

We accompanied Wallace on a tour of the rural Louisiana parishes. He made speeches, generally in front of parish courthouses. He had to dodge a few eggs, but nothing more drastic. Other states were more dangerous. We got on the ballot in Louisiana so fast that we were asked to go to Atlanta to get the Progressive Party on the ballot in Georgia. As we got on the bus to Atlanta, our friends stood waving goodbye. We all sang Woody Guthrie's song "So Long, It's Been Good to Know Ya."

It might have been appropriate. There was a lot more repression in Atlanta than in New Orleans. The situation was complicated by the young volunteers who had come from New York City. All men, they were aggressive, self-righteous, and contemptuous of the South and of southerners—not helpful and indeed a dangerous attitude. Several of them were beaten up and thrown in jail. One was nearly thrown off a railroad bridge but managed to run fast enough to get away. I think I was the only one who stayed out of trouble while collecting lots of signatures. My FBI files claim that I complained about being arrested and thrown into jail with prostitutes, and that I tried to present myself as a martyr. They ordered a search of the arrest files in Atlanta for clarification but found nothing because I was never arrested. In the end, we got Wallace on the ballot in Georgia, too.

An Interracial Party in the French Quarter

After the election, which went to Truman, the Young Progressives continued functioning throughout the city, maintaining essentially the same type of membership and activities as the NOYC. We canvassed door to door, helping African Americans register to vote. That took dogged determination. A few people resisted, saying they were not supposed to vote. But most people received us warmly, especially returning veterans from World War II. One of them told me that if I had taken the trouble to come and teach him how, he should take the trouble to go register to vote. But getting there was only the first step. The voter registration form asked for applicants' exact ages in years, months, and days. We calculated the answer for each person. Their applications were always turned down, and we told them we would take them back to apply again. Instead of getting discouraged, they got angry. They went back with us over and over again, until the voter registrar got tired of seeing them and finally registered them, often after six or seven tries.

We registered thousands of African Americans, years before the Freedom Riders of the 1960s. The African American voter bloc in New Orleans was courted by rival candidates. A few months before my father died, he and I had the satisfaction of watching a TV news report of a street celebration of the election of Dutch Morial, the first Black mayor of New Orleans. He was a junior partner in the law firm of my father's old friend A. P. Tureaud. Morial won with 90 percent of the Black vote and 20 percent of the white.

We held interracial parties at various people's homes, as serious young people trying to get to know each other. Students from all the colleges and universities in town and people from the community came. Our parties were never rowdy but were usually crowded. If there was enough room, we danced. In February 1949, we held one of our parties at a home on Orleans Avenue in the French Quarter. Our party occupied one side of a classic New Orleans "shotgun double" rented by Alice LeSassier, a woman from a very old Louisiana family, and Arlene Stitch, a social work graduate student at Tulane from New York City. So many people came that there was no room to dance.

A man living in the other side of the double had a city government job and some pull. He saw our African American guests coming in the front door and called the police. Several cops showed up. I asked them what they wanted. One of them said, "We ain't got no civil rights here yet. What are you people trying to do?" I explained to them that segregation laws only applied to public places. We weren't violating any law since our party was in a private home. I suggested they check with their precinct captain to see if I wasn't right. I asked if we were making too much noise. The policeman replied, "Oh no, this is the quietest party in the French Quarter tonight. But maybe you should turn down the radio." We did. The police then walked all around the house, staring hostilely at everyone, and then left. Some of our guests got the message and left, too. But others kept showing up.

I called my father and told him what happened. He said, "Break up the party and go home." I got legalistic, insisting that we had a right to have an interracial party in a private home. But the police didn't see it that way. They returned in force and arrested all of us for disturbing the peace by making loud and unusual noises. We were carted off to the jail in the 400 block of Chartres Street, in a building that now houses the Williams Research Center of the Historic New Orleans Collection.

All of us were carefully segregated by race and gender into four patrol wagons and then into four separate jail cells: African American men, African American women, white men, and white women. They took the belts and ties of the men so they couldn't hang themselves. The cells were crowded. There were sixty-five of us packed into four small cells, each designed for two people. I was too young to be afraid, and I found our arrest exhilarating, as this was our most open, public, defiant challenge to Jim Crow segregation yet. I soon found out almost no one else shared my attitude, and they blamed me for our arrest.

The first person released was Carolyn Dejoie. Her husband, Prudhomme Dejoie, was the scion of an old, elite Afro-Creole family. Then, Oakley Johnson, director of the Civil Rights Congress in New Orleans, came and bawled us out for getting arrested. He said he didn't know if they were going to defend us or not and refused to bail us out. My father showed up and bailed all of us out on his signature.

Judge Edwin Babylon presided at our trial. The back of the courtroom was lined with taxi drivers in uniform, shouting about taking all the white women out and raping them. The judge didn't stop this disturbance in his courtroom, because the New Orleans taxi drivers operated as a goon squad for the mayor's office: a paramilitary force that backed up the violent, antilabor, racist New Orleans Police Department. One of the arresting officers testified: "You know, Judge, when you get a bunch of [n-word]s together, they talk loud and laugh loud and make a lot of noise. That's what happened." Our lawyer objected and asked for a dismissal of the charges based on race prejudice. Judge Babylon replied, "What do you mean, race prejudice? Everybody knows that's true!"

I insisted that I should testify that the police said it was the quietest party in the French Quarter that night. But our lawyers wouldn't let me testify at all. They put a few of us on the witness stand and asked them what they were doing when they were arrested. They all said they were having quiet conversations while listening to the radio. No one was dancing. It was a small house, there were a lot of people, and there was no room to dance. A Newcomb professor showed up in court to defend his students. He told a reporter for the *New Orleans Times-Picayune* that he had assigned his students to go to our party as a "sociological experiment." The poor fellow had recently arrived in the South and had no idea what impact this statement would have. The newspapers reported it, and he got in deep trouble at Newcomb.

Judge Babylon found all of us guilty, of course. The next-door neighbor who called the police got a big promotion in his city job. We appealed our conviction, except for two Newcomb students who refused, saying it was a "pink party." We soon won our appeal, and they were left with criminal records. We weren't.

CATHOLIC SCHOOL WORK IS STARTED

Ground Breaking Celebrated by St. Dominic's

OPERATING A PILE DRIVER to start construction on the new school for St. Dominic's parish is the Rev. H. A. Hall, O. P., pastor. In picture at right, school children march to the groundbreaking ceremonies for the Lakeview school.

Raided Inter-Racial Party Leads to $5 Fines for 64

Sponsored by Junior Size Wallace Organization

46 PROVOCATIONS CHARGED TO TITO

Albania Radio Lays 'Incidents' to Neighbor

For several days, every edition of every newspaper in the city printed a list of everyone who had been arrested at the party, including our names, addresses, and occupations or which colleges we attended. I was followed around by the same taxi drivers who had sat in the back of the courtroom demanding that all the white women be raped. I carried a hammer and a wrench next to me on the front seat of my car. The whole city was buzzing about our arrest. I heard people talking excitedly on the streetcar, saying they found all of us dancing in the nude. Twenty of us were Tulane and Newcomb students. At first, Tulane's administrators acted reasonably calm. They tried to dismiss the party as the act of recently enrolled, still-unsocialized Yankee students. In fact, we were overwhelmingly locals.

My first contact with the Tulane administration was when Fred Carrington Cole, the dean of Arts and Sciences, stopped me on campus and asked me very sweetly what had happened. But a few days later, he was more agitated. He told me many alumni donors were calling in to cancel their pledges. Some were withdrawing their daughters from Newcomb. He asked me and several other students to meet with a group of administrators. I did most of the talking. They asked me if there were any Communists at the party. I said we didn't ask about people's political beliefs or affiliations at the door. They wrote in a memorandum that I was "very outspoken about race."

Rufus Harris, the president of Tulane, sent a letter to the parents of Tulane and Newcomb students and to alumni, boasting that only twenty of their students had been arrested, testifying to the good sense of the overwhelming majority. Dean Cole told me that the Tulane Board of Trustees wanted to expel us all, but President Harris threatened to resign if they did. The board backed down. For several years, Tulane had great difficulties with fundraising because of our arrest.

Some of my Communist comrades—probably instigated by FBI agents, or maybe they *were* FBI agents themselves—tried hard to get me expelled from the CP because they blamed me for our arrest. My FBI files show that Irving Goff defended me. A few months later, the legendary William L. Patterson, national leader of the Civil Rights Congress, told Oakley Johnson that our case was important, and we were right to defy the police. I was out of the doghouse for a little while after that.

One night, a Tulane student brought his date to one of our uptown parties. She got hysterical when she saw African Americans there and shouted, in tears: "Arthur, take me out of here! In Bessemer, Alabama, where I come from, I'm considered a liberal, but you people are a hundred dred yeeears ahead of yooour tiiime!"

Her timing was a little off, but that was par for the South in those days. When Hodding Carter II, a famous liberal Mississippi newspaper owner and editor, spoke at Tulane, some of us went to talk to him after his lecture and asked him if he thought racial segregation would ever end. He got very flustered, took us aside, and whispered, "Well, maybe a hundred years from now."

It only took twenty.

To Paris and Back Again

During our campaign to elect Henry Wallace, Michel Yuspeh showed up at a meeting at Tulane. We had met once as children—we studied classical piano with the same teacher and both attended a quiz sponsored by the city's music teachers. One of the questions had been to identify the instruments of a string quartet. I answered correctly and Michel didn't. He said sullenly, "I got it wrong, and she got it right. And she's a *girl*!"

Michel's family considered themselves aristocrats because in Russia they were among the few Jews allowed to go to Moscow. They proudly claimed that their ancestors were loyal Confederates during the Civil War and maintained that the family was reduced to eating shoes and rats during the Union siege of Vicksburg.

Before Michel went to Tulane, he was a student of classical piano at the Juilliard School of Music in New York City. But when his mother discovered he was in love with another male student, she dragged him back to New Orleans. It was rumored he'd had a nervous breakdown. His cousin, their family doctor, prescribed a cruise to Havana and a visit to a whorehouse. The prescription didn't work; Michel's emotional involvement remained almost entirely with gay men. He performed a Schumann piano concerto with the New Orleans Symphony Orchestra and was considered the best classical pianist New Orleans had produced, but that wasn't enough for a successful performing career. He lacked the brilliance and sensitive introspection of great classical musicians.

Michel and I began making Students for Wallace posters together, tacked them up all over campus, and distributed leaflets in various New Orleans neighborhoods. I infused Michel with my optimism and activism. But he was not political. Classical music was his whole world. He wanted to live a safe, secure, uneventful life devoted entirely to classical music and a few other aesthetic pursuits, confining his friendships and experiences to people of similar tastes and largely to people with similar sexual preferences. His mother had convinced him—or forced him—to give up his musical ambitions and study pre-med at Tulane. During his last semester he flunked both physics and chemistry. That settled that.

After the arrests at the interracial party in the French Quarter, we all received threatening letters. Michel's letter arrived when I was visiting his home. It was addressed "Dear [n-word]-Jew" and said he should be tarred, feathered, and run out of town on a rail. It went on with similar sentiments and was signed "Jew Hater." His mother grabbed the letter and yelled at me, "It's Jews like you and your family who get Jews like us in trouble!"

His parents threw Michel out of the house and gave him a small stipend to live on. I think they feared he might undermine their Confederate credentials. I helped him find a tiny apartment in the French Quarter, which was not easy because no one wanted to rent to us. Michel was informally adopted by my parents. They figured he was my last chance for a respectable Jewish marriage. My mother's plan was to talk him into giving up music, studying law, and entering the family law firm.

I was not attracted to Michel sexually, nor he to me. But he was one of the few intellectuals and artists in New Orleans with whom I was on friendly terms. I valued his mind, his ironic sense of humor, and his companionship. He was clearly repulsed by sexual relations with women. But he did manage to function sometimes with me. My mother promised to pay for both of our educations for three years if we got married. I finally agreed but so reluctantly that Michel used to tell me I married him for *my* money. I was miserable at home and wanted to be on my own. I didn't want to leave New Orleans, but New York City was attractive. It was an entirely new, intellectually stimulating world where I could finish my BA in history at NYU in a year and Michel would get his degree in classical piano at Julliard.

None of these plans had much to do with Michel. We were more good friends than lovers. I had a lot of qualms about him, especially his bouts of paranoia. I knew so little about mental illness, but nobody knew much in those days. Freud was all the rage then, and schizophrenia was supposedly caused by emotionally distant mothers. But we now know that it is mainly neurophysiological and hereditary.

We were married civilly by the justice of the peace in Arabi, Louisiana, on my twentieth birthday. Then, on Bastille Day, we had a Jewish wedding under the chuppah in Chevra Thilim Synagogue.

Michel was readmitted to Juilliard School of Music. I was admitted to NYU with senior status in history. One day Dean Cole stopped us on the Tulane campus. He was excited, almost dancing a jig. He said he had heard we were getting married and going to New York, and he offered to get us fellowships. This seemed implausible to me since Michel had just flunked physics and chemistry. But Dean Cole might have come up with a fellowship as a bribe to make sure I left.

Michel was still obsessed with the young man he had fallen in love with at Julliard, Sylvan Fox. When we got to New York, he found out that Sylvan and his new bride, Gloria, were headed to Paris. Michel insisted we go with them instead of staying in New York to get our degrees. In late October 1949, the four of us left for France on the *Queen Elizabeth II*, traveling tourist class. That was the cheapest way to go. It turned out Gloria was pregnant. I talked her out of having an abortion, something for which she later expressed gratitude.

Sylvan quickly ran out of money in Paris. Michel loaned him some of ours—or, better said, my parents'—to get home. Sylvan never returned the money, which cooled Michel's obsession with him.

Nothing we had agreed to do materialized. Despite my mother's wishes, Michel was incapable of becoming a lawyer and entering the family firm, even if he wanted to. He couldn't get admitted to any prestigious classical piano program in Paris, so he studied privately with Jeanne Blancard, who taught at the École Normale de Musique. He was admitted there but never got his degree. Before we left France, he went to a diploma shop and had a fake degree printed. His insistence on staying in France stopped me from getting my BA, and I later spent a decade pounding manual typewriters to make a living after teaching myself office skills.

But we both loved Paris. It was only four years after the war when we arrived. Not many people owned cars. The air was clean. From its beautiful bridges we could see clearly the magnificent Gothic architecture all over the city and the water flowing down the Seine. Although Paris was poor, it was elegant.

Twice a week, farmers trucked in their fruits and vegetables and displayed them at street markets, arranged like works of art. There were no supermarkets, only specialized food shops. The meat stores were a bit gruesome, with chunks of horse, cow, lamb, rabbit, and chicken—sometimes entire carcasses—hung out in front of the stores. The neighborhood restaurants had good food, and if you had US dollars, they were cheap, just like in New Orleans. We learned to like new foods—artichokes, snails (escargot), cheeses we had no idea even existed—and to eat our salads and cheeses last. And French wine—it was always good, even table wine. Breakfast meant going to the bakery (*boulangerie*) to buy freshly baked and hot baguettes, *ficelles*, and croissants, or the *patisseries*, with beautifully decorated, unbelievably delicious pastries. The *charcuteries* were delicatessens with cooked meats and vegetables in bundles and piles. Shopping was an aesthetic experience.

Paris was the artistic and intellectual capital of the world. It had special meaning to New Orleans intellectuals, who identified themselves as French because France was our first colonizer. The feeling was not mutual, however. France was not fond of remembering all the American colonies she had lost, and they were largely ignored by French historians. Nor were we esteemed as liberators; France had been humiliated by her rapid fall to the Nazis, thanks at least partially to large contingents of collaborators in powerful places. Except to famous foreign intellectuals like Ernest Hemingway and Ilya Ehrenburg, French artistic and intellectual life was a closed club, and we had to learn about France on our own. We walked all over Paris, visiting the art museums, historic buildings, cathedrals, castles, and architectural sites. We took boat rides on the Seine as it flowed through Paris, and we walked along its banks, shopping at bookstalls and buying sheepskin pages of medieval music and book manuscripts.

I'll never forget our first winter in Paris. There was no heat at all in our building in Saint-Mandé, right past the Porte de Vincennes. Electricity was cut off several days a week. Being from New Orleans, I had only seen snow once before, when I was in elementary school. Now, in wintry Paris, I read French history textbooks while hovering over a small, smoky woodstove. Michel practiced the piano with baked potatoes in his pockets, trying to keep warm.

Although living in Paris was great, I had a big problem. I couldn't get my BA, much less a graduate degree in history, without first getting a *license de lettres*. Everyone we knew said I could not possibly do that because I would be competing with highly qualified French students in a language I had never studied. I probably could have done it, but that was before I learned not to pay attention to what people said I couldn't do. I wanted to return to New York to finish our degrees, but Michel refused. He had the solution for me: I should switch to music to give my parents a reason to continue supporting us in France, and I was to study privately with Michel's teacher, Jeanne Blancard.

He managed to parlay the three years my parents had agreed to support us into four. My mother thought she cut us off, but my father somehow managed to sneak money to us behind her back. My mother complained I was getting the short end of the stick. But this was one of the few times my father prevailed about money. Everyone had their own agenda. My father went along with Michel because music was sacred to him. He hoped Michel would become a great concert pianist. My parents were making great sacrifices trying to help me, which to them meant helping my husband. I was totally insignificant, invisible, a non-person. It never occurred to anyone that I might become anything except a housewife and mother. Meanwhile, I wanted to be more without knowing what.

I was by far the worst of my piano teacher's students. As much as I love music, I am neither a creative nor a performing musician. Trying and failing to master music was among the greatest challenges of my life, and that was good for me. At last, I had found something that didn't come easily.

In other ways, my years in France were priceless. Michel was a good companion. We traveled all over the country together and learned about the stunning variety of languages, cooking, wines, and architecture of the many regions of France. The medieval architecture, especially the magnificent Gothic cathedrals with their huge stained-glass windows, gargoyles, and religious sculptures, was an inspiration for my sense of history. Historical architecture is visual history. Images are often much more powerful than words.

And I learned French! Aside from a few days of tutoring to pass a high school–level exam, my only prior knowledge of French was from memorizing Gounod's opera *Faust* from a phonograph record. Since I had learned French by listening to singing, I thought I was supposed to hold the final "e," even in spoken words. It was a hard habit to break, and I sounded ridiculous. I finally mastered the language by reading in French and looking up words I didn't know in a French-English dictionary until I hardly needed it. I read history textbooks—first high school–level, then college-level history. I learned more than I wanted to know about Louis XIV. Then I read French literature in French, including almost all the novels of Gustave Flaubert and most of Honoré de Balzac. Years later, I taught myself how to read eighteenth-century French historical documents that very few native-born French historians and archivists can read.

I quickly learned how the French hate to hear their language butchered by overconfident foreigners. I once heard someone say disparagingly of a foreigner, "Il ne parle pas," implying that anyone who could not speak French was mute. At first, I was afraid to speak. When I was under anesthesia at the American Hospital of Paris in March 1951, while giving birth to my son Leo, the nurse complimented me on my "perfect French." After that, I lost my inhibitions and began to speak French. I never lost the language. When I returned to France for a brief visit in 1973, I had not spoken French in twenty years, but I was still so fluent that people thought I was a native French speaker with a slight provincial accent.

Knowing another language means knowing another world. Now I know Spanish, too, with some of its regional and national accents and vocabularies: Madrid, Seville, Mexico, Cuba, Puerto Rico, Dominican Republic, Colombia. Today, I speak Mexican—or, more specifically, Guanajuato—Spanish most of the time.

I learned to deeply respect the French version of liberty. It focuses more on freedom of thought, which our own tradition often neglects or violates. The French version is much less conformist and involves a strong sense of right and rights. The French version of liberty goes beyond the intellectual world. Creativity is given more breathing room. Workers and students are quick to pour out into the streets to overturn unpopular government decisions. Broad boulevards had to be built in Paris to prevent her rebellious population from barricading the streets.

My years in Paris were a great relief from the mean, racist police state I grew up in. But French liberty had its limits. I lived in Paris before the great migration of Black Africans and other nationalities to the country; the intense French hatred of the peoples it colonized focused across the Mediterranean Sea on the Algerians, who wanted to control their own country and were already driving out French settlers. During this period, in contrast, Black American writers, artists, and musicians flocked to Paris and were greeted warmly.

The French government maintained close surveillance of foreigners. The police came to our home several times to tell us to report to the police station in our neighborhood. There was no explanation except that we were foreigners. I only recently discovered why the French police were so interested in me. My latest declassified FBI files revealed a letter from J. Edgar Hoover, with a copy to the CIA, summarizing my political history and calling for a close surveillance of my activities in France.

From: John Edgar Hoover, Director - Federal Bureau of Investigation

Subject: GWENDOLYN MIDLO SAMUELSON YUSPEH,
nee Gwendolyn Charmaine Midlo, was.,
Mrs. Michel Herbert Yuspeh,
Mrs. Morais Samuelson
SECURITY MATTER - C

The captioned individual who has been the subject of an investigation by this Bureau has been reported by confidential informants, of known reliability, to have attended Communist Party meetings at New Orleans, Louisiana, during 1947, 1948 and 1949, and to have been a card-carrying Communist Party member. The subject was also reported to be a member of the Executive Board of the Southern Negro Youth Congress as of July 12, 1948, and to be listed in the records of the Civil Rights Congress as of February 13, 1950. The foregoing organizations have been cited by the Attorney General as coming within the purview of Executive Order 9835.

The subject was reportedly born at New Orleans, Louisiana, on June 27, 1929, the daughter of Herman Lazard Midlo, a New Orleans attorney. She is the former wife of Morais Samuelson whom she divorced in 1949, and is presently married to Michel Herbert Yuspeh. Yuspeh is reported to be a native of New Orleans, Louisiana, having been born there on June 20, 1929. The subject is described as follows.

As a foreigner, I could not become involved in politics in any way. We went to political parades and demonstrations, but we could not belong to any political organization without risking our being kicked out of the country. Still, I got a vicarious thrill from the French politics of those years. The whole country was traumatized by the long Nazi occupation. The CP of France had emerged from World War II with high prestige because it had played a major role in the heroic underground resistance movement. Working-class towns with elected Communist mayors and city councils ringed Paris. The working class was a powerful, autonomous force. The General Confederation of Labor (Confédération Générale du Travail), the Communist-led trade union movement, sponsored frequent, powerful strikes. Government responsibility for social welfare was a given.

On May Day, Bastille Day, and other working-class holidays, the streets of Paris exploded with hundreds of thousands of workers parading to the Place de la Bastille and the Porte de Vincennes. They waved signs and banners and shouted slogans, demonstrating for workers' rights and against France's wars in Algeria and Vietnam. Contingents of Algerians brought up the rear. The demonstrators did not march in lockstep, military style. They were joyful and ebullient, expressing with their gestures and body language: "This is our Paris! These are our streets!" The police hovered disconsolately in the side streets in their patrol wagons, trying to make themselves as inconspicuous as possible.

~

I gave birth to my first child in Paris. I was desperate to have a child after having had two abortions, one of them illegal, with a coat hanger, from which I nearly bled out. Our son Leo was born in the American Hospital in Neuilly-sur-Seine on March 14, 1951.

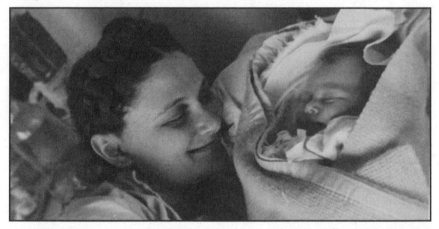

Motherhood was a joyful, humanizing experience. I quickly learned that babies are not blank pages upon which to write. They are born with clear temperaments. They are real, distinct people who can teach us profound truths if we are willing to listen, observe, and learn instead of trying to socialize them into what we are told they should be. For better or worse, I adopted French methods of baby care, using cloth diapers, which I washed by hand in the bidet and then boiled. I started out by picking Leo up and holding him every time he cried. But the French system was to just let the baby cry and, if he didn't stop, put him out on the balcony so you didn't hear him.

Who taught me that? At last, we had become close friends with a French couple, Janine Netter and Henri Alcalay. Michel and Henri both studied piano with Jeanne Blancard. Janine was then an aspiring high school English teacher. Their little boy, Jean-Jacques, was about two years older than Leo. They were Jews who had met while hiding from the Nazis among French peasants in Vichy France. According to Janine and Henri, almost all the French peasants hid Jews and didn't betray them. They had a hard time passing themselves off as peasants while Henri played classical piano, but no one exposed them.

Living in Paris gave me a lot. Although I could not get my college degree, I am not sure how much good it would have done me during the McCarthy era. I was better off learning how to type.

Paris, 1952. My father, Jean-Jacques, Leo, Janine

Coming Home to the Red Scare

In the summer of 1953 we returned to the United States. The US Embassy in Paris had refused to renew our passports a few years earlier, so our temporary passports were valid only for a few days to allow us to return directly to the United States. My parents came to Paris so we could travel together. As the ship pulled away from shore, my father asked me if I was happy to be going home. I said I would be happier if the ship turned around. We arrived in New York City in August, during a heat wave. It was like being trapped at the bottom of an oven.

After staying briefly in a friend's apartment, we moved into the Seville Hotel Apartments on West 58th Street, across from Carnegie Hall and a block from Central Park. I walked with Leo in Central Park and taught him how to say "squirrel" and "pigeon" in English, singing him songs and reading him nursery tales in English instead of French. But Leo continued speaking French. After he tasted American Cheddar cheese, he said indignantly, "Ce ne pas du fromage, ca!"

Leo, age 3

While Michel and I lived in France, information about the ravages of McCarthyism had been scattered and indirect. We had received a hysterical letter from Michel's cousin, saying we had to remove our books from her basement because they were dangerous and subversive. This was the era when Ethel and Julius Rosenberg were tried and executed for espionage because they allegedly gave atomic secrets to the Soviet

Union. The day the Rosenbergs were executed, we watched a wreath of flowers float down the Seine in their honor.

J. Edgar Hoover personally made sure the FBI knew when we returned from France. They couldn't find our new home, so an FBI agent went to South Rampart Street in New Orleans to find out from one of my cousins where I lived now. They finally found us after asking the neighbors about us in both places in New York. The pretense was that they wanted to be sure we were really there, but in the context of Red Scare hysteria, it was also to get us evicted from apartments and fired from jobs. This tactic worked more often than not. After a few months in Manhattan, two FBI agents—playing good cop, bad cop—came to ask us to hand over our canceled passports. We refused. I had the honor of being put on the FBI's Security Index shortly thereafter.

FROM : SAC, New York (100-114961)

SUBJECT: GWENDOLYN MIDLO SAMUELSON YUSPEH, was
SM-C

ALL INFORMATION CONTAINED
HEREIN IS UNCLASSIFIED
DATE 04-03-2009 BY 60324 UC BAW/SAB/LSC

Card Filed
9-18-54 acw

X It is recommended that a Security Index Card be prepared on the above-captioned individual.

___ The Security Index Card on the captioned individual should be changed as follows: (Specify change only)

NAME GWENDOLYN MIDLO SAMUELSON YUSPEH

ALIASES Mrs. MICHEL HERBERT YUSPEH, GWENDOLYN CHARMAGNE MIDLO, GWEN MIDLO, GWENNIE MIDLO, GWENDIE MIDLO, GWEN MIDLO SAMUELSON, Mrs. GENICE SAMUELSON, Mrs. GUINNE SAMUELSON, GWENDOLYN SAMUELSON, Mrs. MORRIS SAMUELSON, Mrs. MORAIS SAMUELSON.
NATIVE BORN X NATURALIZED ___ ALIEN ___

COMMUNIST x SOCIALIST WORKERS PARTY ___ INDEPENDENT SOCIALIST LEAGUE ___

MISCELLANEOUS (Specify) ___

TAB FOR DETCOM ___ TAB FOR COMSAB ___ RACE White SEX Female

DATE OF BIRTH June 27, 1929 PLACE OF BIRTH New Orleans, La.

BUSINESS ADDRESS (Show name of employing concern and address) ___

___ Music Teacher, uses residence for teaching.

___

NATURE OF INDUSTRY OR BUSINESS (Specify from Vital Facility List) ___

RESIDENCE ADDRESS Hotel Sevilla RECORDED - 72 100 - 375336 - 14

117 W. 58th Street, NYC (apartment 9F)

JJM:EAF

EX 122

Another little problem: we had nothing to live on. While applying for a sales job at Gimbels department store I passed out from hunger—they had already turned me down for being overqualified. I wanted to move back to New Orleans, but Michel insisted on staying in New York. He was right. The repression in New Orleans during the 1950s became more and more intense, and it got much worse after the US Supreme Court outlawed school segregation in 1954. The US Congress and the FBI were deeply involved.

On a trip back to New Orleans, I visited Bill Sorum in his apartment in the French Quarter. Bill was about to crack. He told me the CP had instructed everyone to leave town and change their name and identity. He had just finished his residency in psychiatry. "How can I do that?" he asked in a panic. I had no answer. He told me the FBI came to see him the day Ethel and Julius Rosenberg were executed and threatened him.

In the end, Bill survived by publicly and privately informing on everyone, ruining many lives. The Senate Internal Security Subcommittee hearings in New Orleans went into executive session as Bill identified students he had recruited into the CP. I know he identified me because my FBI files refer to his testimony several times to establish that I was a Communist. He was generally accurate and quite informative about the CP in New Orleans, reporting that it had about 250 members, many in waterfront workers' unions with almost entirely Black officials.

Judy Modigliani Jenkins told me the CP had been formally dissolved in the South, and all members had been ordered to leave town, change their names, and go underground. I soon discovered this to be the case across the country. The CP national office in New York gave the same instructions to dissolve to the leadership of every Communist organization arbitrarily placed on the US Attorney General's List of Subversive Organizations without even an investigation or hearing.

According to Judy, James Dombrowski, director of the Southern Conference for Human Welfare (SCHW), told the CP representative who gave him this instruction to go to hell. Instead of dissolving the SCHW, he adopted the name of its nonprofit wing, the Southern Conference Educational Fund (SCEF). Its headquarters remained in New Orleans for at least a decade. It survived arrests, police raids of its offices, and seizure of its files. The SCEF played an incalculably important role in promoting interracialism in the Deep South. It recruited and supported southerners, including whites, to participate in the Civil Rights Movement. Its newspaper, the *Southern Patriot*, continued to expose and protest both vigilante and open state terrorism. The SCEF eventually moved to Louisville, Kentucky, under the leadership of Anne and Karl Braden. Dombrowski stayed in New Orleans and inspired generations of people fighting for racial justice and the rights of southern workers.

The Red Scare took a terrible and sometimes deadly toll among the Communists I had known in New Orleans. Left-wing and CP members of the NMU were screened off ships by the US Coast Guard. The New Orleans cold warriors went after the TWU and the ILWU. Among the African American leaders of the ILWU, Andrew Nelson died of a heart attack and Lee Brown did hard time in a state prison in Louisiana for several years for refusing to become an informer. He had been convicted of perjury for signing a loyalty oath swearing he was not a member of the Communist Party. Lee published his moving story in the 2001 book *Strong in the Struggle: My Life as a Black Labor Activist*.

When Raymond Tillman was voted out of the union leadership of the TWU, he and Grace moved to Chicago. Grady Jenkins, a Mississippi farm boy turned merchant seaman and Judy Modigliani's husband, was arrested under a Louisiana state antisubversive law while he was suffering from tuberculosis, which was hard to treat then. He was kept chained to his hospital bed, with two armed state policemen watching him to make sure he would not "escape." His doctors said he needed to get up and move to recover, but he was chained to his bed anyway. Grady survived, and after he recovered, he learned to be a printer. He slept on our couch in Los Angeles in 1960 until he got a job and could bring Judy and their two kids to Los Angeles. They opened a printing shop and lived in LA for the rest of their lives. I was told Joseph Mouledous slit his wrists, and I assumed he was dead. But he phoned me in 2000 after my *Louisiana Slave Database* was reported on the front page of the *New York Times*. A Vietnam War draft resister, Joe moved to Canada and became a sociology professor.

There is a long history of southern whites supporting the Black freedom struggle, all the way back to abolitionism, the Civil War, Reconstruction, the Knights of Labor, the agrarian populists of the late nineteenth century, and the Industrial Workers of the World (IWW) of the early twentieth century. My earliest memories are of white organizers of the CIO defying segregation and being systematically tortured by the New Orleans police. It was the CP in the South that, almost alone, took up the challenge of building Black and white unity during the 1930s and 1940s. The SCEF did manage to recruit some southern whites during the height of the Civil Rights Movement, but only a few—and even fewer were white workers. Five decades before Katrina, there was an exodus of almost all the New Orleans white people who were ready to lay down their lives for racial equality.

On the other hand, most African American CP members in New Orleans stayed to face the music. Why did they stay? Just like during Katrina, more white people than Black people had the money and means of transportation to pack up and leave, as well as places to go. But it was also the enormous attachment of African Americans in Louisiana to their home.

The destruction of the left-led unions during the Red Scare drastically weakened the Black freedom struggle and the struggles of all workers, and we are all still paying the price. The left-wing waterfront unions were smashed. The interracial youth movement was destroyed. Even as McCarthyism began to diminish in the North, it took on new life in the South. Anyone who opposed segregation was considered a scheming Red spy. Congress was deeply involved in the witch-hunts. The House Un-American Activities Committee (HUAC) and the Senate Internal Security Subcommittee held highly publicized public hearings throughout the South. Victims who were subpoenaed to testify had to denounce others as Communists, take the Fifth Amendment (as protection against self-incrimination), or go to jail. But unless they fingered others, they would surely lose their jobs and could not get other work.

My old friend from the founding of the New Orleans Youth Council, Alvin B. Jones Jr., was another victim of the Red Scare. He died mainly because of FBI persecution. Alvin wasn't just one of the best minds to come out of Louisiana, he also had the most integrity. I visited him every time I returned to New Orleans. He became a partner in Benjamin Smith's civil rights law firm in New Orleans but was kicked out after some of his clients brought complaints against him with the Louisiana Bar Association. I have little doubt these complaints were instigated by the FBI or the New Orleans police. The Civil Rights Congress attacked Alvin for refusing to sell out one of his clients. He was defending two Black men in a case involving the rape of a Black woman. After a national campaign was launched by the Civil Rights Congress claiming the defendants had been framed, each of them told Alvin that one of them was guilty and the other stayed in the car and knew nothing about the rape. Alvin got the charges dropped against the innocent man by encouraging the guilty man to confess. What remained of the left denounced Alvin as a traitor because he spoiled their cause célèbre by encouraging his clients to tell the truth.

Shortly before he died, I asked Alvin if there was any interracialism left in New Orleans. He said, "Well, there are a few meetings of people officially representing groups of whites and Negroes. But not like us. We knew each other. We loved each other." The last time I saw him, he asked bitterly, "Where were you? Maybe you went to get help?"

I told him I did. I was trying.

Harry Haywood in our home in Brooklyn, 1956

PART THREE

BLACK REDS, REVOLUTIONARY NATIONALISTS, AND BLACK POWER

Harry Haywood was a pioneering Black intellectual who deeply influenced several generations of fighters for African American liberation and Black Power. He emphasized self-determination for what he defined as the oppressed African American nation in the Black Belt South, and he challenged legal and de facto segregation, discrimination, oppression, and super-exploitation of African Americans throughout the country. He was brilliant, creative, original, charismatic, a great networker, a man of complete integrity, a thinker and writer of enormous and enduring influence, who was too honest to survive in the Communist bureaucracy.

Before I met him, I admired his brilliant writings about the African American liberation movement. His book *Negro Liberation*, published in 1948, guided the devoted antifascist generation that joined the reconstituted CP after World War II and mostly left it during the mid-1950s when the CP was infiltrated and then taken over by the FBI. I had direct experience with this important, still largely invisible history, and I attempt here to connect the dots while sharing my memories about some of the pivotal people and their times.

Harry and I first met briefly at a May Day parade in Paris in 1950. We began to work together in Manhattan in 1953 and to live together in 1955. We married legally in 1956, had two children, and remained married until his death in 1985.

As soon as I first walked into his apartment in Manhattan, we exchanged two sentences that summed up much of our political relationship. I asked him, "If Negroes are an oppressed nation in the United States, why don't they have their own revolutionary leadership?"

Harry replied, with surprise and enthusiasm, "Where did *you* come from?"

We shared a deep appreciation for Black folk culture, faith in the power and potential of the African American revolutionary movement, especially in the Deep South, and devotion to revolutionary internationalism. We both had grave and realistic doubts about the CP leadership, and as we began to work together we devoted ourselves to freeing the party's highly trained and experienced Black Red organizers from the dead hand of the CP bureaucracy, which by then was almost completely dominated by the FBI.

Although I had rejected stereotypical roles for women since early childhood, I still didn't believe I could accomplish anything important on my own—only by standing by my man. I believed that, through Harry, I could help save the radical Black working-class movement. As bad as it sounds today, this was probably realistic then, given the social norms even on the left.

Ours was a passionate political love affair. But our love went far beyond politics. I perceived and supported the best in him. I don't think he actually perceived me, except as someone who appreciated him and who was "useful," his highest compliment. When we met, I was stuck in a failed marriage to Michel. Harry was in a rocky marriage to Belle Lewis, a devoted Communist with a heroic past. I believed I could give Harry the emotional and intellectual support he badly needed.

I quickly discovered he was on the verge of suicide, talking about jumping out of his sixth-story window. I was driven to save him. We fell deeply in love. I wooed him by appreciating him, encouraging him, giving him hope, calming him down, being thoughtful and original, and— the greatest gift of all—helping him write. He wooed me by telling me the stories of his amazing life. Almost all his stories were published in 1978 in his influential autobiography, *Black Bolshevik: Autobiography of an Afro-American Communist.*

We once met clandestinely in April 1955 in the only hotel in Washington, DC, where Black people were allowed to stay. The FBI informed the CP national leadership, and they called Harry in, demanding to know who I was. Harry refused to give them my name and demanded to know how they knew about his trip to Washington. The FBI had discussed arresting Harry for violating the Mann Act—for taking a woman across state lines for "immoral" purposes. I found out about this after reading Harry's FBI files, which were declassified after J. Edgar Hoover died. Harry never told me about it. But he warned me about the dark forces that would victimize me because of our love and told me to consider carefully what might become of me if our relationship continued. I told him I would take my chances.

HAS ADVISED ON 4/20/55 THAT HARRY HAYWOOD WAS QUESTIONED BY CLAUDE LIGHTFOOT, MEMBER NATIONAL ADMINISTRATIVE COMMITTEE, AT CP HEAD-QUARTERS ON SAME DATE, REGARDING A RECENT FIVE DAY TRIP HAYWOOD MADE TO WASHINGTON. HAYWOOD AT FIRST REFUSED TO ADMIT SUCH TRIP, BUT UPON ADMITTING MAKING TRIP DENIED ANYONE WAS WITH HIM. HAYWOOD WAS ASKED IF THERE WAS NOT A WOMAN WITH HIM. HAYWOOD AT FIRST DENIED THAT BUT LATER ADMITTED THAT THERE WAS A YOUNG WOMAN, 25 YEARS OF AGE, MARRIED WITH ONE CHILD, FROM NEW ORLEANS, WHO BY COINCIDENCE WAS IN WASHINGTON AND WHO HAD COME TO HIS HOTEL ROOM SEVERAL TIMES TO DO TYPING. HAYWOOD SAID SHE WAS IN WASHINGTON VISITING FRIENDS AND A PROFESSOR OUTSIDE WASHINGTON. HAYWOOD WAS EXTREMELY UPSET AT LIGHTFOOT'S QUESTIONING AND STATED TRIP WAS ABOVEBOARD AND THAT BELLE (PHONETIC - PROBABLY HAYWOOD'S WIFE) WAS AWARE OF IT. HAYWOOD DEMANDED OF LIGHTFOOT THAT HE BE TOLD HOW INFORMATION GOT BACK TO LIGHTFOOT BUT GOT NO ANSWER. HAYWOOD SAID ONE OF THE REASONS

Harry struggled with alcoholism all his life, but he straightened up and stopped drinking during the first few years we were together. Those were happy, productive times. We started to live together in Brooklyn in 1955. Our son Haywood was quickly conceived. At fifty-seven, Harry was thrilled because this was his first child. We couldn't get married until both of our divorces were final. Our legal marriage took place on April 10, 1956, a few months before Haywood was born. At first, we tried to get married by the justice of the peace in Brooklyn, where we lived. He refused without explanation to marry us. The Manhattan justice of the peace finally married us.

Our son Haywood, six months old, at a Christmas Party at the Brooklyn home of William L. Patterson

Harry Haywood

Harry was a man of great courage and integrity. A self-educated worker-intellectual, he first earned his living as a teenager shining shoes. He worked as a waiter on Pullman railroad cars running out of Chicago and then waited tables in elite Chicago restaurants. He fought on the front lines in France in one of the few Black combat units during World War I.

His political life started during the Red Summer of 1919. A few months after he was discharged from the army, he was working on a

Pullman train out of Chicago. He had returned home to find the city in flames, with white racists driving trucks through the Black community and shooting people at random. Black veterans went to the US Armory and got weapons, including machine guns. Harry joined them, waiting to ambush the white racist terrorists behind a machine gun that he had learned how to use on the front lines in France.

His older brother, Otto Hall, soon recruited him into the African Blood Brotherhood (ABB). The ABB was founded in 1919 in New York City by Caribbean immigrant Cyril Briggs and other Black radicals, in large part in response to the Red Summer of 1919. The group published and distributed Briggs's journal the *Crusader*. Its first issues chiefly promoted revolutionary Black nationalism, with an emphasis on the need to defend the Black community with arms against racist massacres. Under the influence of Black socialists like Hubert Harrison and inspired by the achievements of the Russian Revolution, the ABB gradually identified with socialism and Marxism, leading its members toward the CP.

The Harlem members of the ABB were mainly intellectuals from the Caribbean. The Chicago members were mainly workers from Midwestern shops. In his autobiography, *Black Bolshevik*, Harry described how some members of the ABB opposed the group's absorption into the CP, arguing that the African American movement needed its own autonomous revolutionary leadership. Harry argued that the oppression of African Americans was so intense that a revolutionary nationalist movement could not survive without substantial help from the world Communist movement. He always believed this, even after the Soviet Union nearly destroyed the Comintern and formally dissolved it during World War II.

Harry became a member of the Communist Youth League first and then the CP, where he quickly became a leader. He had dropped out of school in the eighth grade in Minneapolis, so he was educated in Moscow at the University for the Toilers of the East and then at the Lenin School during the last half of the 1920s, at a time when the Soviet Union was strongly supporting the worldwide struggles against colonialism and for independence. Harry got to know the leaders of the African, Latin American, and Asian Communist and independence movements, as well as artists and intellectuals throughout the colonial world. He mastered the Russian language—no easy task—which increased his clout within the Comintern.

The theory of an African American nation with the right of self-determination emerged from the Sixth World Congress of the Comintern, held in Moscow in 1928. It was part of the world Communist movement's thrust toward supporting anticolonial struggles, making Marxism and Communism more relevant to the most important popular struggles and revolutions of the twentieth century. Although the theory was rigid, its core of truth had an enormous, lasting impact.

Harry helped develop and fight for the theory that African Americans were an oppressed nation within a nation, and that the Black Belt South of the United States should have the right to self-determination. African Americans living outside the Black Belt were defined as an oppressed national minority, which the Black working class would lead. This concept forced the CP to take the African American struggle seriously indeed, especially in the South, where many Communists were afraid to work—for good reasons.

Throughout most of the 1930s, Harry served on the Central Committee of the CP in charge of "Negro work." He became general secretary of the League of Struggle for Negro Rights in 1930; Langston Hughes was its honorary president.[1] Harry worked closely with William L. Patterson, then leader of the International Labor Defense. They supported the Sharecroppers' Union in the Alabama Black Belt and launched and developed the fight to save the lives of the nine Scottsboro defendants, with much international publicity supported by the Comintern.[2]

In 1934, the last time Harry was in Moscow, he was aware that something was very wrong and was relieved to get out of there alive. But he always believed a revolutionary Black movement could not survive without a "real" Communist Party in the United States. He devoted his entire life to trying to create, restore, or recreate one that would fight uncompromisingly for African American freedom.

Looking back on what he achieved within the CP, Harry, his brother Otto Hall, Cyril Briggs, Richard B. Moore, and other distinguished Black revolutionary leaders were perhaps right to support the absorption of the ABB into the CP during the early 1920s. They got a lot of support from the CP and above all from the Comintern at a time when support was not likely to come from anywhere else. During much of the 1930s and 1940s, the CP substantially helped and supported Black freedom fighters in the United States, along with many Black artists and intellectuals, including nonparty members.

A thinker and a writer, Harry had few talents as a bureaucrat. He was quick to escape from the closed world of the CP's national headquarters in New York City. He went to organize coal miners of West Virginia and western Pennsylvania, where he became known as the Black Slav because he was fluent in Russian, returning to Chicago in 1934 to be close to the burgeoning workers' struggles there. His sister Eppa, a stockyard worker, helped organize Chicago's growing trade union movement. Harry organized massive street protests against the invasion of Ethiopia by Mussolini's fascist regime. Then he volunteered to go to Spain to fight with the International Brigades as a commissar and captain in the Abraham Lincoln Battalion. Harry and his comrades were fighting against General Francisco Franco and his Italian and German fascist allies, who together devastated Spain with air raids, troops, tanks, and artillery, and finally destroyed the freely elected Spanish Republic after a horribly destructive war lasting several years.

Harry's experiences during the Spanish Civil War were the most painful to him. He could hardly talk about them. He had the courage to lead a delegation to present a formal complaint to Lt. Col. Vladimir Ćopić, the commander of the International Brigade, about the useless slaughter of hundreds of US volunteers at the Battle of Jarama. Ćopić had ordered the untrained, lightly armed American volunteers to attack fascist machine-gun posts with no cover; promised Soviet tanks never showed up. Harry challenged this Red Army officer, who was finally called back to Moscow and executed. Only once, when he was very drunk, did Harry tell me how he walked across a battlefield at Brunete and saw hundreds of torn-up corpses of young American volunteers. He knew many of them; some were his recruits.

Harry returned from Spain and was removed from the Central Committee of the CP. According to an FBI agent's account, Harry had become the victim of the Soviet secret police's desire for "goats to take the rap for various Russian moves." He was mostly relegated to being a rank-and-file CP member.

After the United States entered World War II, Harry joined the Merchant Marine. He worked as a steward, cook, and pastry chef, first on an oil tanker to the Pacific and later on the extremely hazardous Murmansk run, bringing a railroad engine and military supplies to the Soviet Union. He continued to ship out after the war until he was screened off merchant ships by the US Coast Guard. He started working again as a waiter. His economic autonomy gave him more freedom than most of the CP's leading African American functionaries. In those days, with few exceptions Black people could get only the most menial jobs, even if they had advanced degrees and weren't Communists.

When we first met in France in 1950, Harry was again in deep trouble with the CP. He had been accused of being an agent of the US State Department. William L. Patterson advised him to return to New York. Harry and Leon Josephson, a lawyer known for having financed and participated in heroic missions to save Jews from the Nazis, led an inner-party faction opposed to anyone going underground. In a report, another FBI agent quoted Harry as saying, "The USA is not Czarist Russia. Everyone has his day in court."

Hoover's private FBI file about Harry got longer when James E. Jackson Jr. (Jack from my New Orleans days) and six other leading Communists convicted of subversion under the Smith Act went missing. An FBI agent's report on Harry quoted him as saying that Leon Josephson was in contact with the seven men. The agent wrote that Jackson was part of a "colored group headed by Harry who opposes going underground." One report said someone from Birmingham was living in Harry's apartment. It was probably Jack.

The FBI targeted Harry as part of a new program called TOPLEV, in which its agents would approach top-level CP members and try to talk them into becoming informants. They investigated every weakness in him they could find or imagine and sent two agents to approach him twice, at the most public place possible: the entrance to a subway station at rush hour. The agents got nowhere with him, so the FBI closed its file.

Writing and Organizing with Harry in New York City

The main thing I did was help Harry write. That was quite a challenge. We talked things out and I typed up the conclusions of our discussions. He would look over the typed page, make corrections, and then want to see a clean copy. At first, I didn't know how to type. I hunted and pecked slowly, typing and retyping every page. Electric typewriters were new, high-tech, and expensive. I pounded on Harry's big, heavy Woodstock manual, typing each page over and over again as best I could. He taught me how to mark up manuscripts for editing, including cutting and pasting. The result of this early work was an influential pamphlet, *For a Revolutionary Position on the Negro Question*. I mimeographed it, and it was widely circulated hand to hand.[3]

Now that we were married, I had to decide which name to use. Harry's legal name was Haywood Hall. But everyone knew him as Harry Haywood. I decided to use his legal name Hall because it seemed a bit more anonymous than Haywood. Ironically, just about everyone who knew me or knew of me for the next few decades believed I was married to Gus Hall, a white man who was the leader of the CP for many years. When Gus Hall died, several people expressed their condolences to my children. Aside from the confusion between Harry's legal name and pen name, few white people could wrap their minds around my being married to a Black man.

Above all, I had to figure out how to make a living. My father had taught me how to do title searches in courthouses. I got a job as a file clerk in a large entertainment law firm on Broadway in midtown Manhattan. I memorized thousands of file numbers to save time and taught myself touch typing during my lunch break. My piano training helped, and I became a very fast, accurate typist. Throughout my pregnancy, I went to night school several times a week to learn the stenotype machine. I was fired by the entertainment law firm when I was six months pregnant with my son Haywood. They told me it was because I was pregnant, but it was the FBI again. I got another job as an editorial assistant on a manuscript for a mail-order catalog. Travel time from our home in Brooklyn to my workplace in Manhattan was an hour and a half each way. They finally asked me to leave, explaining they didn't want me to give birth on their office floor.

When Haywood was born one week later, I was in a large ward in the Brooklyn Women's Hospital with Jewish Holocaust refugees who had also just given birth. They were speaking to each other in Yiddish. I understood every word. They talked about the murder of their parents. When their children asked why other children had grandparents but they had none, they didn't know what to say. They saw the look on my face and asked me if I understood. I nodded yes.

I went back to work one month after Haywood was born, leaving him in the care of a neighbor. Within a short time, I became a top-notch legal secretary. After a few more inexplicable firings, I did temporary work. Whenever I went out to look for a job, I had one by the next day. By the time the FBI arrived to get me fired, I was already gone. Harry bribed his way into a waiters' union and worked weekends at the Sabra, an Israeli nightclub in Manhattan. Since he was a union man, the FBI could not get him fired.

My last job in New York was for a real estate law firm on Nostrand Avenue, close to our home in Brooklyn. They were busy exploiting African American homebuyers. None of the buyers could get mortgages because of racial discrimination. The law firm bought cheap houses in bad condition, put some cheap paint on the walls and linoleum on the floors, falsified the appraisals, and sold them for twice the price they paid, writing mortgages for much more than the houses were worth. The law firm kept the mortgages, which paid a high interest rate.

That's where I first met John Hope Franklin, chair of the history department at Brooklyn College. At the time, he was one of the first African American historians to get a job at a white higher education institution. We talked about his book *From Slavery to Freedom*, which was first published in 1947. He told me he couldn't buy a house in Brooklyn because of racial discrimination, so he had to resort to the law firm where I worked. Of course he knew he was being badly cheated. We had such a fascinating conversation that we went out on the street corner for privacy and continued talking away under our umbrellas after it started to rain. Thirty years later, he remembered that very conversation when he gave the Midlo Lecture at the University of New Orleans in 1988.

John Hope Franklin shortly before he died in 2009 at age 94.

~

African Americans in the United States have a long, deep experience of organizing within the realm of the possible. What Communists offered them was international, outside support, which they largely lacked. Harry helped teach the younger generations how to organize and turn the repression of African Americans into an international scandal that eventually forced the US government to make important concessions to African Americans' fight against segregation, lynching, and racist violence. But by the early 1950s, the CP leadership was, under the pretext of "going underground," destroying the CP and every other left-wing organization it controlled or could influence, including Black organizations that had many loyal, devoted, highly trained, experienced organizers rooted in their shops and communities,

I encouraged Harry to become more openly outspoken and critical about how the CP leadership was destroying the radical Black Communist movement. We accomplished a lot. Almost all the African Americans, Puerto Ricans, and waterfront workers left the CP. Some of them left formally, going to the organization we helped create, the Provisional Organizing Committee to Reestablish the Communist Party (known as the POC), led by Harry, Al Lanon, Admiral Kirkpatrick, and Armando Ramon, a Puerto Rican merchant seaman. Many others were deeply influenced by what we wrote, which was mimeographed and passed around hand to hand. Many Black militants trained in the party left the CP on their own. Most were highly skilled community organizers freed from the discipline of the CP. Except for those on salary, few minority members remained.

Like Harry, these militants worked together harmoniously and taught others how to organize. We were strong in Harlem, Brooklyn, and the Bronx. Charles Loman, the district organizer of the CP in Brooklyn, and Isadore Beagan, district organizer in the Bronx, left the party with us. Al Lanon, a founder of the NMU and leader of the waterfront section of the CP, was our most effective spokesman. Mae Mallory, an active member of the POC, was a Black woman powerhouse who fought for quality education for the children of Harlem and supported the armed self-defense movement against the Ku Klux Klan founded by Robert and Mabel Williams in Monroe, North Carolina. Admiral Kirkpatrick, who, like Harry, had been a political commissar during the Spanish Civil War, organized coal miners in Williamsport, Pennsylvania.

Our members included experienced Detroit autoworkers led by Coleman Young, a Tuskegee Airman during World War II and a militant of the UAW. In the 1970s, he became the first elected Black mayor of Detroit, serving for twenty years. We had longshoremen all the way from the West Coast to the Port of Newark, New Jersey. The Newark club became active in city politics and helped get some of the first Black politicians elected. Theodore W. Allen, a worker-intellectual and former coal miner from West Virginia, was an active member. He later developed the influential concept of white skin privilege, which he first published in 1965.[4] Ollie Leeds, leader of CORE in Brooklyn during the 1960s, also left the CP with us and was active in the POC. CORE knew about Leeds's Communist background, but he was elected its leader anyway.

During the POC's brief history, I worked with Harry in our apartment on Lincoln Place in Brooklyn. I was the typist, of course. I did all the national communications and kept all the records. Local communications took place face to face or cautiously by telephone. But the POC was a national organization. Long-distance calls were expensive then, so there was a considerable amount of correspondence by mail.

Armando Ramon lived in a cold-water walk-up on the Lower East Side of Manhattan, where we sometimes met. Armando became suspicious of me because I kept incoming letters and carbon copies of outgoing mail, concluding that I was a spy. Of course, I was keeping everything because of my instincts as a historian. (All these documents are now in the Harry Haywood Papers at the Bentley Historical Library in Ann Arbor.) Armando first accused Al Lanon and then me and Harry of being government spies, expelled us all from the POC, and grabbed the organizational apparatus, such as it was. Each tiny faction within the POC accused the other of being spies, shattering the group. There was some real basis for being suspicious. By then, I think there must have been more FBI agents than real members in Communist organizations. My FBI files have whole redacted pages that list the names of their secret agents.

Still, thanks to the POC, during the 1950s the Communist Party could not force its Black members down the road to self-destruction. Breaking discipline as a member of the party was nearly unthinkable. An expelled comrade was ostracized. But we gave many Black Communists a political home, at least long enough to help get experienced, trained organizers out from under party discipline. Black comrades kept in touch with each other and worked well together. Very few went underground. They stayed home where they were known, continued to organize in their unions, shops, and communities, and taught others how to organize. Many of them emerged as leaders of the Civil Rights and Black Power movements of the 1950s, '60s, and '70s. Many of these leaders concealed their Communist backgrounds, so the role of Communists in those movements is only slowly becoming known. The POC played another important political role as a pioneering organization among Communists who were becoming critical of the USSR and drawn toward Mao's China. Harry's influence grew within the international Maoist New Communist movement.

Black Reds in Harlem

Harlem was the political and cultural center of the Black liberation movement for generations. It set the example for the rest of the country and much of the African-descended world, including Latin America, the Caribbean, and Africa. Why, then, is Harlem hardly mentioned in the histories of battles for civil rights in the North? I think this is a legacy of the Cold War. In reality, the Black Reds were strong in Harlem and influenced generations to come.

Shortly after I returned from France in 1953, I sought out John Henrik Clarke. Then a leading figure in the intellectual community in Harlem, he told me he was working as an elevator operator but was really an office cleaner. He came from a family of sharecroppers in Alabama. Self-educated, he never attended high school, much less college. Like many other Black writers, scholars, musicians, artists, and public intellectuals of his generation, he got effective help from the CP. There was no place else to turn to at the time. As an associate editor of *Freedomways*, he took advantage of his extensive global contacts to make it a truly international publication.

The first time we met, we stayed up all night in his apartment talking about the dead hand of the CP on the radical African American movement. He made the point to me several times that the African American freedom movement was the only one in the world denied the right to choose its own leadership. John later helped me get my first essays published in *Freedomways* and *Negro Digest* (later renamed *Black World*), an influential monthly publication. He was a pioneer in agitating for and promoting African and African American studies at Cornell University and elsewhere. By 1969, he had created and chaired the department of Africana and Puerto Rican studies at Hunter College. He wrote, edited, and published many influential books and articles and lectured nationally and internationally.

John and I remained close friends throughout all the miseries of his life. He got glaucoma and quickly became blind. I bought him a telephone for the visually impaired, which he could use for a while, and I urged him to use a computer, which he eventually did with the help of a young assistant.

By the early 1980s, all of his CP associates turned on him and accused him publicly of being an agent of the US State Department because he gave a talk saying the Soviet Union's engineering projects in Africa were not as efficient as those of the United States. He resigned from *Freedomways* after twenty years of devoted work.[5] When he told me he'd had a stroke in response, I said, "John, these people are not worth a sneeze, much less a stroke." He continued to fly alone all over the country and throughout the world, navigating with his cane while he gave lectures and participated in programs about African and African American history. Shortly before he died, he married his young assistant, Sybil Williams, who helped him remain active and productive until the end.

Harry knew the Black ex-CP members active in Harlem very well. When they shipped out together during World War II, Harry was the mentor of Jesse Gray, then a teenager. They led wildcat strikes aboard the ships. By 1963, Jesse had become the main spokesman for the Harlem Tenants Council and led highly publicized rent strikes, presenting City Hall with dead rats the tenants had collected from their homes. Gray also supported the Harlem branch of the National Welfare Rights Organization: women fighting for greater help for the poor. He was a major spokesman for the Harlem uprising in the summer of 1964, the first urban rebellion of the decade.[6] At his request I answered the phone at his office in Harlem, fielding calls from desperate journalists begging for interviews with Jesse, who was incommunicado. In 1972, he was elected to the New York State House of Representatives from Harlem. He worked with Harlem Fight Back, which made substantial gains for minority workers in the New York City construction industry by organizing demonstrations at construction sites.[7]

Josh Lawrence was a port agent for the rivers and Great Lakes and the second highest-ranking Black official in the NMU, after vice president Ferdinand Smith. Like many of our Black working-class friends who were merchant seamen, he had been screened off the ships by the US Coast Guard. Josh was a quiet, unassuming, effective organizer. With his old shipmates Harry and Jesse Gray, along with James Haughton, he was also part of Harlem Fight Back. Together, those four worked with Malcolm X's Organization for Afro-American Unity. They helped him write the OAAU's platform with extensive input from John Henrik Clarke. Malcolm was prepared to make a public presentation of this program the day he was assassinated in February 1965. Later, Josh became a carpenter to make a living, but his knees gave out. Then he became a sculptor. His wife, Vicky, was an office worker, like many Communist women.

Vicki Garvin was an extraordinary radical leader during World War II and after she joined the reconstituted CP. She coordinated spontaneous Black workers' protest movements in the factories and was the most outspoken fighter for the rights of Black women workers. Vicki was a founding officer and national vice president of the National Negro Labor Council and executive secretary of its New York chapter until the organization was dissolved by the CP in 1955. She admired Harry a lot and was one of many highly trained and motivated Black CP members who left the party for the same reasons we did. She resigned from the party in 1957 and lived in Nigeria and then Ghana, where she welcomed her old friend Malcolm X and introduced him to the ambassadors from China, Cuba, and Algeria. In 1964, she was invited to China. Both Malcolm X and W. E. B. Du Bois encouraged her to go. She spent years teaching writing, editing, and speaking throughout China.[8]

James Haughton led Harlem Fight Back. He devoted his life to trying to create a powerful, autonomous national organization of Black workers to fight for their rights. His family was from the Virgin Islands, which he jokingly called the "Prostitute Islands." An African-style storyteller, he kept his audiences mesmerized, and especially loved telling stories to children.[9] When my son Haywood was an adolescent, Haughton took him under his wing, got him a job reading electric meters in Brooklyn, and was an invaluable presence while Harry was largely absent. Haughton became the male figure in Haywood's life and helped make it possible for our son to rise to distinguished heights in the field of international emergency medicine.

James Haughton of Harlem Fightback. A wonderful organizer and family friend.

Haughton's wife, Eleanor "Happy" Leacock, was an outstanding anthropologist. She had four white kids from a previous marriage. None of her anthropologist colleagues took her seriously because she was not just a woman but also a mother. She told me all they would say to her was, "Hi, Happy. How are your kids?" She ended her career at CUNY as chair of the department of anthropology and a world-famous scholar. Her reputation keeps growing even decades after her death. She is best known for her thorough repudiation of the once widely accepted idea that Black people were poor because of their so-called culture of poverty, which became a great substitute for discussions of structural racism and discrimination and instead blamed the victims for the miserable circumstances of their lives.

During the 1964 Harlem uprising, a protest meeting was scheduled in a big church in Harlem. Happy Leacock phoned and asked, "Gwen, are you going to the protest meeting?" I said, "Hap, if you don't go, and I don't go, ain't gonna be no white folks at all at that meeting." We went together. I carried my daughter, Rebecca, who was about eighteen months old, in my arms. There was a big, angry crowd in the church. One man yelled out, "She brought a fucking baby!" A speaker started pointing at me from the podium, saying in a rage, "All these white women and their half-breed children should leave. We don't want them here." I didn't flinch. He repeated this demand several times until Jesse Gray, his face still in bandages from a police beating, walked up to the speaker and told him something—probably that we were Harry Haywood's wife and child. The speaker changed the subject.

Tragically, Jesse later had minor elective surgery in a small-town hospital in upstate New York and never came out from under anesthesia. He remained in a deep coma for years. Jim Haughton and Josh Lawrence were devastated by his incapacitation. They both spent months trying to talk him out of his coma with no success. He finally died in 1988. I attended his funeral in Harlem, where US Representative Charles B. Rangel gave a moving tribute to Jesse.

Getting to Know and Learning to Love Mexico

After the POC fell apart in late 1958, Harry decided we should leave New York and move to Mexico. During the McCarthy era and the Cold War Red Scare, Mexico was a refuge for persecuted US left-wingers.

They had an informal support group in Mexico City. The FBI named it ACOM, the American Communist Organization in Mexico. I didn't want to leave Leo, who lived with Michel, but Harry just told me we were going. Michel agreed to send Leo for visits, but he never did. My contact with Leo was severed for years, which nearly drove me crazy and turned out even worse for him.

Our closest friends in Mexico were Elizabeth Catlett (Betty) Mora, an African American sculptor who became world famous, and her Mexican husband, Francisco (Pancho) Mora, an outstanding and prolific painter, lithographer, muralist, and mariachi performer. They had three little boys. The FBI considered them the link between the ACOM, the Mexican CP, and the CP of Cuba. They were good, talented, creative people who were wonderful friends and generous with their time. Betty Mora taught me a lot about Mexico, which she loved deeply, especially its ethnic complexity, which she eagerly sought to know and understand. I encouraged her to buy her oldest son his first drum set. He became a famous musician and spiritual leader in New York City.[10]

I saw in Mexico and the people I met there a depth of perception, a sweetness, a quiet wisdom, an exaltation of beauty, an otherworldliness, and a tradition of violence and acceptance of death that was foreign to all my prior experience. The Mexican people I knew had a love of beauty that was overwhelming. It manifested in their plants and flowers, amazing foods, fiestas, original architecture, murals, buildings, bridges, highways, and even airports.

I had grown up seeing images of Mexican people depicted as dozing, doing nothing, while sitting on the ground in the shade of tall cactuses. But the Mexican people I know are the opposite of this racist stereotype. They are the hardest-working people I have ever known. In the United States, they will do the most difficult and dangerous work that no one else will. I was reminded of that after Hurricane Katrina destroyed New Orleans. Mexican people replaced the roofs and rebuilt the roads and bridges under dangerous conditions with no workmen's compensation or medical insurance. Their bosses told the Mexican roofers, "If you fall off the roof, you are fired before you hit the ground." Some bosses refused to pay them because they knew they couldn't legally complain. But my white Mississippi contractor went with some of them to one boss and said menacingly, "We don't do things like that in Mississippi!" He paid.

I had learned many years before that if you assign a job to Mexican workers, they will often collectively figure out how to do it and have fun doing so, no matter how hard and complicated the task, because they love challenges and never give up. I learned from studying Mexico's amazing history that Mexican people can be patient with brutal exploitation for years but then suddenly say to each other, "¡Basta!" (Enough!). Then their exploiters better watch out!

How did we live when we moved to Mexico? Harry had a small disability pension from the Veterans Administration. My uncle, Charles Midlo, convinced my parents to provide me with a modest stipend of about a hundred dollars a month. But that wasn't enough to live on, so we moved from Mexico City to the beautiful town of Cuautla, Morelos, about sixty miles from Mexico City, beyond a huge mountain. There was a big statue of Emiliano Zapata on his horse in the center of town. I loved this tropical place with its stunning flowers and fruit trees and the magnificent sulphur springs called Agua Hedionda. However, although people in Cuautla seemed very sweet and calm, it was all on the surface. Cuautla was in the state of Morelos, which had the highest murder rate in the country. When our neighbors invited us to one of their many fiestas, in an attempt to reassure us, they said that only two people had been killed at the last one. I was not reassured.

Harry did not learn Spanish, partly because of his age, partly because he was a bit hard of hearing. He told me it was my fault because I spoke it too well. But he also had problems with cultural insensitivity. Both Harry and his brother, Otto Hall, spoke in deep, booming voices. They gesticulated wildly and touched people to get their attention. When the two of them were in the same room telling stories, the walls shook. Mexican people, especially in Cuautla, spoke very softly and sweetly. Harry's gestures and tone of voice frightened them, and they couldn't understand what he was saying. They expected him to turn violent. I had to constantly remind Harry to keep his voice down, stop gesturing, and, above all, never touch Mexican women.

During the fall of 1961, I started attending the Universidad Nacional Autónoma de México (UNAM) in Mexico City. Several times a week, I drove over the steep mountains from Cuautla to Mexico City, often through tropical downpours. There were precipitous drops along the sides of the road and few guardrails. Many of the other cars on this narrow, winding highway did not have lights, horns, or brakes, and the drivers seemed to think they were in a race to get where they were going first. By some miracle, I survived.

Later, I found an apartment in Mexico City, where we lived for two years while I attended Mexico City College (now known as University of the Americas) and got my bachelor's degree in history and master's degree in Latin American history. I did well at Mexico City College. Some of the scholars I met there changed my life forever. Because of Mexico's wise old policy of welcoming refugees, it was a magnet for refugees from the political disasters of the mid-twentieth century. They were the finest, most socially responsible, and committed scholars in the world. Many were loyalist refugees from the Spanish Civil War. I first studied with Concepción Muedra, a Catalan loyalist who was the first woman to receive a PhD in history in Spain at the University of Madrid. She was a brilliant, creative woman, an outstanding archivist and paleographer, who saved much of the Archivo Historico Nacional from being destroyed during the war, bringing irreplaceable documents to Valencia. She had been outrageously exploited by her lover, who took her research, published it as his own, and promised to marry her after his wife died. (He married a better-connected woman instead.)

Muedra taught me medieval European history. She taught in English, and though her English was pretty bad, the effort to understand her was more than worth it, and I listened attentively. Her best course was the history of Spain. The highlight was Islamic Spain and the transmission of Arabic, Greek, Hebrew, and Roman culture and technology to Western Europe via Iberian translation centers, which became the intellectual foundation for the Renaissance in Europe. This history is rarely taught except in Spain. At the end of the course, she cried as she spoke about the flight of Loyalist refugees who tried to get into France over the Pyrenees but were mowed down by machine-gun fire from fascist aircraft. I told her my husband had been a member of the International Brigade that fought for the Loyalists during the Spanish Civil War. Moved, she became my friend and ally.

During the Christmas break, our daughter, Rebecca, was born, on January 4, 1963. When I went into labor, I drove myself to the hospital, with Harry in the passenger seat because he didn't know how to drive. The birth was easy: absolutely painless. When I regained consciousness, there was Harry, his eyes shining in wonder, saying, "It's a girl!" She was marvelous. As soon as she could get on her feet in her playpen, she shook her rear end to the sound of Mexican popular songs. Her favorite was "Despeinada."

A few weeks after Rebecca was born, I went through a sudden change of perception. It was so powerful that I understand what people mean when they say they were born again. The transformation is not easy to describe. I was walking across the campus of Mexico City College and suddenly saw people and their interactions in an entirely new way. Everyone seemed to be wearing a cold, unemotional mask, and they were telling themselves and each other lies. There was, at the same time, an intense, emotional, nonverbal communication among them, which I was perceiving directly. This nonverbal communication was intense. Something that I can only describe as spirit shook the people I encountered, leapt into their eyes, flashed there for a moment like a prisoner begging to be freed, and then died. I had intense, enlightening dreams during this time. Looking back, I realize that I'd always had such dreams, but they had become more frequent and more intense. I still don't know if this can be described as a religious experience. It was unlike anything I knew.

I asked myself if other people were perceiving the way I had started to. After watching them for a while, I concluded they perceived only the self-deluded, lying masks, but did not know they were lying and being lied to. The masks were the limits of their consciousness. These people were interacting with each other, arriving at a consensus they accepted as reality, and acting based on this consensus. My impression was that very little of what existed in the real world got past the masks.

I was left with no preconceptions, not sure if anything I had ever known or believed before was true. Before this sudden perception change, I believed we could only know truth through logic, and logic could only be based on what we could perceive. But what I was suddenly perceiving could not be fit into patterns of logic. Much of the intellectual baggage I had picked up over the years was gone. The greatest influences in my life had been based on rationality as the only means of arriving at truth: Marxism, with its grand sociological theories that reduced people to small cogs in a great wheel, and Freudianism, which viewed the unconscious mind, the id, as a pit of irrational destruction kept under precarious control by the ego and superego. My belief in these ideas was gone.

I looked to philosophy to give me some answers and took two advanced undergraduate courses with Ramon Xirau, another Catalan refugee of the Spanish Civil War and son of Joaquim Xirau, a Catalan specialist in the philosophy of education. I was privileged to be taught by him when he was still a young scholar and poet in his late thirties (he was born in Barcelona in 1924). He and Muedra both had a decisive influence on my life and work. And I relied on the library of the Colegio de Mexico, founded by Spanish Loyalist refugees in Mexico, for my research.[11]

Ramon arrived from Barcelona with his parents in 1939, fell in love with Mexico immediately, and eventually became a leading educator, philosopher, and poet. Some of my questions were answered in Xirau's courses. Among the things I learned was to value concrete perception, fellow feeling, and how the self is undermined by socialization, which can destroy the freedom to make ethical choices. The unsocialized, ethical self rejects the rewards and punishments offered by society. I knew this during my childhood but became more conscious of it based on what I learned from Xirau. I finally came to understand that I was always the same person. All that changed was that I became conscious of my mental processes.

The first impact this change had on me was to help me write. I felt free to express myself in writing without the strong self-doubts I had once felt. I knew that I could write and that I had something important to say. When I was writing intensely, my unconscious thought process continued all night long, even while I slept. When I woke up in the morning, I typed page after page, quickly and spontaneously, without ever consciously thinking about it.

My Last Writing with Harry

My growing autonomy put a serious strain on our marriage. When Harry and I began working together, I was twenty-four years old and he was fifty-six. Our age difference did matter. I could look to a world beyond the CP, but he could not. Harry had been a loyal CP member for more than thirty years and was one of a handful of Black revolutionaries from back in the early 1920s. Although ideas about women in the CP were enlightened for the times, no one saw anything wrong with women doing much of the intellectual work, as well as the typing, while the men got all the credit. Women intellectuals know this still happens. Men have no idea.

Harry considered himself "good" on the "woman question" because he recognized my intelligence and therefore my ability to help him with his work. I was his typist, then his secretary, then his editor. He never recognized the active, creative role I played in his work until a decade into our marriage, when I refused to go on doing it. I finally told Harry I would never help him write again, and he should find someone else to do it. At first, he declared that anyone could do what I was doing for him. After spending about six months traveling around the United States trying to find my replacement, he came back and admitted he had underestimated my role in his work.

Harry asked me to give him just two more weeks of typing, which he probably assumed would become a lifetime. I told him I had my own work to do. He said, "That's okay. You can do your work after you finish mine." I agreed but insisted that first I needed three weeks to write my master's thesis. He stopped nagging me for three weeks, and that was a big help.

The two weeks of typing turned into five months and a short book manuscript, *Towards a Revolutionary Program for Negro Freedom*. Most of this time, Harry's contribution to the writing process was to lie asleep on the bed in the room where I was typing (by then, mercifully, on my IBM Selectric typewriter), occasionally opening one eye, not two, and saying, "How is it coming, Gwen?"

Harry saw our task as ensuring a correct line about the Black freedom struggle within the Communist Party. My concern was ensuring independent Black revolutionary leadership. From my experience in New Orleans during an escalating period of repression, I saw the CP abandon its work and its most vulnerable, mainly Black members in the Deep South. I had serious doubts that the CP had much to offer the Black working class at this point. And the more I learned about history, the more I began to question the orthodox views of the Communist world. Every society I studied, regardless of time or place, had its own form of exploitation. There have been few successful revolutions, and those—including the French Revolution of 1789, the Haitian Revolution of 1791, the Mexican Revolution of 1910, the Russian Revolution of 1917, and the long

Chinese Revolution—had to be defended by bloody means. I sympathize with pacifism but have yet to be convinced it is at all realistic. As for the silenced, downtrodden masses, I learned to admire them more and more in the long-ignored documents I was studying as a historian.

I am proud of the Soviet Union's role in defeating the Nazis, and a main reason for their victory was the role of the massive quantity and superior quality of the weapons they produced, which few people talk about. I am proud of the great advances of the People's Republic of China against poverty and its assertion of China's self-determination after centuries of domination and humiliation by foreign powers. I am also aware of the drastic flaws of both these forms of socialism. But neither neoliberalism nor Cold War "scholarship" can dismiss their enormous achievements. As Leonard Cohen sang, we should ring the bells that still can ring and know that the holes are where the light comes in. So I am still thrilled when I see the red flag with the hammer and sickle and hear the *Internationale* sung in any language. Despite all the faults of the Soviet Union, its collapse and fall dealt a severe blow to the international working class.

The FBI knew Harry and I were writing together and expressed concern about the impact of our work on the Black protest movement of the 1960s. No snoops knew anything about its contents. The FBI was reporting ridiculous rumors about our purported beliefs. Their informants in Mexico were extremely imaginative. They had us writing things we never would have, including advocating senseless violence and terrorism. One of their informants reported that Elizabeth Catlett Mora said the Chinese government was subsidizing the Progressive Labor Party (PLP) to publish our new book to the tune of $1,300. I doubt she said that, but maybe she did, and maybe it was true.

Several months into my "typing," I said to him, "Harry, this book I am writing for you: I want my name on it, or I won't finish it." He was shocked and indignant and accused me of blackmailing him. He said he was famous but my name meant nothing. I asked how I could ever get a reputation if I never published. He finally, reluctantly agreed to my name appearing as "collaborator."

By the early spring of 1964, the manuscript was finished. It was liberated from stereotypically Communist language and presented the core of Harry's original thinking without the illusions of recreating a "real"

Communist Party. It explained the revolutionary potential of the African American protest movement and distinguished between revolutionary nationalism based on working-class interests and nationalist separatism based on the interests of the ghetto Black petty bourgeoisie. It called for the creation of a third trend with the best elements of nationalism and integrationism. The manuscript argued that the African American protest movement must pose its own potential threat to order and stability to counter the massive resistance campaign unleashed by the southern oligarchy and its Ku Klux Klan paramilitary. It was dedicated to Robert F. Williams, the initiator of the armed self-defense movement against the Ku Klux Klan in Monroe, North Carolina, during the 1950s.

I made five carbon copies and mailed them to various people, all in California. Harry expressed approval of the language. But he was less pleased with some of the content, especially its call for an autonomous Black working class–led movement rather than the reconstitution of a real CP.

Later, I accepted a job teaching in North Carolina and returned to New York to get my kids and my belongings. Harry had been nagging me all year to remove my name from our manuscript. I finally said, "You take the manuscript, I'll take the kids."

Back to the USA and Harry's Last Years

During the spring of 1964, Harry convinced me to meet him in New York City instead of going to Stanford University, where I had been accepted into the PhD program in Latin American studies. It wasn't hard to do. I was too ignorant of academia to know what a big deal it was to be admitted to a PhD program at Stanford. I always had great reservations about academia and firmly believed that radical politics, especially supporting the Black freedom struggle, was much more important. And I didn't know how I was going to pay for Stanford while supporting myself and our two kids. Later I learned, again from my FBI files, that Stanford was ready to give me financial aid, but I didn't even know what that was.

I drove my car with the kids from Mexico City to New York, where Harry and I rented a big, beautiful apartment on Riverside Drive and 97th Street, overlooking the Hudson River. The FBI had our address and phone number, and they knew who our landlord was. They made a few pretext calls to our apartment to find out where we worked in order to get us fired. When our nine-year-old son Haywood answered the phone, they pumped him for information. Once, the FBI came to our neighbors' door to ask about us. They refused to let the agents in. We overheard them say, "These people are our neighbors. Go away!" Times had changed.

Harry worked as a waiter at a foreign pavilion at the New York World's Fair. That made him safe from the FBI. I did my usual thing as a temporary legal secretary, this time as a summer vacation replacement at a law firm in the Empire State Building specializing in divorce.

At this point, Harry was enthusiastic about the Progressive Labor Party, one of the first of a number of Maoist aspirants to the Chinese franchise in the United States. Mao's Cultural Revolution was already devastating China. A lot of left-wingers in the United States supported China, and China supported them. In New York City, Milton Rosen led a pro-Chinese faction out of the CP and founded the PLP. They wanted to publish our manuscript, although they disagreed with the premise. Harry and I met with the PLP leadership for about half an hour. Rosen told us that only class struggle mattered; racial discrimination was a minor issue. I asked Rosen if he would feel the same way if he, as a Jew, was forced to wear a yellow star in Nazi Germany. After we left, I told Harry I wanted nothing to do with the PLP.

All kinds of strange people started to show up in our apartment. To Harry, they were all "good guys." One man came often, plied Harry with alcohol, and pumped him for information. But he got nowhere with Harry, even when drunk. Others started talking about blowing up the Statue of Liberty. All of them ignored me, which was fine. When obvious spies and provocateurs showed up, I went into my bedroom and closed the door.

During the 1970s, Harry continued to be an idol of the Maoist movement. I was never a Maoist, although I greatly admired Communist China. When the Chinese-Soviet alliance broke up during the 1960s, my sympathies were with China. I agreed with the CP of China's criticism of Nikita Khrushchev's 1956 report denouncing Stalin, which denied Stalin's extraordinary role in defeating the fascist onslaught during World War II, grossly exaggerating his own role. The Chinese Communists pointed out Khrushchev's enthusiastic participation in the purges in the Ukraine and his fatally destructive impact on the world Communist movement. But I never accepted the Cultural Revolution during Mao's final years. I was and still am too much of a civil libertarian. And yes, I believe in constitutional rights; in the rule of law, including the rights of the accused to defend themselves; and, above all, in controlling the arbitrary powers of the state and the church.

Harry was courted by and then joined the October League, which evolved into the Communist Party Marxist-Leninist (CPML). There were sincere, idealistic, self-sacrificing, hardworking members of these Maoist organizations, which flourished during the period of the Great Cultural Revolution. Their rituals of criticism and self-criticism weren't as deadly as in China, but they weren't pretty. I heard about them indirectly from some of the victims who accepted their "guilt." These Maoist splinters were organized and controlled by white radicals, some of them former leaders of Students for a Democratic Society, which led the student protest movement against the war in Vietnam. Many of the enthusiasts of the New Communist Movement were happy to have the support of China for their politics, which were far to the left of the Moscow-backed Communist parties. But they spent much of their time and energy tearing each other apart, with much provocation from the FBI.

The October League recruited Harry and a few other prestigious Black Communists but treated them largely as tokens. Harry was aware of this. He once told me each Maoist group had its own "Negro." But Harry had a strong practical streak. Writing came hard to him, mainly because of his self-doubts and insecurities. He had to "talk things out" with the person who was typing for him. I resigned from that job by early 1964 after doing it alone for a decade. The October League supplied him with an endless stream of typists and editors to help him write his autobiography. But it cost something. If you read *Black Bolshevik*, you would think Harry was a detached observer of the Black upsurge of the 1960s and early 1970s. The book omits his entire role in inspiring the founders of the Black Panther Party in Oakland in the mid-1960s, his organizing with the amazing radical Black working-class movement in Detroit during the late '60s and early '70s, and his work at the Institute of the Black World in Atlanta in 1970–71.

My doubts about Maoism were confirmed when I went to China twice during the 1970s, a time when few foreigners, especially Yankees, were allowed in. I went with a women's delegation sponsored by the October League in 1976, the year Mao died. They expected me to come back and make propaganda speeches about China. But I wasn't impressed. The Great Cultural Revolution was still going strong. I didn't see starving children, which had been the stereotypical image of China when I was growing up. But I saw an incredible amount of backwardness that was pointed to with pride. I saw crowds of workers in Chinese factories doing nothing. I saw places in the countryside where there were no cows, oxen, horses, mules, goats, or carts. Humans were the only pack animals.

We were invited and greeted in China by Defense Minister and Vice President Geng Biao, an old revolutionary comrade of Xi Jinping's father Xi Zhongxun. Geng later educated and mentored Xi Jinping as party secretary for Guangdong province, implementing economic reforms in an area that was to become the engine of the New China.

Then, during the summer of 1978, the Chinese government invited Harry and our family to China for a five-week tour as guests of the state. By then, the Cultural Revolution was over. Our hosts gave us an earful about its horrors. The stories we heard were very moving and, unfortunately, entirely credible. What impressed me most was the lessons they learned from that terrible experience, their determination to make sure such a thing would never happen again, and how they expected to do this. I met with the International Relations Commission of the Higher Education Department of the People's Republic of China in June 1978. They informed me that China's graduate education and research institutes were destroyed by the anti-intellectualism of the Cultural Revolution. Professors and scholars had been denied access to foreign scholarship, denounced as bourgeois, and sent to do hard labor in so-called reeducation camps. There were few academic survivors who could do up-to-date research, teaching, and administration, much less reconstitute higher education. But the repression had ended, and the government's plan was to send Chinese students to study abroad, bring foreign scholars to China to teach, keep education open with no enforced conformity, and thus give China the best, most up-to-date global knowledge. China obviously succeeded. (In 1980, I published a chapter about this in a volume about international human rights.)

I differed with Harry about politics, but he often didn't realize it. I hid my doubts about Maoism from him because I didn't want to hurt him. He finally developed a deep respect for my political judgment, though he never acknowledged it to anyone, especially after the Maoist movements fell apart when China abandoned them. Harry always believed that only the CP could lead the struggle for Black liberation and self-determination; if not the old CP, then a new one. To me, neither the old white guys in the CP nor the young white guys in the New Communist Movement could claim the right to lead the Black liberation movement or decide who should lead it.

The CPML did their best to erase me from Harry's life. They referred to me as a bourgeois professor, and they even edited my image almost entirely out of a photo they published of Harry standing with me while I was holding our son Haywood. But Harry insisted on dedicating his influential autobiography *Black Bolshevik* to me and our two children.

Family photo circa 1976, Brooklyn, New York, that appeared in *People* magazine, 2000

~

Harry was in his mid-eighties when the CPML fell apart. He was flown all over the country to back one splinter group against the other. Finally, when he was terminally ill and utterly deserted by his CPML "comrades," he asked me, "What happened, Gwen? You know what happened."

I said, "Harry, I'm going to say this only once, and I don't want to discuss it again. Any revolutionary movement in the United States must be validated by the people of the United States. It can't be validated by the Russians, the Chinese, Fidel Castro, the Vietcong, the Shah of Iran, or Pol Pot."

There were good reasons why I couldn't talk to Harry about politics near the end of his life. He was a good, devoted, scrupulously honest man. We loved each other. He was old and weak and very proud. I didn't want to hurt him or argue with him about his deepest beliefs when I was questioning many of them.

In early 1985, I got a phone call from the VA extended care home where Harry had gone to live. He had severe pneumonia and had to go to the VA hospital in Manhattan. His immune system had been destroyed by the systemic steroids he needed to breathe. Our daughter Rebecca stayed with him in the ambulance, and I followed in my car. The last thing I heard him say was, "I should get full compensation now from the VA."

When I arrived at the hospital the next morning, I realized I'd forgotten to bring him the *New York Times*. I went outside and bought him a copy. When I got to his room, he wasn't there. The staff told me that after we'd left the night before, he had gone into cardiac arrest. They revived him, but he was in a coma in the ICU. Although I sat beside his bed, the doctors didn't recognize me as a loved one. When one doctor asked the other how Harry was doing, the reply was, "He needs a coffin." Even after I explained that I was his wife, I had to wait all day before they would talk to me. They finally said they could get him through the pneumonia, but he would not regain consciousness. I told them I knew he would not want to live like that. The hospital phoned me early the next morning and told me he had died. It was January 4, 1985, our daughter Rebecca's twenty-second birthday.

I had been trying to prepare myself for Harry's death. My greatest emotional expertise was in repressing my feelings. I was wondering if I would cry. I couldn't stop crying for a week. I was in so much physical pain that I was prescribed muscle relaxants, which sent me into a deep depression, so I had to stop taking them. It took me six months to return to emotional stability, more or less. Harry was always an enormous influence in my life, and I in his. I still miss him and always will.

PART FOUR

A PUBLIC INTELLECTUAL
IN THE BLACK FREEDOM
STRUGGLE

H arry and I lived separately during most of the last twenty years of his life, though we visited each other and lived together for weeks and even months at a time. I remained closely connected to the Black freedom struggle, both through my own friends and acquaintances and those I knew through Harry.

This was the era in which the struggle was reaching new heights. While the CP was busy dissolving itself and every other organization it influenced, the Black freedom struggle hit the streets and exploded with the Montgomery Bus Boycott, which began in December 1955. Dr. Martin Luther King Jr. emerged as a great political and spiritual leader after the successful boycott. Water hoses and dogs were unleashed against Black children on the streets of Birmingham, Alabama.

The conformity of the 1950s was over. McCarthyism was dead, even in the South. An autonomous Black working class–led struggle had emerged in 1957 with the armed self-defense movement in North Carolina led by the Williamses. The Student Nonviolent Coordinating Committee (SNCC) emerged in 1960 from the sit-ins at lunch counters defying segregation laws. Ella Baker urged the students to organize separately and maintain their independence from Martin Luther King's Southern Christian Leadership Conference (SCLC), and they did. They soon embraced armed self-defense and Black Power. Autonomous Black revolutionary leaders formed the Revolutionary Action Movement, the Republic of New Africa, and the Black Panther Party. The Revolutionary Union Movement began at the Dodge Main assembly plant in Detroit in 1968 and spread to other auto factories before evolving into the Black Workers Congress. I participated as much as possible, but my main contribution was developing some pioneering concepts about structural racism, published mainly in *Negro Digest/Black World*.

Reds and the Civil Rights Movement

Though the CP did not participate in the early years of the civil rights movement—and in fact opposed its militancy—the Black Communists whom Harry and I encouraged to leave the party during the 1950s had a great influence on Martin Luther King Jr. and his organization SCLC.

To understand what happened, we must discuss the little-known, quiet, patient work of the self-effacing Stanley Levison. He had been treasurer of the American Jewish Congress in New York City after World War II and then a secret account manager, fundraiser, and business manager for the CP. Levison was reputed to collect and distribute subsidies from the Soviet Union to the CP. He had contacts among wealthy capitalists with bad consciences, some of whom contributed more than $100,000 a year to the CP. Levison was a skilled fundraiser, attorney, promoter, speechwriter, and editor with important ties with commercial publishers in New York City. He was the main fundraiser for the campaign to stop the execution of Ethel and Julius Rosenberg and retained a list of generous contributors after the Rosenbergs were executed in 1953.

Levison left the CP in 1956 and immediately transferred his money, contacts, and skills first to the Montgomery Bus Boycott and then to the SCLC. He was King's main fundraiser and an important adviser and political strategist, and he continued to support King's widow and children after King was murdered. J. Edgar Hoover continued to claim Levison was a secret member of the CP, but, according to Ben Kamin's book *Dangerous Friendship*, "there never appeared, in any statement or assertion by the US government, a shred of conclusive evidence that Levison had been involved with, or given a single dollar to the Communist Party after 1956." Kamin related an anecdote from Andrew Levison, Stanley's son, about his father's reaction to being told by FBI agents that he could "serve his country" by being a mole in the CP.

"I could not have asked the agent for a better setup line," Levison would tell friends, according to Andrew. "I drew myself up and said: 'I think I'm serving my country a whole lot better by helping Martin Luther King to dismantle southern segregation than by going back into the CP to spy on a pathetically isolated and irrelevant bunch of guys, half of whom are already working for you."

Like all of us who were active in the CP right after World War II, Levison understood the crucial importance of the African American freedom struggle and the right to self-determination of Black people, especially in the Deep South. When Levison left the CP, it was attacking Martin Luther King in print for taking the struggle to the streets. Levison also became concerned about growing antisemitism in the Soviet Union. He was horrified by the suppression of the Hungarian Revolution by Soviet troops and tanks in 1956 and was totally shocked by the revelation of Stalin's mass murder of his opponents or people he believed might oppose him.

Another figure close to King was "Jack" Hunter O'Dell, whose political life closely paralleled my own. Born and raised in Detroit, he moved to New Orleans to attend Xavier University. We both joined the CP in the South after the war when the theory of an oppressed Black nation with the right of self-determination in the Black Belt South was going strong. O'Dell began shipping out as a member of the NMU, where he got his political education from Jesse Gray, who got his from Harry Haywood. O'Dell and I were elected to the national board of the Southern Negro Youth Congress at its Southern Youth Legislature in 1946, where we were inspired by W. E. B. Du Bois's great speech "Behold the Land." We were both active in the Henry Wallace campaign. And we both published in the influential magazine *Freedomways*, where he was associate editor for years and wrote many of its editorials.

O'Dell started to work with the SCLC in March 1960 as a volunteer in New York City helping with fundraising, and in less than a year, he was asked to serve as SCLC's director of voter registration in seven southern states. He focused on the Black Belt counties. In March 1962, attorney general Robert F. Kennedy authorized the FBI to begin surveillance of both Levison and King. The following year, shortly before the famous March on Washington, King and other civil rights leaders were invited to meet with president John F. Kennedy at the White House to discuss civil rights legislation. Prior to the meeting, King was taken aside for one-on-one conversations with Burke Marshall, Robert Kennedy, and the president himself. All three told King that he should cut ties with O'Dell and Levison.

Two weeks later, King wrote to O'Dell asking him to resign from the SCLC, explaining that he wanted to avoid the implication that "the Southern Freedom Movement [is] Communist inspired." O'Dell resigned, but he was hard to replace. He continued to work with the SCLC behind the scenes, and he resumed his job with the organization several years later. King never broke his ties with Levison. They stopped meeting directly and continued close communications through others. J. Edgar Hoover had wiretaps everywhere and gleefully reported their ongoing communications.[1]

Learning to Teach and Fighting the Klan in North Carolina

After living with Harry in Manhattan for most of 1964 amid FBI agents and provocateurs, I grabbed the first chance I got to move back south, where the Civil Rights Movement was exploding—and so was the Ku Klux Klan. My old friend Carolyn Dejoie was a member of the NOYC and had been arrested with us in New Orleans in 1949. We had kept up with each other ever since. She visited me at just the right time and place: Carolyn was teaching Spanish at Norfolk State College in Virginia and told me that Elizabeth City State College, a rural, historically Black college in northeast North Carolina, was looking for a history teacher. They were having a hard time finding anyone who wanted to teach there, especially on short notice. It is about forty miles south of Norfolk, across the Dismal Swamp, a historic refuge for runaway slaves.

John Henrik Clarke sent a warm letter of recommendation— something that was noted several times in his FBI file. I was invited for an interview. First, I met with president Walter Ridley, a serious, distinguished, athletic Black man. He told me they had been hiring white teachers for only a year. The Board of Education was afraid that any white teacher who would go there would be a Communist.

Toward the end of the interview, he asked me if I had a left-wing background. I said I was from New Orleans—only left-wing whites were against racism there. He nodded gravely. Finally, he asked, "Is there anything you have to tell me? I might as well know now."

I said, "Yes. My two children are Negroes." He asked me if they were adopted. I said they were my natural children. He asked if my husband was a foreigner. I told him no; he was an American, would be remaining in New York City, and would not accompany us. He told me interracial marriage was still illegal in North Carolina, but a case was pending before the US Supreme Court to overturn that law, hopefully within a few months.

Then he said, "I have some relatives who look as white as you do."

I replied, "I have sometimes been taken for a Creole. I'm from New Orleans, and I speak French."

He said, "Whatever I say around here is like speaking through a megaphone. All I have to say is, 'Have you met our new Creole history teacher from New Orleans?'"

I said, "That's fine with me."

He told me that when I got my driver's license, "Be sure to get the race right." I did.

I went to North Carolina with our two children and taught from January through July 1965. It was my first experience teaching. Elizabeth City used to be a teachers' college, and the students had earned their keep by working in the fields of the plantation where it was located. They grew food for the college, and the surplus was sold. The crop rows were still visible when I arrived, but the students weren't expected to do field work anymore. The college was only a few brick buildings. The tallest was three stories high and housed the administrative offices, some classrooms, and the library. President Ridley told me the students' average reading level was sixth grade, and they needed to practice reading and writing.

Dorms for the students were spread around the campus. There was a row of houses rented by teachers. President Ridley moved us into a faculty house, which I rented from the school. It was like living on a remote island. After I had been there for a week, it was hard to remember any other world. Everything was provided by the school. I got my meals in the faculty dining room across the road from my house, where I got to know my fellow faculty members. The food was made from fresh ingredients and was deliciously cooked. Credit was opened for me in furniture and department stores in town.

All the teachers except for one, an astute sociologist named Harry Gamble, believed I was an Afro-Creole from New Orleans. Gamble told me he didn't believe me, but he wouldn't make trouble. Other faculty members said I looked typically Creole. Some had been purged from teaching at Southern University in Baton Rouge for supporting their students' protests, and they asked me where I had lived. I told them the Seventh Ward, which was the Creole district where many people of indeterminable race lived. I invited Carolyn Dejoie to visit and introduced her as my cousin.

The teachers were convinced, but not the students. They weren't fooled. They decided I was a foreigner: a GI bride. They told me there were debates about me in the dormitories: "She's Irish. No, she's German. No, she's Italian." I showed them my passport to prove I was born in New Orleans. They still didn't believe me. "Why do you think I'm a foreigner?" I asked. "I don't have a foreign accent." They said, "No, but you don't act like an American."

When it came to accents, the students spoke with one I had never heard before. It took me about two weeks to understand them. Most were children of tobacco sharecroppers from northeast North Carolina. But the college was in a lumber town. The family who owned the lumber mill owned the town and everyone in it. They wouldn't allow an anti-poverty program because they didn't want any interference with their cheap help.

The campus was an isolated community. The teachers lived in their own little worlds and were afraid to talk openly with each other. They treated fellow faculty members with the greatest formal respect, perhaps to compensate for the lack of respect they received in the outside world. No one was on a first-name basis with colleagues. It was always Mr., Mrs., or, best of all, Doctor. The college community was a weird world of make-believe. There were teachers who had worked there for ten years and had never been to town. They didn't even know where Main Street was. They were the ones most likely to talk about what a lovely, advanced, progressive town it was, how important the college was to the town, and how much our teachers were esteemed there. I soon discovered the only way to maintain the illusions about the prestige, power, and status that faculty enjoyed in town was not to go there. African American PhDs would find themselves addressed by their first names by white store clerks. Then again, one of our teachers said he didn't mind being called by his first name if he got the bank loan he applied for. My kids and I were nearly assaulted for trying to buy a take-out pizza from a white restaurant. When I told my fellow teachers about it, I was advised not to file a complaint if I wanted to keep my job.

My first ten minutes in a classroom were memorable. I had never taught before, and on one day's notice, I was teaching history I hadn't studied in years. I had to learn how to teach, fast. I started lecturing about comparative slavery, using many words the students had never heard before. They were puzzled to the point of panic. Not knowing what to write, they held their pencils poised above their notebooks. I read the same expression on every face: "What in the world is this woman talking about?" I stopped and said, "You don't understand what I'm saying, do you?" They shook their heads no. "Okay," I said, "let's start over."

We spent a lot of time on words. Once they understood a word, they understood a concept. I used the word "paternalism" in class, and no one knew what that meant. I explained: "Paternalism is when somebody makes you do what they want by acting nice—and you better do it or else!"

The students had been taught to obey, to learn by rote. They couldn't understand why I objected to them quoting the textbook word for word on their exams. "I didn't copy it," they would tell me. "I memorized it." They were used to the teacher giving them all the questions and all the pat answers. Once, we discussed something in class, and I closed the discussion without giving them an answer. They were upset. "But what's the answer?" I was asked.

I said, "There is no answer." They laughed in delight. They had never heard of such a thing.

One of the favorite topics of conversation among teachers was the students: how stupid and ignorant they were. Students were leaving the class before mine with tears in their eyes after being humiliated by their teacher for not knowing the answer to a question. Many teachers complained about the students' lack of spontaneity. "They never smile," I heard them say. "They never show a spark of life." After a while, we had to close the windows and doors in my classroom because the discussions were so animated.

Teaching was hard work, and I had a heavy teaching load. My specialty was Latin American history, but I had to teach the history of just about everywhere else. My classes had about fifty students each. I gave essay exams every other week and spent long hours correcting them and writing long comments and suggestions on each exam.

Although this was a state college, there was something called Religious Emphasis Week. Sermons were preached in the auditorium. The social order was thoroughly identified with God. The students were exhorted to feel eternally grateful for the opportunity to get a college education. Right after Religious Emphasis Week, we had a class discussion about Napoleon Bonaparte's opinion that the only way to make the poor and downtrodden submit to their lot here on earth is to promise them rewards in the hereafter. One of the students said Napoleon was right. The other students indignantly stared her down.

Only a handful of students were from outside North Carolina, and most of them were on athletic scholarships. A basketball player from Indiana was determinedly hostile to me, and he influenced other students. But on the day Malcolm X was murdered, we both found ourselves explaining to the class who Malcolm was. One of the students asked, "Didn't Malcolm preach hate?"

We answered in unison, "Malcolm didn't preach hate." Before the semester was over, the basketball player was carrying my books to class.

I asked him, "Aren't you afraid the other students will make fun of you?"

He said, "I don't care anything about that."

When president Lyndon Johnson began sending large numbers of combat troops to Vietnam, my students were enthusiastic. I explained that there was a lot of popular support for the Vietnamese National Liberation Front. We were invading their country and would be resisted by guerrilla warfare. It would be a nasty, dirty war aimed at helpless civilians, and we would probably lose. One of my students said we should not back down. I told them, "You have to take low sometimes."

The students were patient and long-suffering. The campus was several miles out of town, and there was no public transportation. Girls were expelled for riding in boys' cars. They had to be in their rooms by 7 p.m. and couldn't sit on the porch, even in the summer. The dorm had iron bars on the windows. The president's dogs were released from their kennel to roam the campus at night. The administration had absolute power over the teachers, and the teachers had absolute power over the students. The college had funds for student jobs that teachers could give to their favorites. As the saying goes, power corrupts. Some of the students were conditioned to this corruption. Around final exam time, some of the girls offered to clean my house for free and couldn't understand why I refused. Students complained to me about teachers flunking students who rejected their sexual advances.

In March 1965, President Ridley projected onto a big screen in the auditorium live TV broadcasts of the nonviolent march from Selma to Montgomery, led by Martin Luther King Jr. We watched as the marchers were attacked by violent white racists. Normal activities at the college stopped while everyone watched.

In the late spring and early summer, it was harvest time on the nearby truck farms. Migrant workers arrived from Florida on open-bed trucks. Some of my students told me they hid migrant workers who were trying to escape from their camps. As time passed, the recruiting of workers to get in the crops became aggressive. Students were stopped on the streets, and recruiters even approached small children. One morning at four o'clock, I found my nine-year-old son Haywood dressed and ready to pick corn for four dollars a day. I had a hard time stopping him.

The kids who worked in the fields told me they had to look out for the tractors because the tractors didn't look out for them. The farms were swampy, with poisonous snakes. The children were transported on open truck beds, and three small boys had been killed on the highway the year before. Some of the little kids told me they were beaten up. I asked if they told their parents. They said, "They won't do anything about it." I didn't know what to tell them. I couldn't do anything about it, either. One little boy with terror in his eyes was mute. Haywood tried to teach him to speak.

~

By late spring, 1965, the Ku Klux Klan was obviously active. Lines of cars with Confederate plates paraded slowly down Main Street, blowing their horns. I got worried about my kids. My son went to school right across the street from the campus. I told him to keep away from white people, especially people with Confederate plates on their cars. He paid me no mind. He'd bring white boys onto the campus to play. One day, he told me, "Mom, you were wrong about those people with Confederate plates on their cars. I made friends with some of them. I went to their house. They were very nice." Kids can make you feel humble sometimes.

I watched as the Klan demonstrations got bolder and bolder. The last day of my class in American history, I explained that there were two points of view about how to deal with the Klan. There was the passive resistance of Martin Luther King Jr. and the armed self-defense of Robert Williams, who was from farther south in North Carolina, near Charlotte. Harry and I had strongly supported Rob since he had started loudly advocating armed self-defense.

I wrote the name of his book on the blackboard: Robert F. Williams, *Negroes with Guns*.[2] My students didn't have to see it or read it. They got the message from the title. They went home for about a week. When they returned, lots of them signed up for my summer course. The first day of class, they said, "Robert Williams's way works." They gave me no details, and I didn't ask.

My students worked hard. Their writing improved so much that I asked some of them if someone else had written their essays for them. They said no and that they had worked hard on their writing. I gave out many A's for the essay exams written in that class.

After my summer classes ended, we headed for Detroit because I wanted to get to know the Black working class everybody was talking about. I drove there with my two kids. Segregation had recently been outlawed in public places, and we stopped at a Holiday Inn in Pennsylvania for the night. When we got into the swimming pool, everybody got out except for the kids. Their mothers yelled hysterically for their children to get out. I told mine, "Okay. Now there's a lot more room for us to swim. Let's jump in."

Right after I arrived in Detroit, I got a Western Union telegram from the administration of Elizabeth City State College saying my contract for the fall of 1965 was canceled and I should not return. That was a blow. I loved my students, and they loved me. By then I knew I was doing a good job teaching them, and I'd made a few friends on the faculty, too. In that isolated, backward place I felt at home.

It turned out that President Ridley had renewed my teaching contract for the fall, but then the FBI showed up. One of their agents had gone to see the president and bawled him out like he was a wayward child for hiring me. At the time, I didn't know. In fact, I didn't know for sure why anything bad happened to me during these years. When I was fired from jobs, evicted from apartments, blacklisted, I asked myself, *Was it my fault?* But I always did good work. It could have been race; it could have been gender; it could have been the local police. But after I got my FBI files, I discovered it was always the FBI.

When I returned to Elizabeth City in the fall to pick up my belongings, I saw a poster announcing a meeting to protest the war in Vietnam. One of my students jumped into my car. She said they were told I was fired because I was a Communist, and then she told me how my former students were defeating the Klan. They were sending white spies into Klan meetings with hidden tape recorders to find out where and when they would meet next. My students then showed up in a group and pulled the sheets off the Klansmen.

The FBI knew something I didn't at the time: the armed self-defense movement against the Klan was expanding throughout northeast North Carolina. It lasted for four years until an armed confrontation with Black students drove the Ku Klux Klan out of northeast North Carolina in 1969. There was a news blackout. I knew nothing about this until I went to Robert Williams's funeral in October 1996 and met historian David Cecelski. Along with conducting oral history interviews about the Civil Rights Movement, he had studied state police documents. He told me the armed self-defense movement, which began to escalate throughout northeastern North Carolina in 1965 and 1966, was spearheaded by students from North Carolina State and Elizabeth City State College.

My students were not alone. They were the northeast wing of a movement that stretched all the way from Texas to Maryland by 1965, at the height of Klan violence to intimidate and destroy the Civil Rights Movement. Self-defense is a deep tradition among Black southerners. The Deacons for Defense and Justice began in Jonesboro in northwest Louisiana in 1964 and expanded into Bogalusa, Louisiana, in February 1965. It then spread all over the South. Whatever name these groups took, they all did the same thing: they armed themselves and defeated the Klan. This history has been silenced.

Robert and Mabel Williams

Robert F. and
Mabel R. Williams

When Robert Williams loudly proclaimed the right of Black folks to defend themselves with arms against the Ku Klux Klan, in 1955, I was deeply impressed. I never believed desegregation could win without decisively confronting racist terror in the South. While the media gave greatest exposure to passive resistance as a principle, that is not the whole story. In the South, the level of terror was so intense that the African American freedom movement could not get off the ground without armed self-defense. The right of African Americans to defend themselves physically from racist terror was elementary, but it was considered violent and subversive by most white people and by many Black people. No other peoples in the United States were denied the right of self-defense.

When Rob and his family fled North Carolina in 1961, after he was framed on a kidnapping charge, Harry and I were living in Mexico. I asked Elizabeth Catlett Mora to use her contacts to help Rob. She did, defying the CP, which was then opposing Rob and any kind of street demonstration against segregation. The Mexican press published articles about Rob and Mabel's struggles against the Klan and their flight, which helped them get from Mexico into Cuba, no doubt with the help of Catlett's husband, Francisco.

FBI poster signed by J. Edgar Hoover trying to get Robert F. Williams killed by describing him as heavily armed, extremely dangerous, violent, and schizophrenic.

I first met Rob in 1969, after he flew from London to Detroit, where he was arrested for extradition to Monroe, North Carolina. I had published a letter about Rob and his struggles in the *Michigan Daily*, the student newspaper of the University of Michigan, where I was studying for my PhD. After his extradition hearing, I stepped out in front of his phalanx of security guards from the Republic of New Africa and held out a letter addressed to him. His guards tried to push past me, but Rob stopped them and took the letter.

A few weeks later, I received a phone call from the Center for Chinese Studies at the University of Michigan, with the message that Robert F.

Williams had asked that I meet with him and the center's director, Professor Allen S. Whiting. Whiting had come to the University of Michigan after he was kicked off the China desk at the US State Department for advocating normalizing relations with China. While Rob and I talked about the Black protest movement, Whiting kept trying to steer the conversation to China. The Center for Chinese Studies gave Rob a one-year fellowship. Rob later told me that Chou En-lai had sent for him shortly before he left China and asked him to do what he could to normalize relations with the United States. Rob spent the year briefing the China experts at the State Department to prepare for president Richard Nixon's trip to China. Rob taught them how to approach the Chinese and the pitfalls to avoid. Normalizing relations went a long way toward ending the war in Vietnam.

Rob, Mabel, and I became close friends for the rest of their lives. We visited each other's homes over many years. I attended their family reunions in Monroe. When Rob was extradited to North Carolina, I organized his defense committee. Famed defense attorney William Kunstler defended him. All the charges against Rob were dropped after a broad range of local and outside protesters arrived.

Robert F. Williams, Gary Goff, me, and my daughter Rebecca in Monroe, North Carolina, for an extradition hearing, 1976

Rob was a brilliant, original thinker. He avoided projection and getting caught up in false images. He was never a Communist, but he knew how to use the Cold War and the Communist world to promote the Black liberation struggle. At Rob's request, Mao Tse-tung issued a detailed, well-informed statement supporting the Black freedom movement in the United States.

Rob summarized his attitudes about the Black liberation struggle in *Negroes with Guns*:

> When Afro-Americans resist and struggle for their rights they also possess a power greater than that generated by their will and their hands. With the world situation as it is today, the most racist and fascist United States government conceivable could not succeed in exterminating 20,000,000 people. We know there is a great power struggle going on in the world today and the colored peoples control the true balance of power.... Racists consider themselves superior beings and are not willing to exchange their superior lives for our inferior ones. They are most vicious and violent when they can practice violence with impunity.

Rob was never a nationalist separatist like Elijah Muhammad and his followers. He was a revolutionary internationalist:

> As for being a "Black Nationalist," this is a word that's hard to define. No, I'm not a "Black Nationalist" to the point that I would exclude whites or that I would discriminate against whites or that I would be prejudiced toward whites. I would prefer to think of myself as an Inter-Nationalist. That is, I'm interested in the problems of all mankind. I'm interested in the problems of Africa, of Asia, and of Latin America. I believe that we all have the same struggle, a struggle for liberation. Discrimination and race hatred are undesirable, and I am just as much against racial discrimination, in all forms, every place in the world, as I am against it in the United States.

Rob was brave but avoided martyrdom. As Rosa Parks said at his funeral, he was one of our few great leaders who died in his bed of natural causes. He was no ideologue. He was an African American revolutionary internationalist guided by deeply felt spiritualism with strong African roots; a moralist who hated lies and self-deception and refused to embrace them, including those that might have seemed politically expedient. As John Bracey points out, the Revolutionary Action Movement inspired by Rob survived because of its flexible, quiet tactics, unlike the Black Panthers, whose visibility put its members in constant danger.[3]

The civil rights movement could not have survived without the armed self-defense movement against the Ku Klux Klan. Even Martin Luther King relied on armed self-defense. His home was well armed. During the James Meredith March Against Fear in Mississippi in 1966, which was defended by the Deacons for Defense and Justice, a prominent armed self-defense movement formed in Louisiana, Dr. King entrusted his children to my friend Henry Armand Austan, a Deacons member who had shot a Klansman in Bogalusa to protect a young girl injured in an anti-Klan demonstration.

Rob and Mabel Williams returned to the United States only a year after Martin Luther King was murdered. J. Edgar Hoover believed that Rob was the most likely charismatic new leader of the Black liberation movement.[4] Rob was effectively slandered and accused of being a government agent. I became one of the Williamses' closest friends at a time when they had few others because the slanders worked so well.

When I visited Rob and Mabel in their home in Baldwin, Michigan, Mabel was working, shopping, cooking, washing the dishes and clothes, ironing, mopping the floor, looking after her kitchen garden, typing and editing for Rob, sorting his mail, and caring for their dog. That's what was expected of women of our generation. But I came to understand that my dear, unassuming friend Mabel was at least an equal partner with her husband. He was the great promoter. She was the organizer who maintained a tight circle of women friends who got things done. She never promoted herself and didn't think of herself as an individual or even a leader. I understood the sacrifice it was for her to follow Rob and live abroad, isolated from her friends and family. Her mother died while Mabel lived abroad. Mabel was a social person and suffered deeply from isolation. Another terrible blow came after they returned to live in Michigan: the death of their oldest son, Rob Jr., leaving his two young sons fatherless.

After Rob died, in 1996, I helped organize the only university program in the country commemorating his life, at the Midlo Center of the University of New Orleans. Mabel and I became even closer after that. Hoping to distract her from her grief, I took Mabel with me to conferences in Jamaica and Senegal. We traveled together and visited each other often. Throughout our lives, we lived together for weeks at a

My mother signing to establish the Midlo Center for New Orleans Studies and Herman Midlo endowed chair at the University of New Orleans, 1991. My nephew Lawrence Lehman seated on her right and me standing.

time and got along well. When I moved from Mexico to East Lansing, Michigan, in June 2010, she and her son, John Chalmers Williams, met me at the airport, and we moved in together into a condo I rented in East Lansing. We lived together until late 2011, when she got so sick that she required constant care.

Mabel, Grace Lee Boggs, and I were each the wife of an influential Black Power leader. Mabel was Black, Grace was Chinese, and I am Jewish and defined as white. At one point Mabel and I visited Grace at her office and home in East Side Detroit, where I had lived in 1965. Almost nothing was left standing except for Grace's house on Field Street.

No one I knew dressed as elegantly as Mabel. She carried herself like a princess in gorgeous African-style clothes. What she loved most was being helpful, in her later years mainly to the neglected elderly. She died in her son John's home in Detroit in 2014. I held her in my arms for two hours a few days before she died. John died shortly after his mother. That's the hardest part of living so long. You lose so many of the people you love most.

My last photo with Mabel R. Williams, with Helen Hornbeck Tanner at her home, 2011.

Living and Working in Detroit

When the kids and I first arrived in Detroit, in August 1965, I rented a furnished apartment by the week, and we had nothing with us but a few clothes. I didn't expect to be there long—until I received a telegram saying my contract at Elizabeth City State College had been canceled. I quickly came to love Detroit, mainly because of the autoworkers and their rich union culture. They were hardworking, proud, and generous. Once, my car died at a traffic light. The autoworker in the lane next to mine jumped out of his car with a screwdriver and fixed it before the traffic light turned green. He refused to accept payment. I liked the single mothers, too. Sometimes their kids' fathers would show up with a little money. The women said the guys were doing the best they could. The kids of single mothers created their own street society. They helped one another and were loyal. I used to feed the neighborhood kids out of my scanty resources. I would leave my door unlocked so kids escaping from the problems of their families could find refuge.

I worked in downtown Detroit as a temporary legal secretary. When that job ended, I went to a temporary agency to look for a new job and always had one by the next day since legal secretaries were a hot item on the job market. But most of what I earned went for child care. Grace Lee Boggs was a good friend, and got me a longer-term job working with her for some lawyers she knew. We visited her house in Detroit, which was a center for Black working-class organizing. Her husband was the autoworker, intellectual, and writer James Boggs. James died in 1993, and Grace died in 2015, at age one hundred. She was busy writing, lecturing, and filming until she died.

I applied for a job as a substitute teacher in the Detroit Public Schools, scored high on their exam, and was hired. Then the Detroit Board of Education phoned and said I would have to be interviewed by their psychologist. The interview was very brief. They told me I had failed the psychological exam and withdrew the job offer. An anonymous sympathizer mailed me a copy of a letter from the Detroit Public Schools to the FBI stating that I had been blacklisted from any type of job.

CE 100-10098

The 1964 City Directory for New Orleans, Louisiana, lists the resident of 4216 Vincennes as HERMAN L. MIDLO.

It is noted that the name of subject's father is HERMAN LAZARD MIDLO.

MARGARET PATRICK, Apartment 1, 5404 Concord, Detroit, Michigan, on January 21, 1966, advised SAs [   ] that subject formerly resided in Apartment 4 at this address; however, she moved approximately one month ago and did not leave any forwarding address. Mrs. PATRICK identified a picture of subject and advised that subject resided in the apartment at this address with her two children. She stated that subject informed her that she had secured employment as a teacher in the Detroit Schools System.

On January 24, 1966, Miss ADELAINE CALLERY, Supervisor, Records and Certifications, Detroit Board of Education, Detroit, Michigan, advised SA [   ] that subject during December, 1964, and November, 1965, applied for a teaching position in the Detroit Public Schools System. She advised that both of subject's applications for employment as a teacher were turned down inasmuch as subject did not meet the requirements for a Michigan Teaching Certificate. Miss CALLERY advised that subject's file contains a notation that subject not be hired in any capacity by the Detroit Board of Education.

According to Miss CALLERY, subject's address in 1964 was 250 Riverside Drive, Apartment 44, New York City, New York, and as of November, 1965, was indicated as 5404 Concord, Detroit, Michigan.

Miss CALLERY advised that in the event she received any subsequent information regarding subject's present location, she would advise the Detroit Office.

We later moved to an unfurnished, monthly rental apartment in a somewhat better neighborhood. Ultimately, my two small children and I were evicted from both apartments I rented in Detroit and a third in Ann Arbor, after the FBI visited my landlords. My FBI files remind me that the second apartment in Detroit was on Inverness Avenue. If you want to know the exact address, how much rent we paid, who our landlord was, our telephone number, and where we worked, it's all in our FBI files.

I spent much of my spare time with the children in my neighborhood. They all called me Mommy. I even got to know the neighborhood people who were addicted to heroin, too. I treated them like they were human beings—that's all it took to win their confidence. They weren't violent. They stole because they were desperate for money to get their next fix. One of them told me there was a drug called methadone that would help them. I wrote to Marie Nyswander. She and her husband had developed methadone maintenance treatment at Rockefeller University in New York City. The program had not yet been used elsewhere. I approached the institutions responsible for dealing with drug addicts in Michigan about getting methadone maintenance treatment. Guess what? None of them believed there were heroin addicts in Michigan, although many veterans were returning from Vietnam strung out.

The conditions that I witnessed in Detroit were among the root causes of the Detroit Rebellion, the most widespread of the late 1960s urban uprisings. These uprisings have been portrayed in the media and history as irrational acts. I wrote an article for *Freedomways* magazine, drawing on my personal experiences in Detroit, to counter that story:

> All of us are trapped by the collective consciousness; by a kind of cognition by consensus which screens out much of reality. Our limited perception is shaken only when data contrary to the consensus are forced upon us in the most dramatic manner. Detroit in flames; tanks rumbling down her streets; helicopters shooting it out with rooftop snipers. Her total indifference to symbols of force and authority. Madness, yes. But madness closely akin to revelation. Before Walter Reuther plants that grass he promises to plant to hide the scars of the revolt; before the self-satisfied bureaucrats and politicians reconstruct their delusions of their own perfection—if these delusions were measurably shaken by the insurrection in Detroit—let us look at the city; at the daily lives of her factory workers, Black and white, and at the system that pushes them over the brink.
>
> The consensus is, everything is fine in Detroit. Plenty of high-paying factory jobs. Lots of overtime. What more can a worker want? The truth is, workers, especially Black workers, are treated like dogs, cheated on every side by a swarm of parasites, work crazy hours, and stagger under such a burden of usurious debt that no matter how fat their paycheck is, they often don't know where their next meal is coming from.
>
> I spent a year in Detroit, living with my two children in some of the areas affected by the riot, working as a temporary legal secretary downtown. That's a good way to get to know a city. I moved to Ann Arbor from Detroit in July 1966. And to those who prided themselves on conditions in Detroit, and on the lack of riots there, my response has been: "If it ever starts in Detroit, it will never stop."

I learned some quick lessons about the status of the poor in Detroit, from my own experience. Here are a few incidents. I was living in the ghetto on the East Side and enrolled my son in the third grade in the neighborhood school. The children were forbidden to play on the playground, which, although quite large, was used as a parking lot for the teachers' cars, and the teachers were afraid their cars might be hit by balls. They kept the playground equipment locked in the basement. A number of children in the neighborhood complained to me that one of their teachers was selling school supplies (which were supposed to be given to needy children) at 50 cents per child per day. They were not allowed to bring their own supplies because the principal had a rule against children carrying school supplies in the hallways. Each day the children failed to buy supplies from the teacher, they got a failing grade. . . .

My landlord used to break into my apartment while I was at work and verbally abuse my son. One day, he pushed my son down the stairs. I went to the police to complain. They had to place me socially before they could respond: "Where do you live? Furnished or unfurnished? Do you pay by the week or by the month?" Since my apartment was furnished and I paid by the week, evidently I had no rights at all. They treated my complaint like a big joke, and said, "It's his house. He has a right to do whatever he wants in it. If you don't like it, move."

For my pains, I was evicted.

I saw the kind of bind my neighbors were in, and how the legal system operates to keep the workers in a state of urban peonage. It's a tightly knit system in Detroit: a handful of big employers, easy credit, uncontrolled usury in installment buying. And not even God can help the worker if he doesn't pay. His wages are attached. If they are attached twice, he loses his job. The unions won't lift a finger to protect his job. Blacklists circulate among the big three auto manufacturers of workers who've been fired. He can't pay his traffic tickets? Ten days in the Detroit House of Correction. He loses his job? Too bad for him. He can't keep up child support payments? Too bad. Back to jail. He has to keep up a car to get to work. He pays for the car, interest on the car, astronomical insurance rates, interest on the insurance. The big food chain stores sell him leftovers from the white suburban stores; they tend to stock only the highest-priced items. The little groceries steal pennies from children. Home improvement racketeers commit outrages with impunity. He is overworked and kept at a marginal existence by swarms of parasites who take his last nickel. He is preyed upon and unprotected, pushed around, outraged, insulted, and then told he lives in a perfect city. And the City Fathers cannot understand why many of the youth aren't panting to be incorporated into this great system and prefer to live by their wits.

If we examine the specifics of the rebellion, I think we will find that it reflected a magnificent grasp of reality; that it was not inspired by irrational hatred, but by legitimate resentment of exploitation. And considering the amount of property damage and widespread sniping, remarkably few lives were taken by the rioters. The same cannot be said for the National Guard, who fired indiscriminately into crowded buildings and committed other atrocities.

The word is that resentment against the police had been building up on Twelfth Street because of the shooting of a prostitute by a policeman two weeks before the riot broke out. Twelfth Street—street of pawn-shops and vice—sucks the lifeblood of demoralized victims of ghetto life and converts it into hard cash for big-time vice operators. The police, as many other municipal institutions, play the opposite role of what they are supposed to be playing in this situation: they protect the profiteers and persecute the victims. Tearing down Twelfth Street was a triumph.

Furniture stores charging high interest rates and overcharging for shoddy goods were particularly singled out for destruction. Notes of indebtedness were burned, wiping out a vast burden on the people. It brings to mind the peasants burning down the chateaux and destroying the feudal dues records during the French Revolution.

I am afraid that the response to the insurrection in Detroit has been far from appropriate. There has been much buck-passing and an attempt to create hysteria about Black racism, which was conspicuously absent from the rebellion. The rioters showed exquisite respect for life, if not for property. Hostility was directed not against "whitey" but against the establishment. It is greatly to their credit that they made the distinction.

Governor Romney and Mayor Cavanagh called for more feder-al funds and denied their own responsibility for the situation. In my opinion, unless the workers are protected from the ravenous parasites who swarm all over the ghetto, federal funds will continue to be wasted.

I have three specific proposals to make, all within the competence of state and municipal government, just as a step in the right direction:

1) Apply laws against usury to consumer credit.

2) End wage garnishments (attachments of wages for debts). This practice is illegal in many states.

3) End all forms of imprisonment for debt.

These three measures, in themselves, would be more effective than any of the so-called anti-poverty programs so far devised.

Detroit is a beautiful town because it is full of intelligent, humane workers with a good grasp of reality, even though the political structure is a self-righteous sham. If Detroit rises from the ashes without learning anything, the Fire Next Time will only be that much brighter.

Meanwhile, Harry had followed me to Detroit and moved in with me during the spring of 1966. Someone showed him a copy of *Soulbook* magazine, which was serializing the manuscript we wrote in Mexico. Harry phoned their office. An editor, the eighteen-year-old poet Ernie Allen, answered. Harry told him it was okay that they published the manuscript, but they should have asked his permission. Ernie said, "But we thought you were deceased." Ernie told us the manuscript had been mimeographed and widely circulated, especially in California and the Deep South. Harry went to Oakland to work with the *Soulbook* editors, who were among the first in the Bay Area to call themselves Black Panthers. Bobby Seale was their distribution manager.

When Harry returned to Detroit, he lived in the home of Edna and John Watson of the Dodge Revolutionary Union Movement (DRUM). John Watson was editor of the monthly newspaper *Inner City Voice*, the organizing center for the Black worker-led protest movements in the auto plants beginning with DRUM. Of the activists, I knew Watson best. He protected the Detroit movement from ambitious outsiders, whom he called "sky people." The Black Panthers sent in their organizers from the West Coast with little success. The movement spread to other auto plants, universities, libraries, and high schools. Harry was highly respected by all sections of the League leadership. The movement led to the formation of the League of Revolutionary Black Workers, but it was torn apart by rigged union elections and divisive tactics used by police agents of various kinds.

The Black autoworkers' culture of resistance frightened the establishment. I believe the deindustrialization of Detroit was mainly carried out to dispense with the Black autoworkers. The system preferred to destroy Detroit rather than work together with its vibrant community of autoworkers to build a better society.

Ann Arbor Years

While living in Detroit, I tried applying to Wayne State University for admission to its PhD program in history. I met with the chair of the history department, bringing my daughter Rebecca along. I figured I might as well know what I was dealing with. His attitude was dismissive. He said, "It would take extraordinary ability to get through this program."

I said, "How can you tell by looking at me that I do not have extraordinary ability?"

He said, "Even if you do get through it, you are a woman, you are in your thirties; when you graduate you will be in your forties and menopausal and no one will hire you."

I said, "But I thought there is a shortage of college teachers."

He said, "There is a shortage of bright young men from Harvard."

So I went to the University of Michigan instead and talked to Charles Gibson, the greatest Latin American colonial historian of his generation. I told him the advice I got at Wayne State. He said indignantly, "That is the worst kind of professionalism!" My application was accepted at Michigan, and I was admitted to the PhD program in Latin American history. Gibson sent me to talk to Helen Hornbeck Tanner, director of the Center for Continuing Education for Women. She gave me much practical advice, emotional support, and encouragement; I couldn't have made it without her. We remained close friends until she died in 2011 at age ninety-six.

During the spring semester of 1966, I commuted from Detroit to Ann Arbor to attend a heavy schedule of classes. My adviser said I should not take so many courses because I had to pass two foreign language comprehension exams. I told him I already knew both foreign languages well.

We moved from Detroit to Maiden Lane Apartments in Ann Arbor in July 1966. When I got a notice of eviction a short time later, this time I fought back. There was a hearing in which the landlord claimed my three-year-old daughter had stolen newspapers from another tenant's doorstep and that my dog had defecated in the hallway. I thought it was racism, but it turned out to be the FBI again.

That was the last dirty trick they played on me in Michigan. They soon had their hands full with the 1967 uprising in Detroit and the terrorist group the Weathermen in Ann Arbor. I rented a small house on Hillcrest Avenue from an African American hairdresser. She rented me the house because she was grateful for my helping her stop a city housing inspector from shaking her down. He had claimed the electric wiring in her house needed to be completely replaced and recommended his brother-in-law to do the job. I encouraged her to file a complaint. The city of Ann Arbor sent an independent inspector to her house, and he reported there was nothing wrong with the wiring.

I earned a fellowship in the University of Michigan's new comparative history program, and my parents helped me financially during my doctoral studies, but it wasn't enough. These were hard, lean times. I had to live in a tent at Friends Lake, a Quaker community, for a few weeks while my kids lived with their friends.

Since the youth movement operated under the principle of "Don't trust anyone over thirty," my political impact was certainly limited in Ann Arbor. Occasionally young organizers would stop by my house to ask for advice, and sometimes we would talk in the student cafeteria. Once when Harry was living with us at our house on Hillcrest Avenue, Sheldon Stark and some students came by and asked us where they should organize. I suppose they thought we would say in factories. I said they should organize where they were: at the University of Michigan.

By 1965, though, the spread of television as the major source of news was having an impact. Visual images are much more powerful than print. They made the public quickly and deeply aware of our torture of helpless children in Vietnam with napalm as well as the racist violence against the Civil Rights Movement in the United States. But there were drawbacks. The media ended up choosing movement leaders: too often the most dramatic, flamboyant, and sometimes self-appointed ones. Self-dramatizing sensationalists became the heroes. The patient, day-to-day work of devoted organizers, rooted at the workplace and in the community, the greatest strength of the old left, was lost. Continuity was largely destroyed.

When I started graduate school in the spring of 1966, student protests against the war in Vietnam had already started with teach-ins against the war. The protests escalated when the military draft was extended to students. Although my hands were more than full, my children and I participated in antiwar demonstrations, including a protest against the production of napalm at a DuPont shareholders meeting in Midland, Michigan. We traveled to the huge peace rally in Washington, DC, in October 1967, where at least 250,000 people protested against the war in Vietnam, forcing president Lyndon Johnson onto the defensive.

I knew the counterculture hippies well. I had met John and Leni Sinclair at their commune in Detroit in 1965 when the counterculture movement there was starting. Their definition of love was a bit too broad and indiscriminate for my taste. Their commune moved from Detroit to Ann Arbor about the same time we did. We agreed strongly about the need to change consciousness, but strongly disagreed about the promotion of illegal drugs.

When the Black Panthers started getting a great deal of media attention, the commune on Hill Street changed its name to the White Panthers. By 1968, violence became the "in" thing. Young people and even little kids were walking around with *The Little Red Book: The Sayings of Chairman Mao*. I ran into a little kid wearing a T-shirt with big letters saying, "Power Comes Out of the Barrel of a Gun." I told him, "Then you better get ready to run, because the US government has a whole lot more guns than you do."

Mostly it was talk, except for the Weather Underground. I knew its leaders, Bill Ayers and Diana Oughton, well before they organized the Weathermen. They changed their name to the Weather Underground when they started planting and setting off bombs. My daughter Rebecca attended their experimental school in Ann Arbor, the Open Door. It had a good approach but offered little of the content kids needed to learn, so I put Rebecca back into public school. The Open Door soon closed.

They were so young—Bill Ayers was just in his early twenties—and had a lot to learn about being underground. Diana Oughton and two other Weather members accidentally blew themselves up in a Greenwich Village brownstone while making bombs. It was said they were plotting to blow up a dance scheduled at Fort Dix Army Base in New Jersey. This struck me as symbolic and misguided: playing with dynamite when you don't understand the consequences. Diana seemed like a sweet, good, loving person. My son Haywood, then in junior high, had a crush on her and was devastated by her death. The Weather Underground finally managed to explode bombs at a few places without blowing themselves up, including at the Pentagon.

My children got to know the hippies even better than I did. It was an exciting time for Haywood and his friends. We ended up homeless for a while, and our friend Jane Schiller took us in. Her daughters Lisa, Greta, and Tina became our lifelong friends. Haywood, Greta, and Tina organized and led the antiwar protest movement at Forsythe Junior High School, cranking out antiwar leaflets and a magazine on mimeograph machines. They pulled the American flag down from the flagpole to protest the war.

Haywood also played drums in a rock band. He wanted to become a famous rock star. I became known in Ann Arbor as Haywood Hall the Drummer's mother. My main reaction to their music was that I wished they wouldn't play it so loud, but we found common ground with John Coltrane and with the Motown sound. I passed on the family tradition of singing folk songs. Classical music was a hard sell to Haywood. It was Rebecca who learned to love it. Intellectually, I have more in common with Rebecca than with my other children. We share a love of reading, especially literature and history, researching, and writing history, as well as an interest in law and political protest.

Haywood's rock band at Forsythe Junior High School in Ann Arbor, Michigan.

But we got off on the wrong track about the feminist movement. I had been a feminist for as long as I could remember, but in isolation.

It seemed there was no way of sharing, especially with younger women, how oppressed women had been in the past. I couldn't talk about it; it was too upsetting. A graduate student brought me the first book I ever read about feminism: Virginia Woolf's *A Room of One's Own*. I was happy to read that one, as it made me realize the odds I faced as a woman intellectual and writer. I wasn't enthusastic about the other feminist books I came across because I felt they lacked race or class analysis.

Robert M. Warner, director of the Michigan Historical Collections, further enlightened me about the odds I faced at the University of Michigan. The year I applied to the PhD program in history, there were seven hundred applications. I was among only thirty-five admitted. No one could predict who among us were capable of writing their final thesis, but they expected only five or six to complete it. Among those, only two or three would get tenure-track jobs and only some of those would eventually be awarded tenure. I was competing with young men with wives who worked to provide them with a living, did all their husbands' typing, and often helped them with their research. Meanwhile, I functioned essentially as a single mother of three, including one with serious mental illness, while dealing with deep-seated prejudices against women in the field of history.

I am now impressed by the many young African American women who are advancing through the profession based on their voluminous, quality, original work while networking with each other. Some women historians and scholars from several generations have expressed that they have been inspired by me and my work. That means a lot to me.

Raising Biracial Children in the Bad Old Days

My children Haywood and Rebecca with me at the New Orleans Afro-American Museum, January 4, 2013.

One day in Detroit in 1965, I went into a supermarket with Haywood and Rebecca. A young white woman was pushing her African-descended child in a grocery cart. She asked me naively, "Have you ever had any problems raising mixed-blood children?"

My answer was "Yes." My children and I suffered from isolation and lack of a support network of immediate or extended family or friends. Biracial families were rare when my children were born. Interracial marriages were still illegal in many states for a decade after Harry and I married and our first child was born.

One of the most painful things was my mother's rejection of my biracial children. When my sister invited us to my father's seventy-fourth birthday party at her home, my parents both wrote me, asking me not to bring my children. Rebecca, then eleven years old, wrote two amazing letters to my mother, disputing her decision to exclude her from her grandfather's birthday celebration. Here is their exchange:

Dear grandparents,

My mother and I have discussed the situation and have come to a conclusion. I agree it is important to have your daughter to come to your
birthday party. But mom feels that it's equally important that I come to
the party because I'm her daughter and your grandchild.

I'm being so formal because we have never really been that close
because of prejudices in your minds. When you decide to be more
close to me, I will be able to write you like your grandchild, not your
lawyer. Don't take this too harshly, for I still love you, whether you
love me or not.

Love,

Becky Hall

Dear Becky,

We are very sorry that you have been placed in the middle of this situation which neither you nor we created. Nor did we create the attitudes
in the place where we live. But live here we must, and we cannot flout
the taboos in the face of our neighbors and family. As we have told
your mother before, you'll come for a few days, and we'll be left to face
the consequences. It isn't fair for this onus to be laid on us.

This is something that should have never happened. But it did.
It will take many more years before we can have a relationship on our
home ground. Until that time, we're afraid we will only be able to see
you away from here....

You say you love us. Love is only a word unless it has some meaning.
When one truly loves, he will do anything not to cause embarrassment,
pain or misery to this person they profess to love. Very often this is done
by great self-sacrifice. I can't expect you to understand this. Your mother
was much older, and she couldn't understand this word love either. Love
is standing by when every fiber of your being knows that the loved one
is heading for heartache for themselves. Standing by and taking vituper-
ations in return for the kindness and forgiveness offered.

You have a long life before you—ours is a long way behind us. In
time, all this race question may be over, but we doubt if we will live
long enough to see it in our lifetime. You are a very lovable little girl,
and it's a shame that this race problem should be yours, and we know
you have had it elsewhere besides the South. As we said before, we

didn't create this situation. We live here. We hate this whole thing. We hate denying you. We hate hurting you, but these are the facts, and we're too old to start new crusades. We've had one generation of heartache. It's too much to expect us to take on another.

Dear grandmother,

You are perfectly right about you being left with the consequences because you are the only ones of my relatives that feel that way. May I ask what you mean by "This is something that should have never happened?" Is that me being alive?

My mother did not help me with this letter, nor did she tell me what to write. The reason this race question is still around is because people like you are afraid of being socially embarrassed. I do know the meaning of love. If one truly loves, he will not be worried of social embarrassment, just of defending the person who he loves.

It is true that I have a long life ahead of me. But someone is never too old to learn.

Becky Hall

My beloved sister Razele Midlo Lehmann, 1927–2003.

My sister insisted we all come to the party anyway. Haywood refused to go, so I went with Rebecca. During that trip, I slapped my mother when she spoke contemptuously about Harry in front of his daughter. Rebecca later told me that meant a lot to her.

Two years later, in 1976, my mother insisted that I come to my parents' fiftieth wedding anniversary party without my children. My father tried hard to get my mother to relent, without success. Then he urged me to be a "good girl" and come without my children. He said she was concerned about the reaction of her garden club friends, who would soon mean nothing to her. I didn't attend my parents' fiftieth wedding anniversary party. I never learned how to be a good girl. And I never will.

Shortly after my father died, in 1978, my sister dragged my mother to Haywood's wedding celebration in Brooklyn. She came to the memorial for Harry in New York after his death in 1985 and went to Haywood's graduation when he was awarded his MD from Baylor College of Medicine in 1986. During the last decade of her life, she had completely forgotten her earlier behavior toward my children. But they, of course, never

Above: Bea Hammond, wife of my daughter Rebecca Hall, me, and their little son Caleb while Rebecca was awarded her PhD in History at the University of California, Santa Cruz, 2004. Below: Me and daughter Rebecca at her home in Santa Cruz, California

forgot. She finally behaved better toward them, partially because she was old and weak, and also because my sister put pressure on her. My children attended her funeral in 1997 and were upset to see the grief of my sister's children over the death of their grandmother, whom my children never really knew and who never loved them.

~

I tried to be a good mother under impossible circumstances. But I know I have deeply hurt my children. We all suffered: we were constantly spied on and evicted from apartments, and I was fired from jobs when my children were very young. My marriage to Harry led to new gender-role battles against attitudes that were deeply rooted, including in the Communist movement. I ultimately had to bear full responsibility for providing for and raising my two children fathered by Harry, and later also my elder son, Leo, after he became severely mentally ill.

Leo and I were separated after my marriage to Michel Yuspeh fell apart. When I left Michel, he offered to care for Leo until I could figure out how to make a living. But when I had finally settled myself and was ready to take Leo back, Michel refused to give him up. At first, Leo stayed with me frequently, often every weekend. He was with me when I went into labor with Haywood. But Michel, perhaps because of the intense pressure he felt from the FBI, hired a ruthless divorce lawyer who brought up in the proceedings my interracial marriage to Harry and our politics. Michel won custody of Leo; I wasn't allowed to bring Leo to my home and could only see him for a few hours every other week, in a public place.

Leo was seven years old when I moved to Mexico in early 1959. Michel promised to send Leo to visit me, but he never did. When I moved back to New York City in early 1964, Michel only allowed him to visit me once. So when Leo sought me out in 1967, while I was living in Ann Arbor, we'd had no contact for eight years while he was growing up. Hearing from him after all those years was a profound joy. But Leo was suffering from drug use and mental illness. Because he sometimes became violent, it was immediately obvious I couldn't leave him alone with Rebecca and Haywood. The day he arrived, Leo slapped five-year-old Rebecca in the face. When the principal of Rebecca's nursery school sent us to a psychiatrist, he told me that since I had no relationship with Leo and he was creating problems, I should hospitalize him, but I thought I would never have a relationship with Leo if I did that, even if it would have been easier for me.

I tried my best to care for Leo as he suffered through episodes of schizoaffective disorder, a serious and often misunderstood mental illness. By some miracle, he survived into old age while largely avoiding medication, institutionalization, or living on the street. He died accidentally in June 2020 at the age of sixty-nine.

Leo and me at our home in the Mississippi pine belt, 2001

The impact of Leo's illness on my other two children was devastating. Before Leo's arrival in Ann Arbor, Rebecca and Haywood did not even know they had a half-brother because I was so emotionally shattered from losing him that I could not even talk about him. Haywood was just entering adolescence when Leo showed up. Haywood survived some very rough times better than most kids could have, but I did not know how badly he was hurt by those years.

Rebecca was only five when Leo slapped her in the face, and it affected her deeply. She wanted my undivided attention at a time when I was already exhausted and distracted by graduate school, writing my PhD thesis, and dealing with Leo's mental illness. Fortunately, when Leo first returned I was preparing for exams and had no classes, so I could stay home to watch her when she wasn't in nursery school. Rebecca was a marvelous little girl. When my first book was published, she remarked on how small the book was, after all that work. She demanded that I not write anything else until she had grown up. I agreed, and I didn't.

Both Haywood and Rebecca turned out to be amazing, creative, effective, socially conscious, relevant human beings despite poverty, virulent racism, social isolation, eviction from our homes, and the trauma of their encounters with Leo. I hope that some of their great resiliency was learned from me.

Above: Bea, Rebecca, and Caleb. Left: Grandson-in-law Ken Kopp and granddaughter Sajia Kopp, Haywood's daughter.

Snoops, Discrimination, and My Years at Rutgers

The little spare time I had when I lived in Ann Arbor was devoted mainly to writing essays and campaigning for medical treatment for heroin addicts. I agitated for the implementation of methadone maintenance treatment, which worked and even substantially reduced crime, in both Detroit and Ann Arbor. Then Richard Nixon started his so-called War on Drugs, which criminalized drug addiction instead of treating the victims and sentenced mainly Black people to long prison terms without parole.

After receiving my PhD in 1970, I did oral history interviews about heroin traffic in Detroit for the Michigan Historical Collections. I interviewed addicts as well as officials with responsibility for dealing with the drug problem. One of the people I interviewed was James Brickley, then a US attorney and later lieutenant governor of Michigan. He spent his last years as a highly respected justice of the Michigan Supreme Court. Brickley made it clear that he knew exactly who I was. He talked about Robert F. Williams and denied that the US government was conspiring against him. He said the government was so disorganized that they couldn't conspire to save their own lives. I told him the people I talked to said two policemen ran the illegal drug traffic in the East Side of Detroit. He was honestly shocked; he denied it and said that police might be corrupt about gambling and prostitution but never about drugs.

When the interview was over, I asked Brickley if we could copy some documents and then return them. He got out a file, leafed through it, and handed it to me. After I got back to the Michigan Historical Collections I looked over the file and found a letter, several pages long, with a black border around it, marked "VERY CONFIDENTIAL." It was a list of the names, addresses, and telephone numbers of all the undercover narcotics agents in the Midwest. I showed it to my boss, Robert M. Warner, who later became Archivist of the United States in 1980 and fought long, hard, and successfully for the independence of the National Archives from the bureaucratic General Services Administration.[5] "We don't want this here, do we?" I asked.

He looked at the letter and said, "No, we don't want this here. Send it to him registered mail, saying he alone can sign for it."

I enclosed a little note to Brickley that said, "Don't worry. It wasn't copied."

When I got my FBI files, I learned how far Brickley went to protect me after that. He knew I was leaving Michigan in 1971 for a job at Rutgers University, in New Jersey. I had asked him if he could help prevent Robert Williams's extradition to North Carolina and asked him to meet with me and Mabel, Rob's wife. He wrote me back saying there was nothing he could do and wished me good luck with my "new assignment." The Michigan FBI stopped the New Jersey FBI from opening up a file on me, claiming I was still in Michigan even though I moved to New Jersey that July. For several years, an annual report on me stated that I was still at the University of Michigan, which was an outright lie, and the Michigan FBI knew it.

In 1973, as I was coming up for promotion with tenure at Rutgers, the New Jersey FBI did open a file on me, claiming I belonged to a Maoist organization with headquarters in Chicago. I had visited Harry and went to a few meetings with him, but I certainly never joined a Maoist organization. The agents at the Newark office of the FBI were ordered to make contacts at Rutgers. They sent to Michigan for my file and received a letter from the Michigan office saying the report from Chicago about me was false, and they should close their file. I don't know what the New Jersey FBI thought—maybe that I was a mole for one of the shadowy, rival intelligence agencies polluting our country during the Nixon years. But it closed my file until late 1976, after I went to China and then organized Robert Williams's defense committee. They described me, with evident chagrin, as an "old C2," which meant a Communist. All the same, I was promoted to associate professor with tenure at Rutgers in 1973—and, very reluctantly, to full professor in 1992, after I had been an associate professor for nineteen years. I remained at Rutgers until I retired in 1996.

~

As it turned out, I was under surveillance from the start of my tenure at Rutgers, just not by the FBI. I had gone to Rutgers for a job interview in the spring of 1971. It started on College Avenue at the main campus. I thought I was in a time warp, because nothing seemed to have changed since the 1950s. No minorities, no hippies, no women. Then they took me to Livingston College across the Raritan River, and I said to myself, "Oh, that's where they put them all!" I was hired to teach at Livingston

College: the only woman in any of the history departments except for a few at Douglass, the women's college.

As I arrived on the Livingston College campus, I was driving along in my car, and an African American man yelled out, "Hey, Gwen, stop!" I stopped, and he jumped into my passenger seat and introduced himself as Ralph Lopez.

I asked, "How do you know who I am?"

He said, "I knew you were coming, and I saw your Michigan license plates, so I figured it was you."

I soon got to know Ralph well indeed. He was a Black Puerto Rican, affiliated with Livingston as a graduate student in the urban studies department. He had keys to every office on campus but didn't need them. He could open any locked door or window with no problem. Ralph usually slept in various offices on campus. He stuck to me like glue, especially when Harry was coming into town. He was right there to help carry Harry's suitcases. When my washing machine broke, he fixed it. He was at my beck and call. Harry praised him as "useful." Although he was a student with no visible means of support, he kept two Mercedes-Benz diesel cars on campus.

When I took my students to interview prisoners at Edna Mahan Correctional Facility for Women, in Clinton, and the state prison, in Trenton, Ralph tagged along. At Trenton, we met with a group of prisoners, one of whom said to me, "We get mean in here. And when we get out, you'll be in trouble."

I told him, "When you get out, we'll both be in trouble. But I suspect you'll be in a lot more trouble than me."

Everyone was amused, including the prisoners. Ralph was evidently satisfied that I wasn't planning a prison break.

I assumed Ralph was an FBI agent but harmless to me because I wasn't involved in politics. I figured Ralph was hanging around me because of Harry—I was used to FBI agents by then and had come to appreciate their helpfulness—that was how they ingratiated themselves with the people they snooped on, by being helpful.

But Ralph was much more sinister. He was US Army Intelligence. He tried very hard to warn me about what he was doing, but I was too dense to understand. Once, he took me and my kids to the Fort Dix Army Base store and showed the cashier his ID. I hadn't been socialized as a spy, and I respected people's privacy, so I didn't even look at his ID. I figured he had the right to shop there because he was a veteran. When that didn't sink in, Ralph got more explicit. He came into my office, all agitated, talking about the "big computer" in Washington, and he grabbed some books off my shelf and said they had all been read into the computer. He was trying to warn me about what was happening at Livingston College. Evidently, Army Intelligence was active on campus mainly because of the radical sociology department's ties to the Salvador Allende government in Chile. The professors traveled there and then gave public reports on campus, naming all the important people they met. Ralph Lopez was always there, quietly taking notes.

I dismissed what Ralph said as crazy. It was partially his agitated manner and partially because it was hard for me to wrap my mind around what he was trying to tell me. This was only a short time before Allende was murdered and his government overthrown in a bloodbath engineered by Henry Kissinger and the CIA in 1973. The Allende regime was a legally elected government that respected democratic rights, and that's what led to its destruction. I was still enough of a Leninist not to be surprised. But Livingston College was full of naive radical faculty who knew nothing about political repression and violence.

As far as I can find, nothing has ever been mentioned about the role of US Army Intelligence in fingering Allende supporters for torture and murder. After Allende was overthrown, I still didn't make the connection until a few years later, when I discovered that Ralph was a colonel in US Army Intelligence. When I got copies of my surveillance files in 1977, there were US Army Intelligence reports dating from the early 1970s. They were surely from Ralph Lopez. One of my greatest regrets in life is that I didn't listen to what he was trying so hard to tell me. He had a guilty conscience. Evidently, Ralph was present when Viola Liuzzo, a white housewife from Detroit and mother of four children, was murdered by Klansmen in Alabama during the march from Selma to Montgomery in 1965. He never got over it.

~

Livingston College at Rutgers University had been originally planned as an elite college for well-prepared and highly motivated students who needed a looser structure. The faculty was recruited with this emphasis in mind. Then the Newark uprising erupted in 1967. The mission of Livingston suddenly changed to the study of urban problems, although it was in the middle of the woods in a suburban New Jersey community. To quiet things down in Newark—which entailed controlling and destroying the remarkable community-based movement led by writer Amiri Baraka—Livingston College recruiters offered fellowships to the young people who were most likely to cause trouble for the sole purpose of getting them out of Newark.

I never recovered from my initial experiences teaching at Livingston. I had prepared course lectures from materials in four languages. But when my Friday 8 a.m. class met, I was often the only one there. When the students did show up, most of them were stoned. I knew I was a good teacher. After my experience at Elizabeth City State College, I had taught a course at the University of Michigan, and my students handed in excellent work. I asked my colleague Gerald Grob, who had hired me, "What in the world is going on here? Is it me or the students?"

He said, "It's not you. It's the students." A few weeks later, Grob demanded to be transferred to Douglass or he would leave Rutgers and take his large grants with him.

When I won the confidence of a few of the students who came to class, they told me that students had been kidnapped at gunpoint out of the dorms that spring because they had been speaking out against the drug trafficking. The kidnappers were now back on campus—with the written support of ten department chairs appealing on their behalf—and those they had kidnapped were not.

Bryan Blake, the assistant dean of students at Livingston, was a seven-foot-tall, tough, realistic man from East Harlem. When I told him about how badly my teaching was going, he said, "Just walk down the halls when classes are supposed to be in session. The classrooms are empty. No one is there. It's a miracle you are teaching at all." He confirmed what my students told me. He said his job was to buy off potential troublemakers, and told me that after the poet Sonia Sanchez had spoken out against the drug traffic in her class at Livingston, some men in disguise came into her office, pointed to a photo of her children, and told her they knew where she lived. She soon quit her job.

I went to the protected world of the College Avenue campus and complained long and hard to the central administration about the drug traffic at Livingston. I doubt if it did any good. Grob asked my opinion about what they should do. I said centralize the hell out of Rutgers. None of my colleagues at Livingston ever forgave me for supporting centralization, but over time the Rutgers administration did centralize many functions of the various colleges, including the academic departments.

Centralization was a slow process, though. Livingston College remained Rutgers' corrupt secret, tucked safely away across the Raritan River. Its faculty was caught up in the college's image as a great experiment to solve urban problems. Its students were overwhelmed by the illegal drug traffic. Its radical faculty were being used unwittingly to locate key supporters of the Allende government in Chile and finger them for torture and death, as Ralph Lopez was trying to warn me.

Shortly after I began teaching, there was a protest by Black students against Luis Nieves, a Puerto Rican dean who controlled student activities funds. The Livingston Faculty Senate met to enthusiastically support the student protest. I stood up in the meeting and said the protest was provoked by Dean Nieves' refusal to put student activities funds directly into the personal bank account of the leader of the student protest. I was shouted down and accused of slandering the student movement.

Finally, a faculty member called on Bryan Blake to refute my slander. All seven feet of Bryan Blake stood up and said, "She's right." Then all seven feet of Bryan Blake sat down. The leader of the student "protest" got an administrative job at Rutgers, just one example of how corruption was rewarded and used to suppress real student protest.

That was just one of the problems I encountered at Rutgers. I continued to face discrimination as a woman scholar. That first year, one of my colleagues told me that a student asked him why the history department had no women faculty members. After he started to explain, he remembered that I was a woman. He said, "I don't think of you as a woman." I think he meant that as a compliment.

The following year, the Livingston College history department hired more women, one at the last minute without a formal search. I later discovered that the federal government had threatened to cut off Rutgers' funding if it didn't hire more women. One of my prominent colleagues, who evidently didn't know I was Jewish, told me, "First, we had to let in the Jews. Now we must let in the minorities. But I have no problems about hiring women." Indeed, my colleagues in the history department stopped talking about hiring minorities, and "affirmative action" became about hiring white women. To them, that was a lot better than hiring minorities because it could double the family income when they hired each others' wives—the thing to do at the time was to hire couples. Single women or women married to men outside academia were at a disadvantage. Women were pressured to teach and write women's history, even if they specialized in other fields. Women and minorities could teach and write only "their own" history, leaving the "real" history to the white men. When I insisted that women and minorities had the right to study and teach any kind of history they wanted—and were qualified—to teach, my words were indignantly rejected.

My colleague who was so worried about the Jews and minorities suggested that I go into administration. That was how they dealt with women historians who had somehow managed to squeeze past the gender barriers. I told him I had no interest in or talent for administration and would probably lose all the papers.

I did some good teaching at Rutgers. I had been hired as a Latin Americanist and was one of the few who considered the Caribbean as part of Latin America and worth studying or teaching at all. This was at a time when the Latino population of the northeast corridor of the United States had grown rapidly. The Caribbean poured out its eager, ambitious, and usually impoverished daughters and sons, searching for new opportunities. Unlike previous waves of immigration to the United States, their homeland was nearby and transportation was relatively affordable. Puerto Ricans came in the greatest numbers at first because they were US citizens, and flights between San Juan and New York were direct, short, and cheap. Cuban immigrants, many of them subsidized under the anti-Castro policies of the US government, settled in New Jersey. They turned Elizabeth and West New York into Cuban towns. I have always gravitated toward Cubans. My best friend was the great Cuban historian Fe Iglesias.

A fascinating variety of students from the Caribbean began to flow into Rutgers: Haitians, Dominicans, Jamaicans, Trinidadians, and students from Suriname, Guyana, Barbados, Grenada, Nevis, St. Kitts, and other small islands. Their homelands had only recently won independence, and their history had long been treated as a minor part of the colonial history of their European colonizers. They lived largely in isolation from one another because of language and transportation barriers. Airline flights traveled mainly between Miami and San Juan rather than connecting one island with another.

I taught a course about the history of the Caribbean, and students from all over the region got to know each other in my classes. The course emphasized the similarities and differences of their histories and encouraged them to speak to each other in class about their experiences. I got along especially well with Cuban students, who were often caught between their anti-Castro parents, for whom Castro could do nothing right, and their left-wing professors, for whom Castro could do nothing wrong. In my classes, students could say whatever they pleased and ask questions they dared not ask elsewhere.

Over the years, my scholarship played a major role in founding Caribbean history and studies as an important interdisciplinary field in the United States. At Rutgers, I was able to help to launch and later administer the Puerto Rican and Hispanic Caribbean Studies Department. It was during this brief stint as an administrator that I got an inside look at Rutgers's real attitude toward hiring Latinxs and other minorities. The administration didn't want this department but couldn't dissolve it for political reasons. So they held it at a distance and avoided hiring faculty members who were eligible for promotion and tenure. By 1988, when I left my job as acting chair, no faculty member had been awarded tenure since the department's founding. Its faculty had much heavier teaching and advising loads than did other faculty, and they didn't get leaves for research and writing. The department was essentially a revolving door for Latinx faculty members that made Rutgers's dismal record in minority hiring look a little better than it really was.

Rutgers managed to derail the academic career of one of the finest scholars in the field: Andrés Pérez y Mena, who studied with Margaret Mead and wrote what was considered to be one of the five best dissertations ever produced at Columbia Teachers' College. Nobody told him how to get his dissertation published—a prestigious press contacted him. At first, the Rutgers administration refused to renew Andrés' contract, but he successfully appealed that decision. He came up for promotion and tenure when I was acting chair. I solicited evaluations of his work from leading scholars in his field and got very enthusiastic letters back. I recommended promotion with tenure, yet it was denied: Andres was blacklisted by Rutgers. I had to explain the situation to one of his potential future employers, who had received a telephone call from a Rutgers dean explaining that Andrés was a "troublemaker." He has not been able to get a permanent academic job since.

I was discriminated against at Rutgers for defending Andrés. The dean came to a meeting of the full professors of the history department and told them not to promote me or put me up for promotion again. By 2005, a decade after I had retired, Rutgers' Latinx faculty had left for greener pastures, en masse and with much publicity, after protesting their treatment in hiring and promotion. It finally began to sink in to the Rutgers administration that Latinx students and faculty were important.

PART FIVE

MAKING A BETTER WORLD
WITH CREATIVE HISTORY

"The philosophers have only interpreted the world, in various ways; the point is to change it."
—Karl Marx, *Theses on Feuerbach*

M y later life as a creative historian wouldn't have seemed very likely, given my first experiences with college and academia. In August 1947, I graduated from Newman High School by passing a French exam after being tutored for a few days. For the fall semester, I enrolled at Newcomb College, the female division of Tulane University, considered among the finest higher education institutions in the South. "Now," I said to myself, "you're in the big time. You're a college student, and you have to work hard and study for the first time in your life."

Wrong! I went to all my classes for about a week and found them boring. I felt like I learned more by hanging out on the New Orleans waterfront. I never went to class, and I didn't take the midterm exams. I told my parents there was no way I could pass any of my courses. But I read both the Spanish grammar and the logic textbooks the night before the final exams and got perfect scores. I got an A on my final research paper for a course in twentieth-century European history and ended up on the dean's list.

What did I conclude? Not that I was intelligent or good in logic or foreign languages, but that the college was a joke. I figured maybe the problem was that Newcomb was a girl's college, and they taught the real courses at Tulane. I signed up for an introductory economics course at Tulane. As I remember, I was the only girl in the class. Trying to be good, I even went to class for a few weeks and listened while the professor introduced each point with the phrase "under normal conditions." I finally raised my hand and asked the professor to define "normal conditions." He replied, "Not wartime, not prewar, not postwar, not depression, not pre-depression, and not post-depression."

I asked him to give me an example of a time during the past fifty years when "normal conditions" existed. He replied very slowly, "Well, Miss Midlo, perhaps you are asking a more profound question than *you realize*." He paused thoughtfully and said, "The consensus is the year 1924."

So it wasn't just Newcomb, it was the whole place. After two years at Newcomb I decided the only solution was to get this over with as soon as possible. During the two years I was at Newcomb, I took the required courses for two majors, American History and European History, and earned senior status. The southern history courses were taught at Tulane. I couldn't stand the racism of the historian Ulrich Phillips, whose work was treated as gospel, not just in the South but all over the United States. The consensus theory of history—that there had never been any serious social conflict in the United States—was also gospel. This seemed totally absurd to me. I knew better from my experiences growing up in New Orleans and from listening to Leadbelly and Woodie Guthrie songs.

I went to New York City with Michel Yuspeh with the intention of finishing my BA in history at New York University. But we then went to Paris, where it was impossible to get my degree. And when we returned to the United States, I went to work in New York City. I didn't attend college again until 1961 when Harry and I were living in Mexico.

Studying with Some of the Greatest Scholars in the World

The first two courses I took at UNAM (Universidad Nacional Autónoma de México) were both great joys. One was a Spanish language class, and the other was Mexican history with the distinguished, elderly scholar Pablo Martínez del Río. This was the first time I systematically studied a foreign language. Mexican Spanish is especially beautiful, reflecting the musical, aesthetic soul of the country. My professor held up my "eloquent way" of expressing myself in Spanish as an example to the class.

The history of Mexico course was just as thrilling. Mexican history is a breathtaking morality play, a story of challenge and response, full of amazing people triumphing over incredible odds. My favorite figure from Mexican history is Benito Juárez, a leader of the liberal revolution that fought for equality, the rule of law, separation of church and state, and land for the landless, and against the privileges of the church and the military. A full-blooded Zapotec from Oaxaca, he didn't speak Spanish until he was an adolescent. During one period of political exile, he worked as a cigar roller in New Orleans. Juárez was president of the republic of Mexico when Napoleon III of France sent the French Army to invade and installed Maximillian, a remnant of the Hapsburg dynasty, as emperor on Mexico's "throne." Juarez triumphed against the French, restoring the republic and defending the sovereignty of Mexico.

The spring semester of 1962, Harry and I left Cuautla for Mexico City. I enrolled at Mexico City College. I didn't know I had walked into a hornet's nest. Mexico City at that time "was considered by many to be the 'spy capital of the Cold War,'" wrote human geographer Richard Wilkie, "because it was where international espionage could flourish, with agents and informers being able to move through the city to be redirected in all of the cardinal directions—north into the US, east to Cuba and flights on to Eastern Europe, south into the rest of Latin America, and even west toward Asia." Unbeknownst to us, CIA and FBI agents had a big presence at UNAM and MCC, where they could check up on radical students and US exiles. My FBI files from Mexico indicate that the more sensational the information supplied by informants, the more likely the FBI would keep them on their payroll and probably increase their pay. The FBI had a very active and imaginative office operating openly in Mexico City, even though overseas intelligence gathering is supposed to be the province of the CIA. Now it turns out that several Mexican presidents have acknowledged they were on the CIA payroll.[1]

With my high scores on the Graduate Record Examinations (GRE), which I had taken during my last semester as an undergraduate, I was able to enroll in the MA program in Latin American history at MCC, under the careful and attentive guidance of Richard Greenleaf, an outstanding scholar, teacher, and administrator. I had one important adversary among the faculty at MCC: Dr. Lorna Lavery Stafford, the wife of the US consul in Mexico City. She was a professor of Spanish literature and director of the graduate program. Because of her US diplomatic and intelligence connections, she was the real boss at MCC. I had to take a one-credit course with her about the correct form for documenting footnotes: how many spaces, where to put the punctuation. She gave me a B.

After more than a year of coursework and writing and submitting my masters thesis, I faced the great challenge of graduate school: the oral exam. Stafford seized this opportunity to stop me from getting my degree. She sat in the back of the room during my exam and put great pressure on Richard Greenleaf to go along with what she wanted. His voice dripping with sarcasm, Greenleaf opened the exam with this question: "To what extent do you believe that your MA thesis was motivated by detached, scholarly considerations rather than by elements in your *personal life* and therefore marred by emotion?" I said that all good creative work, including history, should be motivated by emotion combined with respect for truth. Otherwise, history becomes a pedantic exercise that no one reads, and it therefore has no impact. Rémy Bastien, a Haitian anthropologist and refugee from the Papa Doc Duvalier regime, covered his mouth to hide his grin, but his eyes sparkled.

After a few similar exchanges, I was asked to wait outside while they decided my fate. I heard Concepción Muedra, my friend and ally, screaming at the top of her lungs. They finally called me back in, all looking exhausted. I had passed my oral exam. But Stafford didn't give up. She managed to get my degree reduced from magna cum laude to cum laude based on what she claimed was the not very impressive quality of my thesis—because I wrote it too fast.

I knew the pressure Richard Greenleaf was under from Stafford, and I never forgot what he did for me in spite of that. He recognized my talent for history before I was aware of it myself. I'm sure he was decisive in getting me admitted to Stanford's PhD program in 1962 and to the University of Michigan's PhD program in Latin American history in 1966. He was proud of many former students, but he was especially proud of me.

I have enjoyed the most support in the academic world not from the young, the ideological, and politically correct but from mature, sometimes conservative historians who judged me for the value and potential of my work. They were almost all white men because women were few and far between in academia then, and nonwhite professors were nonexistent outside historically Black colleges and universities. Richard Greenleaf was the first to support me but not the last.

When I resumed my studies at the University of Michigan, Charles Gibson, the greatest colonial Latin America historian of his generation, advised on my doctoral thesis. What luck! He was the best: a real scholar who avoided the temptations of big grants and programs. He taught me how to become a professional academic historian. His specialty was colonial Mexico, and he researched and wrote brilliant books about the forms of exploitation to which Native Americans were subjected by the Spanish Empire. Gibson exposed me to the excitement of studying large numbers of original documents. Because I knew both French and Spanish and always wanted to learn and write about African slavery in the Americas, my research interests focused on the Caribbean.

Gibson was scrupulously honest, open-minded, and flexible, and he was not overly concerned with mountains of bibliography and historiography. All he cared about was the quality of the creative work of his students. He expressed doubt that I could write a comparative history as a dissertation, telling me that it would be more difficult than writing two dissertations. But he gave me all the rope I needed.

Eric Wolf, the world-famous anthropologist, directed my field in African American anthropology and served on my dissertation committee. He led teach-ins against the war in Vietnam. When I told him that if I had known what was involved in going to graduate school, I would not have come, he replied, "I'm glad you didn't know."

My Major Writings

My experiences as a writer and author began around this same time. John Henrik Clarke was the first scholar and editor who took an interest in my writing and helped me get my articles published in some of the most influential African American publications. These essays often touched on my life experiences, the history I was learning, and its importance as an inspiration to effective collective resistance against the repression, exploitation, and denial of Africans and people of African descent throughout the world. My most important messages emphasized

African slavery throughout the Americas, including denying that slavery was mild throughout Latin America; the resistance of enslaved peoples across both continents; and structural racism, including addiction to illegal drugs and mass incarceration as profit systems.

During these crucial years from 1964 to 1972, I became a well-known, influential essayist, reaching a broad audience of mainly Black scholars, artists, intellectuals, and activists. The article "Junkie Myths" was published in the *Inner City Voice*, a publication of the protest movement of Black autoworkers in Detroit during the late 1960s and early 1970s. As soon as my article exposing heroin traffic and the need for medical treatment instead of incarceration for its victims appeared in *Negro Digest* in 1969, there was a large demonstration in the streets of Detroit supporting the call for methadone treatment for heroin addicts. I watched it on TV from Ann Arbor.

The last essay I published in *Black World*, in 1972, was about Toussaint l'Ouverture, the main leader of the Haitian Revolution. It emphasized his undaunted faith in the people and how careful he was not to reveal himself until he had a solid, well-organized, winning movement supporting him. Toussaint's style, his quiet, careful wisdom, didn't stand a chance at a time when the media was often choosing the "leaders" of the Black liberation movement, overlooking the quiet hard-working local people, especially the women, who got no recognition much less credit for all the good, essential work they did.

While I was writing these essays, I was in the PhD program at the University of Michigan, where my dissertation was about comparative slavery in St. Domingue (Haiti) and Cuba. I loved doing the research, and the writing went very fast. One prestigious member of my dissertation committee phoned Gibson and told him it was the most exciting thing he'd ever read. Johns Hopkins University Press published it without changing one word.

Social Control in Slave Plantation Societies: A Comparison of St. Domingue and Cuba, published in 1971, as many of the last Caribbean countries were becoming independent, was greeted as one of the earliest works to treat Caribbean history "from the inside out." It had a broad, long-lasting impact on scholarship and still does, fifty years after it was first published. The book focused on the people rather than on the history of empire, and it contradicted much of the work of Latin American and

US scholars who claimed that Latin American slavery was mild and that both the state and the Catholic Church had protected the enslaved. I pointed out how these formal protections eroded over time, and I exposed the gap between law and practice, explaining how and why slavery became more deadly as each colony became more prosperous. That prosperity was based on the life-destroying process of sugar production, the main crop in Latin America, with an extremely high mortality rate among sugar-producing slaves. I stressed slave resistance when scholars were denying that enslaved people would or could resist slavery at all. The book discussed the various forms of racism that exist throughout the Americas—something that is still a radical innovation in thinking about Latin America, where racist repression and exploitation are denied on the grounds that race doesn't exist.

In 1992, I published *Africans in Colonial Louisiana: The Development of Afro-Creole Culture in the Eighteenth Century*. It is based on extensive archival research into previously unknown or unused documents found in France, Spain, and the United States. I collected Afro-Creole folklore, poems, and songs, learned some Louisiana Creole, and studied sociolinguistics. My greatest thrill was studying rare documents in the French Colonial Archives, then located in Paris.

I drew some important conclusions in this book. First, I found detailed, concrete descriptions of what went on aboard slave ships headed for Louisiana: where the individuals came from, how many died during the voyage, and how many landed alive. Some descriptions gave information about gender balance and age category. And there were wonderful stories about slave revolts, which were frequent. One rebellion among women so frightened the ship captain that he jumped overboard.

Another important conclusion was about the African ethnicities that had the most influence on the early culture of Louisiana and their impact through words, stories, song, and dance. I found the African ethnicities of enslaved people identified in the documents I studied in Louisiana. Based on this, I concluded that the Bambara/Bamana people were an important representative, resilient culture in Louisiana. They had been shipped down the Senegal River to St. Louis de Senegal before being transported on the Middle Passage. The Bambara were among the few descendants of the old Mali Empire who rejected Islam and maintained their animistic religion. They had a strong military tradition, with a reputation as fierce and effective fighters. Some of their key words survived in the Louisiana Creole language. They were disproportionately represented among runaways and led the first slave revolt in Louisiana.

This book, too, disrupted existing scholarship. I learned quickly that history does not simply exist; it is constantly created and recreated. It is both literature and science, and I made advances in each area. But since I wasn't doing what my colleagues were doing, they thought I wasn't doing anything.

I didn't expect many people to read *Africans in Colonial Louisiana* because it's long and difficult. But boy, did they! When it first came out, in 1992, I got on a St. Charles Avenue streetcar in New Orleans, and everybody was reading their own copy. During 1993, it received nine book prizes. In awarding me the John Hope Franklin prize, the American Studies Association wrote:

> In making its selection of *Africans in Colonial Louisiana*, the committee cited the book's wide range of original research and its certain impact on many fields of American culture. Providing a solid ground for theory in extensive and difficult archival documentation, the book combines work in African American history, diaspora and Caribbean culture, anthropology, linguistics, and colonial American history. It opens to view a new transnational conception of the American culture that grew from slavery and from slave resistance, and describes a process of creolization whose full effects have perhaps only become apparent, at least to scholars, in the present day. More than any of the more than one hundred books submitted to the committee by publishers throughout the country, *Africans in Colonial Louisiana* promises to shape the course of future research in American studies for many years to come.

Although it was published many years ago, *Africans in Colonial Louisiana* is still being widely read and rediscovered by new generations. It has had a special impact in Louisiana, where Afro-Creole as a language and culture is now widely recognized and appreciated. Throughout the United States, the understanding of our regional cultures is going beyond emphasizing the diversity of various ethnicities to embrace the concept of creolization, which explains the way diverse peoples interacted with and influenced each other, creating resilient, flexible, and constantly evolving cultures. My book encouraged regional and local research, which is all-important to revealing the courageous, indomitable struggles of the exploited and oppressed, and to providing important examples of fellow feeling among our diverse peoples.

I never believed the thinking that Africans lost all their ethnic cultural heritage during the transatlantic crossing or shortly thereafter; this was a hotly debated topic for years. I wanted to know who they were, where they were clustered, and why. I dealt with these questions in *Africans in Colonial Louisiana*, but that dealt with only one region. I searched for more universal patterns and then wrote *Slavery and African Ethnicities in the Americas: Restoring the Links*, published in 2005. It is probably the first truly Afro-Atlantic book, because it studies what was going on in the various African regions as well as in the Americas during all the major times and places of the transatlantic slave trade. It is based to a great extent on databases about slaves throughout the Americas at various times and places as well as more traditional methodologies, using scholarship about African regions involved in the Atlantic slave trade and the Western Hemisphere over a time frame of four hundred years.

When I was teaching at Rutgers, historians focused narrowly on more or less important times and places—more and more about less and less. They worked alone. I adopted digital humanities technology. Many of us now seek to work more and more collaboratively, globally across disciplines, asking more and more questions important to the wider world by collecting and studying massive amounts of data, using information technology.

I have always been an interdisciplinary scholar as well as an internationalist. Some of my major ideas I learned from Mexican and Brazilian colleagues, such as the Mexican philosopher and minister of education José Vasconcelos, whose book *La raza cosmica* was first published in 1925. Caribbean scholars have refined these ideas with the concept of creolization as a basis for culture formation. I brought the concept of creolization to my studies of the formation of colonial Louisiana culture.

Scholars from the United States and Brazil have learned from each other for more than a century. To take one example, the anthropologist Gilberto Freyre was inspired by and learned from Franz Boaz, a German Jew who taught at Columbia University in New York during the 1920s. Boaz was the founder of cultural anthropology and a powerful voice for racial equality at a time when what is now called scientific racism prevailed everywhere. Before he studied with Boaz, Freyre believed that all the problems of Latin America stemmed from its darker and mixed-blood populations, and the only solution was to bring in large numbers of white immigrants and encourage the dark-skinned population to die out or be absorbed by racially superior whites. Under Boaz's influence, Freyre abandoned this orthodoxy of Latin American thought and embraced and popularized the concept that Brazil's greatest strength was the biological and cultural mixture of its population.

Earlier in my life, I was torn between studying music and history. I failed to master music, but the structure of music, especially Baroque music, became patterned in my brain. It is not linear. It is not univocal. It is complex, ever-changing, with interacting patterns over time and variations on themes. When I finally became a historian, that was how I wrote. I transcended linear national history and embraced comparative global history.

Every people and nation have largely created their own history. Long before written language, history was told as stories, sung and danced, and passed down by wise men, women, and oracles. History gives coherence to communities, allowing people to identity as part of a whole, making them willing to sacrifice for the common good. But the world has shrunk, and narrow ethnic and national history has become a cursed mythology, feeding destructive nationalisms like Nazism in the '30s and '40s and Trumpism in the United States today. The history I grew up with excluded a vast number of our peoples—Native Americans, Latinxs, and especially Africans and their descendants—from what was defined as the American people and its culture. But that's not who we are. That's not what the world is. This is the main message of my work. My research revealed the indomitable spirit and intelligence of the enslaved, and my scholarship has tried to redefine what American culture is, helping us identify as one people. The process of creolization blends the greatest strengths of all our peoples and cultures, including Native American, African, European, Asian, Mexican, and Caribbean people. I know that white racism, now calling itself white nationalism, is on the rise throughout the world, but it has a much weaker foundation throughout the Americas, and I believe it will die here sooner than most others believe.

Digital Technology and the Slavery Database

One reason I could write in the 1980s even while dealing with the difficulties of caring for Leo and Harry when both were desperately ill was that, in 1984, I discovered computers. The history department at Rutgers University bought an IBM Displaywriter, a rather primitive word processor that was not very good for word processing and useless for any other purpose. Within a week, I had all my research well organized on it under topics, but I couldn't always get access to it, so I invested about four thousand dollars to buy my own, which I kept in my office.

Working on an early PC

I was among the first wave of scholars to use personal computers. Nobody taught me how. I learned fast, through trial and error. I finally got a portable computer small enough to carry into archives, typed my notes, and organized them on my computer. I still have many of these notes after transferring them to newer software versions: from WordPerfect to Microsoft Word and from PC to Apple.

Beginning in 1984 I also began to produce the first original digital database in historical studies. I started my database after I discovered documents in the Pointe Coupée Parish Courthouse containing rich information about enslaved people in Louisiana and, most surprising, their largely self-identified African ethnicities. At that time most historians and other researchers put research notes on index cards. But I found so much detail in these descriptions that I needed a more complex tool for collecting and understanding it.

The Louisiana documents contain a greater variety of African ethnicity designations than any other documents in the Americas. There are extensive data about names, genders, ages, racial designations, family relationships, prices, skills, illnesses, character as perceived by their masters, and testimony by enslaved people about running away and their involvement in conspiracies and revolts. I included all information about each enslaved person, including what type of document we found them in and the identification and location of the original document.

My research assistants and I entered all the documents we studied during research in archives and courthouses throughout Louisiana. Working in archives in France and Spain, I studied and entered all the information I could find about slave trade voyages coming from Africa and arriving in the Gulf South. The *Slave Database* contains more than 104,000 descriptions of slaves. More than 4,000 records are about enslaved people who were freed or in the process of being freed, including how and why they were freed, by whom, how the enslaved person was related to the freer, the price paid when there was a self-purchase or a purchase by another person to free them, the terms and conditions of freedom, and the name, racial designation, and origin of the mother of the freed.

Here is an entry from the *Louisiana Slave Database*:

Antoine [Note: This is surely the leader of the 1811 revolt in St. John the Baptist Parish. The document establishes that he was a Creole of Louisiana and not from St. Domingue and that he was listed as a slave during the 1811 revolt. In history books, he is almost always described as a free mulatto from St. Domingue/Haiti.]

Gender: male
Race: mulatto
Birthplace: Louisiana Creole
Age [when this record was documented]: 15.0

Selling Information
Last Name of Deceased: Rixner

Estate Number: 06-S-084-081-1788
Grouping: sold or inventoried as an individual
Currency of Inventory: piastre = 1p
Inventory Value: 800

Document Information [about the document from which these records were retrieved]
Document Location: St. Charles (old German Coast)
Document Date: 1788-10-11
Document Number [from the document]: 873
Notary Name: Masicot
Coder [person who encoded this record]: Philip McLeod

Type of document:
Any documents involving maroons, including reports of runaways, interrogation of captured runaways, and testimony by slaves about runaways: No
Language: French
Is this document of linguistic interest?: No
Is this inventory or sale of an estate of a free person of African descent?: No

Skill and Trade Information
Skills and Occupations: domestic "domestique"
Skill: domestic, house, domestique, servant, butler, housekeeper, serviente, domestico

Personality

Family Information
Was this slave inventoried with his/her mother?: No
Was this slave sold with his/her mother?: No

Importation Information
Was this slave being emancipated?: No
Slave listed as dead?: No

One advantage of databases is that they can be queried quickly and easily with statistics software, generating calculations and graphs. No prior historians had thought to ask many of these questions because it was assumed they could not be answered. The results of calculations made from databases often refute speculative conclusions and the collective "wisdom" passed on by generations of historians who base their work on less reliable, more subjective sources, including the views and opinions of travelers and officials who lived at the time. Best of all, these databases give rich information about the lives of slaves who nobody thought we could know anything about.

Although I created these databases mainly for my own research and writing, I figured they would be used by other scholars and knew they could be helpful to genealogists in tracing their ancestry. Thanks to a National Endowment for the Humanities Collaborative Research Contract awarded to me and Patrick Manning, professor of world history at the University of Pittsburgh, I spent most of the 1990s completing the databases for all of Louisiana through 1820 and preparing them for digital publication on a CD with the help of a few research assistants I trained. Paul LaChance, professor of history at the University of Ottawa, gave me generous, highly skilled help as usual. He, Ginger Gould, and Jeffrey Gould contributed their databases to the CD.

Left to right: Patrick Manning, me, and Paul LaChance, consulting together about our database projects on my patio in New Orleans, around 1995.

In the mid-1990s, a few years after I had moved back to New Orleans, I got a phone call from John Cummings, a prominent class-action attorney. He said he was looking for Gwendolyn Midlo Hall. I said, "You found me." He said he had been looking for me ever since he read *Africans in Colonial Louisiana.* He had bought a plantation along the west bank of the Mississippi River in St. John the Baptist Parish and wanted my advice about turning it into a museum about slavery. I visited his property during the early stages of its development. It took well over a decade to complete the Whitney Plantation Museum. Cummings followed the best of the advice I gave him in his hiring of Ibrahima Seck, who has been the museum's full-time research director for years. They relied on my database to create a large marble memorial to all the enslaved people documented. It is located in Allées Gwendolyn Midlo Hall, and a plaque with my photo and biography sits nearby. Many thousands of people from all over the world have visited this museum, the only one specifically devoted to slavery.[2]

~

A few weeks after my seventy-first birthday, in 2000, David Firestone, then one of the two southern regional reporters for the *New York Times*, came to my home at 1300 Dante Street in New Orleans to interview me for an article about the *Louisiana Slave Database*. Firestone had experience working with databases and realized their value and potential. He, too, had started using databases on personal computers during the mid-1980s and was teaching other *New York Times* reporters how to create them. He was surprised at how little attention had been paid to mine and asked me if I was disappointed. I said no because, although it may sound immodest, I am usually at least twenty years ahead of my time. "Perhaps if I live to be ninety, I will see my work appreciated," I said.

As Firestone walked out the door, he said, "We'll see about that."

His extensively illustrated article ran on the front page of the *New York Times* on Sunday, July 30, 2000, and continued inside for almost two pages.[3] After that, an Associated Press story, accompanied by a photo of me and my dog on my tropical patio in New Orleans, appeared in newspapers all over the country. *People* magazine published a story about me, my family, and the databases. ABC World News, CNN, and Lifetime Live broadcast segments and interviews. NPR and BBC World News did several radio features.

Later that year, the *American Bar Association Journal* published a cover article featuring Percy Pierre, a famous African American electrical engineer. He had uncovered the ethnicity of his African ancestor through my database before it was published, and he was quoted as saying he wanted reparations for slavery. There was a large story inside about the implications for reparations the database represented. It concluded that my database is a major refutation to legal arguments against reparations because now we can identify the specific victims and perpetrators of the enslavement of Africans and their descendants and assess concrete damages based on the prices paid for them.

I had suddenly become famous because my database revealed substantial details about just about every enslaved person who lived in Louisiana between 1719 and 1820. But the most frequent question asked of me was "Are you really seventy-one years old? Wasn't your age a misprint?" Few people could believe a seventy-one-year-old woman had created a cutting-edge tool in digital humanities. But I had just gotten started. The University of North Carolina digital humanities website ibiblio asked permission to mount my database on its platform. I agreed, if they would create a search engine for it. Thanks to the Center for the Public Domain's generosity in funding the project, ibiblio created an extraordinary platform for the *Louisiana Slave Database*, mounted in 2001.[4]

I made several proposals to find ways to work collaboratively among the many scholars who were by then creating additional slave databases, and to link at least some of them together online. Around 1995, I organized a database conference about this in New Orleans, before the internet was in general use. It was attended by twenty-five scholars from the United States and Canada. Between 2005 and 2010, I wrote several proposals to further develop this project, but they were rejected mainly because I didn't have an affiliation with a university capable of carrying out the project. But in February 2010, I was invited by historian Walter Hawthorne to speak at Michigan State University. While I was there, I met with Hawthorne and Dean Rehberger, the director of MATRIX, Michigan State's center for digital humanities. I detailed my plans and proposals to create a universal slave database. I returned to East Lansing in June and moved into an apartment I shared with my dear friend Mabel Williams. At age eighty-one, I wrote a grant proposal—with help from Hawthorne, Rehberger, and Christine Root—to store and link the many databases about individual enslaved people that had sprouted up after mine. It was enthusiastically approved by the National Endowment for the Humanities, but its funding for that year was slashed to a pitiful amount.

Nevertheless, we did do some important, innovative work.[5] We worked collaboratively to establish universal best practices for slave databases. Paul LaChance, University of Michigan digital archivist Catherine Foley, and I reached out by Skype to fellow scholars throughout the world and held weekly meetings among ourselves for an entire year. We organized an influential conference at MSU in 2013 that brought together the creators of some impressive slave database projects, opening up future collaborations. For our final report to the National Endowment for the Humanities, Catherine Foley wrote an impressive summary of our work toward creating a best practices slave database with controlled vocabulary. But when I left MSU to return to Mexico in late 2014, the project remained stalled at an elementary stage of programing because of lack of funding.

Then the Andrew W. Mellon Foundation offered to help MATRIX and some partner projects apply for substantial funding to resume our collaborative project. In January 2018, Mellon came up with almost one and a half million dollars for an eighteen-month initial period for MSU and its partners to prove they could create a hub that linked records of individual enslaved people on different platforms—with the prospect of more funding after this proof-of-concept period. Mellon encouraged us to work with familysearch.org, and we now have a team to complete the *Louisiana Slave Database* throughout the entire time of slavery. It is led by Kathe Hambrick, founder of the River Road African-American Museum in Donaldsonville. In March 2019, MATRIX held another extensive international database conference.[6]

I am now optimistic that this ambitious project will succeed. As we continue to develop a controlled vocabulary and best practices slave database to link similar projects throughout the world, millions of enslaved Africans and their descendants, whose very existence has been denied and ignored, will be acknowledged and remembered in cyberspace.[7]

Getting a Chance to Travel at Last

After the publication of *Social Control in Slave Plantation Societies* in 1971, I had been invited to attend a conference at Johns Hopkins University in Baltimore to defend its mention of African ethnicities. But attending conferences wasn't doable. I had three children, one of them suffering from serious mental illness, and no support. It wasn't until 1980, when my youngest child went off to college and I was invited to join the Association of Caribbean Historians and attend its annual meetings in different Caribbean countries, that I got to travel and network with other scholars.

Visiting my Cuban colleague Olga Potuando Zuniga in her home in Santiago, Cuba, 2003

Before that, I had made one trip to the Caribbean, in 1977. I was invited by Michel Laguerre, professor of Africana studies at UC Berkeley, to join him on his research trip to Haiti. Baby Doc Duvalier still reigned. That was my first visit to a foreign country where an openly repressive regime ruled. When Baby Doc appeared on TV, there were two soldier-thugs on each side of him with pistols drawn. One day when Baby Doc was traveling, everything shut down: no vehicle moved, and no one was allowed to walk down the street.

There was nothing in the archives but some old, brittle newspapers that were being destroyed by the dust and wind blowing through the open windows. I stayed with a family in their guest house in Delmar, right outside of Port-au-Prince. The little boys who served the meals leaned up against the walls, acting like they did not exist. When I went into the city, I rode on public transportation, which consisted of colorfully decorated extended pickup trucks, their passengers piled up on top of each other. Michel Laguerre and I planned to visit the Haitian countryside. He rented an all-terrain vehicle. But an official document was required to leave Port-au-Prince, and he was denied one. There were armed checkpoints at each miserable, dirt-road highway leaving the capital. That was as far as we could go.

What impressed me most about Haitians is that they keep trying. Nothing stops them. They rebuild their miserable metal huts with anything they can find, search for clean water, and grow food. Above all, though, they try to leave the country. Everyone I met in Haiti asked me to help them get to the United States. Of course, there was nothing I could do.

During most of the time I was teaching at Rutgers in the 1970s, I lived in Brooklyn, which I appreciated more and more for its rapidly growing cosmopolitan working class. Not just Haitians but people from all over the Caribbean were pouring in. The ambitious Haitians did well in Brooklyn. We lived on Eastern Parkway across from the Brooklyn Museum, with the main branch of the Brooklyn Public Library down the block. The office of the resistance movement against Baby Doc was at 333 Lincoln Place, right behind my apartment building. It was run by two priests, Antoine Adrien and Jean-Marie Vincent, who was assassinated in 1994. I volunteered to do some translations from French for Father Adrien. He is credited by Jean-Bertrand Aristide for laying the groundwork for the liberation theology activism that led to Aristide's watershed election as the first democratically elected president of Haiti. After Baby Doc was finally overthrown, Father Adrien became an important figure in the Aristide government. Aristide was later kidnapped and kept in exile in the Central African Republic, later in South Africa, and then in Jamaica after he was crudely overthrown by the US government, defending the "free world."

More and more Haitian students had begun to enter Rutgers. The year 1991 was the two-hundredth anniversary of the outbreak of the Haitian Revolution. But no one paid attention to this landmark historic event. I gave a course about the history of Haiti to honor the revolution. Lots of Haitian students, most of them supporters of President Aristide, signed up.

~

For the 1986–87 academic year, I received a Fulbright research fellow-ship at the University of Paris VIII. This was still a time of great personal difficulties. I spent a total of about four months back home dealing with problems related to Leo's illness, and the fellowship paid only for a sin-gle round-trip airline ticket to France. My salary was reduced for being on leave. Unless I was staying with my old friend Janine Netter in St. Mande, I lived in a walkup room in a damp Latin Quarter hotel, with a bathroom down the hall.

Nevertheless, my time in France, Africa, and Spain that year turned my life around. All of my problems were compensated for by my won-derful experience working at the National Archives of France, where I did much of the research for *Africans in Colonial Louisiana*, and my travels to Africa in the spring.

I presented a paper at an international conference at the Sorbonne and lectured in French at a meeting of the Institut des Études Hispan-iques et Hispano-américaines. A US Cultural Exchange officer heard my lecture and suggested a speaking tour of Francophone Africa, be-ginning with Morocco. It was arranged for April 1987, sponsored joint-ly by the Fulbright Commission of Morocco and the African Regional Services office of the US Information Agency in Paris. I wrote out my first lecture, for an upper-division history class, in French before I left. After I gave it, the students asked many intelligent, deep questions in Arabic, which the professor translated into French for me. I responded in French, and the students understood. With growing confidence in my French speaking ability, I started lecturing without notes.

I was scheduled to fly from Casablanca to Dakar and then catch a connecting flight to Ouagadougou, the capital of Burkina Faso, named Upper Volta in colonial times. The African Regional Services office in Paris allowed plenty of time to catch the connecting flight because planes tended to be delayed. But the plane between Casablanca and Da-kar left two days late, long after the plane for Ouagadougou took off in Dakar. Ouagadougou finally informed us that they couldn't reschedule me until three weeks later. I decided to go to Dakar and wait for three weeks to go on to Ouagadougou, although I had no idea how to pay for it after American Express refused to cash my check.

I was amazed at how my interactions with the people in Senegal—their body language, the rhythm and intonation of their speech—made me feel at home. After living in France, in Mexico, and in many parts of the United States, I expected to encounter a culture at least as unfamiliar as those other places. But it didn't happen. There was a very familiar openness among people, which was truly energizing.

Robert LaGamma, director of the American Cultural Center in Dakar, invited me to attend a lecture by someone he described as an "old Africa hand," whom they had been cultivating for two years. I was supposed to learn from this lecture "how it was done." It was LaGamma who finally gave me the good news. "You have clearance," he told me. "You wouldn't have gotten your Fulbright without it." This was more than forty years after the FBI began spying on me in New Orleans. We drove to Saint-Louis, a city near the mouth of the Senegal River. We were told the lecture was about American literature and that it was to take place at 10 a.m. It was originally slated to be about US foreign policy since 1945 and scheduled for 3 p.m. The audience didn't want to hear about American literature—they wanted to know why the United States hadn't overthrown the South African government. And this nice young man was trying to lecture about *Sister Carrie*! Even his impeccable French didn't help. LaGamma tried to speak about US foreign policy, but it didn't go over well. As usual, the Africans were blamed for the disorder, but I soon learned that the confusion usually stemmed from the inability of our diplomatic staff to speak any language except English.

After the lecture, I stayed in Saint-Louis alone for a few days. When I stopped at a market I was followed around by children. Senegal is a predominantly Islamic country, and charity to beggars is valued in the religion. But these children weren't asking for money or food or candy. They said, "I go to school. I need a pencil. I need a pen—*un bic*." I later met a French educator who was the principal of a high school in Saint-Louis for many years. When I told her about the children who were begging for pens and pencils, she told me that when the school year begins, each pupil is given a pen and a pencil. But since only a few children from each family go to school, the siblings at home take the writing implements away from the schoolchildren.

The flight from Dakar to Ouagadougou finally departed on May 4. The chauffeur of the American Cultural Center met me and took me to an expensive hotel with a dirty swimming pool. It was hot, and the air conditioner hardly worked. The US cultural attaché told me my program was thin. They couldn't reschedule anything at the history department of the University of Ouagadougou. The government was constantly canceling their programs at the last minute, she told me, and I shouldn't be surprised if nothing came off at all. The Peace Corps had just been thrown out of the country. The attaché had been away on vacation for a month and came back to a pile of incident reports about Americans being beaten up by police and soldiers for wandering into security zones. I assured her I wouldn't be upset if all my programs were canceled, but I would regret wasting their money.

All this was the product of the US government's hostility to Burkina Faso's president, Thomas Isidore Noël Sankara, a Burkinabé revolutionary who became president in 1983 after a rebellion against the military government that was supported by France and the United States. Sankara nationalized the country's land and mineral wealth, and Burkina Faso became food self-sufficient in the span of four years. Sankara rejected the imperialist aid industry and encouraged local production and trade against the encroaching power of the World Bank and the International Monetary Fund. Alongside the economic revolution, he began a social-cultural transformation. Civil servants were forbidden from driving luxury vehicles and were required to wear cotton tunics indigenous to the country. The women of Burkina Faso partook in the revolution with action centering on their rights. Sankara outlawed female genital mutilation and polygamy, and women were encouraged to join the military and take government positions.

Sankara's revolution took place within the context of the Cold War, and his visits to the Soviet Union and Cuba, calls for the cancellation of African debts held by Western governments and institutions, and his modified Marxist ideology were controversial, especially in France and the United States, as well as to most of Burkina Faso's immediate neighbors. Sankara was murdered in a coup d'état in October 1987, only four months after my trip to Burkina Faso. The coup was organized by Blaise Compaoré, Sankara's former colleague, who became Burkina Faso's president until October 2014. Most Burkinabé citizens believe that France's foreign ministry, the Quai d'Orsay, was behind Compaoré in organizing the coup. Sankara and his policies are still held to be visionary by many in West Africa. His assassination was a heavy blow to African revolutionaries and reformers during the Cold War.

That was the cauldron I unknowingly flew into. My first event was

.a lecture to a class in linguistics at the University of Ouagadougou. It went well. Next, there was a luncheon at the home of Charles Twining, the deputy chief of the US mission, with a few Burkinabé trade unionists and leaders of the cultural community attending. Twining was a real pro and a human being—my image of what a diplomat was supposed to be. His French was good, too, very unusual among the American diplomatic community in French-speaking Africa.

My next lecture was to an American Studies class, in English this time. It was a large class. They asked me questions about the Black movement in the United States and the conditions of Black people there now, and I told them some things I don't think they had heard before. I told them about the armed self-defense movement against the Ku Klux Klan and the deplorable condition of many Black people in the United States. I pointed out that while legal racial segregation was gone, racial violence went unpunished less often, and a significant Black middle class had emerged, the material and social conditions of many Black people in the United States were, in many ways, worse than ever.

The big event was a cocktail party at the home of the political and economic attaché of the US Embassy. It turned out to be the most successful event they ever held. People from the Ministries of Culture and Education, Communications, and Foreign Relations; professors and administrators from the University of Ougadougou, including the vice rector; reporters from the official government newspaper; and a few Americans turned out. I talked mostly about the runaway slave communities in the cypress swamps near New Orleans. They were fascinated. The discussion was very lively. They asked about interracial families in the United States. I said that now you could see mixed couples and their children walking down the streets of New Orleans, which would have meant a sure and quick death when I was young. I told them that I had two biracial children, one a doctor and the other studying law. They murmured in approbation. No one wanted to leave. The cultural attaché rudely stopped the discussion.

Professors from the history and archeology departments asked to meet with me again before I left. We talked about their research projects in oral history and archeology and discussed some avenues of cooperation with American professors and universities. I told them that I believed the Fulbright program was clean, fair, and nonpolitical, and that decisions were made based on the value of the proposal. Burkina

Faso had no publishing house, and there are no historical documents. The professors gave me some of their work in mimeographs. I suggested computer desktop publishing to Robert LaGamma as a technology that African scholars could use to publish and distribute their work.

When *Sidwaya*, the official government newspaper, interviewed me, the reporter asked what school of sociology I belonged to. I said none, and that I believed in studying the concrete, the particularities of society. That's why I'm a historian, not a sociologist. He asked what I thought his country should do. I said, I don't know your country; you know it better than I do. There are no magic formulas. Things that work very well in one country might not work at all in another. That is why one must understand the language, the history, the culture, and the society as well as the resources and potential of each country before presuming to plan for them. Then one should try out projects on a small scale, and if they don't work, they should be abandoned, because resources shouldn't be wasted. He turned off the tape and told me about a project by a nongovernmental agency to save wood fuel by providing solar-powered cooking stoves in the countryside of Burkina Faso. The planners neglected to find out

Audience at my lecture at l'Ecole Superieure Normale in Dakar, Senegal in 1993

the size of the families. As a result, the stoves were designed to cook for six people, but the average family size was ten. And they ate their meals at night, after sunset. So the solar-powered stoves were never used.

One of the students, Josephine Kulibali, regarded me as her mother. She visited me at my hotel so I could help her understand a poem in English. It was Walt Whitman's "A Strange Vigil I Held on the Battlefield One Night." We read it together. She gave me pictures of her family, and when I left, she brought her baby to the airport to say goodbye to me.

Thus began my love affair with West Africa. I returned to Senegal in 1993 to give the keynote address at the opening of the West African Research Center in Dakar. I also spoke at the École Normale Supérieure. Ibrahima Seck was in the audience. Afterward he asked me for a copy of my talk, and thus began an extremely fruitful, lifelong friendship. He is now doing a fantastic job as research director of the Whitney Plantation Museum, near New Orleans. When I spoke to high school classes in the Muslim-administrated city of Touba, I was amazed by the linguistic abilities of my Senegalese students. They spoke Wolof at home, did their course work in French, and learned both English and Spanish in school. I have come to understand that the reason I felt so surprisingly at home in Senegal is because I am a native of Louisiana.

On my way back from Africa in 1987, I flew to Spain to work in the Archivo de Indias in Seville and the Archivo de Simancas. My colleague Enriqueta Vila Vilar, Spain's leading expert on the African slave trade, was very kind and patient with me until my Spanish came back. When I went through immigration on my return to France, the officer asked me which countries I had come from. I rattled off the list. She shrugged her shoulders, stamped my passport, and said, "Continuez!"

Working in Paris at the National Archives was one of the greatest experiences of my life. Every American historian I met in Paris pitied me when I told them where I was working and complained how badly American historians were treated. But that's not what happened to me. First of all, I didn't butcher their language, which is important to people everywhere in France. My neighbor at the archives was a retired medievalist working with fourteenth-century documents in Latin. He graciously took time out from his work to help me with some particularly unreadable handwriting and became enthused about my documents, especially those about the uprising of the Natchez Indians in Mississippi. Although

French bureaucrats are often hard cases, I tamed them by bringing pilot logs of slave trade ships to be photocopied. Word got around the archives that I was studying very difficult documents. I was treated with great respect. Every door was opened for me and every rule bent.

My fellow historians were interested in the computer I brought into the archives. I happily explained both it and my database. Although tables were not supposed to be assigned to researchers, they assigned me one of the few tables with an electric outlet for my computer. My fellow historians began to tolerate, and even be a little amused by, this eccentric American woman (me) who dragged her computer into the reading room on a rolling platform, calling it her *tou tou* (puppy dog). They even stopped being annoyed when my computer beeped.

I brought one of the first portable computers to Paris: a big Zenith that was too heavy for me to carry. When it broke down, the Zenith agency in Paris fixed it for me several times gratis, even though it wasn't under warranty, which I regarded as evidence of the French respect for the life of the mind.

Conclusion

I always felt like New Orleans was home. I moved away when I was twenty years old. It took me forty-two years to move back. I was hard at work on the *Louisiana Slave Database* and the projects that followed it, and I spent much time with my mother during her final years.

My sudden few months of fame in 2000 and 2001 took an ironic turn. Right before my interview with the *New York Times*, I contracted to buy a thirty-two-acre property in the Mississippi Pine Belt, located twenty miles south of Hattiesburg and forty-five miles north of Gulfport. Everyone I knew was shocked that I would buy property in Mississippi. I told them I would lay low, not make a fuss or get involved in politics, and use it as a retreat where I could commune with the forest and its critters and write. But between the time I signed the contract and the closing, stories about me appeared on TV, in newspapers, and on websites throughout the country. An Associated Press story mentioning my African American husband's leadership of the Communist Party, my biracial children, and my persecution by the FBI appeared in the *Hattiesburg American*, along with a picture of me and my dog.

The main house of my shotgun family compound in New Orleans.

The reaction of white Mississippians was pleasantly surprising. When I arrived for the closing, the seller showed us her copy of the story about me from the *Hattiesburg American* and told us she showed it to her coworkers at the Forrest County General Hospital, telling them proudly that this was the woman who was buying her house. The insurance agent at the closing said he has a hard time reading, but he read every word. What happened? My white neighbors in Mississippi were proud they had a famous writer living among them. I was the most famous writer in Brooklyn, Mississippi, and maybe in Hattiesburg, too.

I commuted between New Orleans and my critter-laden pine forest with breathtaking stars at night that put me in another world. I lectured in New Orleans and throughout Louisiana, as far as Natchitoches along the northwest border with Texas, and I flew all over the world lecturing in French and Spanish as well as English. I expected to live like that for the rest of my life.

Yet, nature showed me once more who's boss. It wasn't the neighbors who drove me away from my Mississippi retreat; it was Hurricane Katrina. Seven trees fell on my two houses. Wind badly damaged both roofs. The houses didn't flood, but winds and tornados split my Longleaf pines in two. Much of the wildlife, already at risk, fared badly. But after I returned, I heard and sometimes saw red-headed woodpeckers, who flew after me from one house to the next. There were blue jays, quails, robins, mockingbirds, sparrows, finches, wild turkeys, foxes, and raccoons. I heard coyotes in the distance. There were two black swamp hawks circling around above my head wherever I went outside, not because they expected me to die, but because I fed them chicken legs. Some of the birds tried to fly into my house, striking the huge glass windows. This was their way of greeting me and telling me they were home.

The forest and the critters that lived there started to restore, even the bees. But I rarely saw deer and saw strangely few squirrels, an overabundant nuisance before Katrina. I was less thrilled with the wasps. An even less welcome visitor was a huge water moccasin slithering along in a rain puddle next to my ground-level porch.

Some of the Monarch butterflies came back. I finally had to follow the butterflies to Mexico, where I went to live with my son Haywood after he insisted I could no longer live alone, either in my forest or my utterly shattered New Orleans. I have nerve damage from a post-Katrina accident in New Orleans and, combined with spinal arthritis for the past forty years and a fall at the airport in Nashville, I can't live on my own. My son Haywood, his wife Blanca Otero, and their two sons Ruben and Hector share the family compound in Guanajuato City with me. We get frequent welcome visits and much help from Blanca's mother, Jacoba Otero, whom I love dearly, and she loves me too. I keep in touch with family and old and new friends on Facebook and Skype, by email and telephone, and sometimes even with some real live visitors. We celebrated my ninetieth birthday at a big fiesta in 2019.

Grandson Hector, Blanca, Haywood, me, and grandson Ruben in our garden in Guanajuato, Mexico, 2021

~

I have lived long enough to receive substantial recognition for my scholarship and activism. At least three of my books are still being bought and used by academics and the wider public. My database projects have taken off since 2010, when I first went to Michigan State University. But much more important than "fame" is the knowledge that my work has a substantial, positive impact on the people I write about, as well as on how history, anthropology, linguistics, musicology, American studies, and other disciplines are written, researched, and taught.

I sought out original manuscript documents in three languages in archives in France, Spain, and Louisiana to try to understand what the lives of the enslaved were like, where they came from, what they thought, how they felt, and how courageously they fought for their rights. This is history that was long ignored. The winds of change finally came. But we could only change the narrative by doing serious archival research. Original documents are the building blocks of creative history and the only way to hear silenced voices.

Since 2001, when most of the *Louisiana Slave Database* became available free of charge on a website with a search engine, I have received email messages and telephone calls from people all over the world searching for their enslaved and slave-owning ancestors. Interest in African American genealogy continues to boom throughout the African American community. Some African-descended people, including some surprised white people, have found the African ethnic designations of their ancestors on my database. It has also stimulated interest in searching for African ancestors using genetic testing. A huge number of southern white people have African ancestors.

Being welcomed at the Louisiana Creole Research Association

Here are a few comments directed to me on Facebook in 2018 [*all sic*]:

Mike Hilton: I've read your book sixteen times, Gwendolyn Midlo Hall, and will probably read it another hundred times before I die, and I appreciate your pioneering work, and the information you gave me some years back about some cases concerning Slaves in Rapides found in Cabildo Cases. I have found a little bit more but it is unfortunate that the Court Records were destroyed.

Rodney Sam: *Africans in Colonial Louisiana* is a pioneering book and

I appreciate the work Gwendolyn Midlo Hall put into it. Since then, I was able to locate my Wolof and Fula ancestors, also using her database. Louisiana genealogists surely appreciate her work.

Ras Akpan: Ms. Hall, you've been my hero since I heard your lecture at the Jazz Fest in the '90s. . . . So many people through me have read and are still reading *Africans in Colonial Louisiana*.

Kongo SQ West Kinship Society: One of the most prolific preservation initiatives that came to the surface in the midst of a Hurricane aka "Katrina" was the tireless works of Dr. Gwendolyn Midlo Hall and her database of enslaved Africans and freedman of Louisiana (1719-1820), Her book *Africans in Colonial Louisiana: The Development of Afro-Creole Culture in the Eighteenth-Century* [includes] names of people, ethnic groups, languages spoken and gives a relational glimpse of their lives. A CD-ROM database was first published in 2000 and is now available free on the Internet. Records combine archives, documents, records of global proportions in several languages, citing the lives of over 100,000 African peoples.

The Gulf Coast Hurricanes were more than a natural phenomenon, the disaster was the displacement of the peoples, the lack of preservation of a levy and diabolical deployment against the spirit of a people. . . . We remember, venerate and continue to preserve in service . . . and say their names. . . . Kongo, Mandingo, Mina, Senegal/Wolof, Igbo, Bamana, Chamba, Yoruba, Kissi, Nago and more.

It is easy for me to choose what I consider my best quality. It is resiliency. I know it is popular for writers, especially female writers, to discuss their inner life in great detail. I don't do that very much. Why? Because I would have been utterly destroyed by intense self-absorption, which easily dips over into self-pity and blaming others for the problems I had because of my own mistakes.

I always knew my life had meaning—I had no conflict about that. So I was always highly motivated. The more obstacles I faced, the more determined I was to overcome them. I usually succeeded, but not always.

I was horrified by the society I grew up in and have spent my entire life doing all I can to make it better. It has not been easy, but looking back on the last eighty years, I did accomplish quite a bit. I learned from experience that I was at least twenty years ahead of my time. I didn't really know why. Now, I have begun to understand that I helped create the best of my times. That's what this book is about.

I used to believe I was a tiny, insignificant cog in the huge wheel of history, moving ever forward toward inevitable progress. Now I know better. Progress is made by people who make ethical choices and inspire others to do the same. That is the powerful role of the individual in history. It's the people who do what is right because it is the right thing to do and for no other reason who finally win, even though it often takes a long, long time. They rarely get the credit. But that's not why they do it. Let's work together across racial, national, and religious lines to save our fragile world by making it a better one.

The enslaved, the tortured, the lynched, the murdered do not lie quietly in their graves. Their spirits wander about, haunting us until we see them and recognize who they are and what we owe them. It is past time to honor them as best we can.

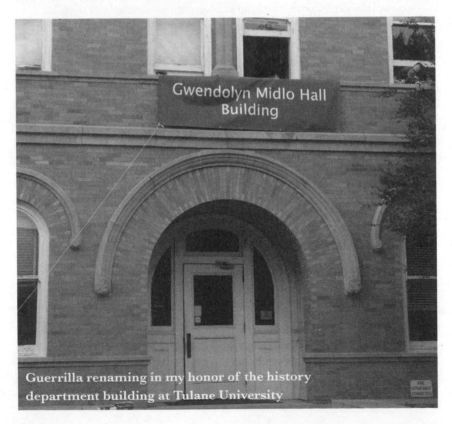

Guerrilla renaming in my honor of the history department building at Tulane University

In my room in Guanajuato, Mexico, 2020

Notes

Part One: Growing Up in New Orleans

1. Daniel Blatman, "Bund," YIVO Encyclopedia of Jews in Eastern Europe, https://yivoencyclopedia.org/article.aspx/Bund (accessed November 17, 2020).
2. Marek Edelman, "The Ghetto Fights," in *The Warsaw Ghetto: The 45th Anniversary of the Uprising* (Interpress Publishers, undated), 17–39, http://www.writing.upenn.edu/~afilreis/Holocaust/warsaw-uprising.html)
3. "Circulars Hostile to State Charged," *Town Talk* (Alexandria), September 20, 1937; see https://www.newspapers.com/image/?clipping_id=10244769.
4. "Judge Voltz Assaults and Jails Attorney Herman Midlo," *Town Talk* (Alexandria), June 19, 1941, https://www.newspapers.com/clip/10268158.
5. Bruce Raeburn, "Satchmo and the Jewish Family," 64 Parishes, 2020, https://64parishes.org/satchmo-jewish-family.
6. "Sugar Strike Spreads Wider," *Town Talk* (Alexandria), October 15, 1953, https://www.newspapers.com/clip/10542380.

Part Two: A Revolutionary in the Deep South

1. US Holocaust Museum, Holocaust Encyclopedia, "Kiev and Babi Yar," https://encyclopedia.ushmm.org/content/en/article/kiev-and-babi-yar.
2. Hymen Samuelson, *Love, War and the 96th Engineers (Colored): The World War II New Guinea Diaries of Captain Hyman Samuelson*, ed. Gwendolyn Midlo Hall (Charleston, SC: BookSurge Publishing 2008), https://www.amazon.com/Love-War-96th-Engineers-Colored/dp/B01F822X0O.
3. The International School for Holocaust Studies, Shoah Resource Center, "Black Book of Soviet Jewry," https://www.yadvashem.org/odot_pdf/Microsoft%20Word%20-%206102.pdf
4. "Youth Organization Sponsors Prom," *Pittsburgh Courier*, November 9, 1946, https://www.newspapers.com/clip/10260495.

5. Historical estimates of the gulag population size (in chronological order)

Gulag population	Year the estimate was made for	Source	Methodology
15 million	1940–42	Mora & Zwiernag (1945)	–
2.3 million	December 1937	Timasheff (1948)	Calculation of disenfranchised population
Up to 3.5 million	1941	Jasny (1951)	Analysis of the output of the Soviet enterprises run by NKVD
50 million	total number of persons passed through gulag	Solzhenitsyn (1975)	Analysis of various indirect data, including own experience and testimonies of numerous witnesses
17.6 million	1942	Anton Antonov-Ovseenko (1999)	NKVD documents[
4–5 million	1939	Wheatcroft (1981)	Analysis of demographic data.
10.6 million	1941	Rosefielde (1981)	Based on data of Mora & Zwiernag and annual mortality.
5.5–9.5 million	late 1938	Conquest (1991)	1937 Census figures, arrest and deaths estimates, variety of personal and literary sources.[a]
4–5 million	every single year	Volkogonov (1990s)	

Note: Later numbers from Rosefielde, Wheatcroft and Conquest were revised down by the authors themselves.

Chart reproduced from "Gulag: History of Gulag population estimates," Wikipedia, accessed February 6, 2021, https://en.wikipedia.org/wiki/Gulag

6. Elwood Watson, "Highlander Research and Education Center (1932–)," BlackPast, December 9, 2010, https://www.blackpast.org/african-american-history/highlander-research-and-education-center-1932/.

7. W. E. B. Du Bois, "Behold the Land," BlackPast, May 7, 2009, https://www.blackpast.org/african-american-history/1946-w-e-b-dubois-behold-land/.

Part Three: Black Reds, Revolutionary Nationalists, and Black Power

1. Daren Salter, "League of Struggle for Negro Rights (1930–1936)," BlackPast, January 19, 2007, https://www.blackpast.org/african-american-history/league -struggle-negro-rights-1930-1936/.

2. Trevor Goodloe, "William L. Patterson (1891-1980)," BlackPast, April 26, 2008, https://www.blackpast.org/african-american-history/patterson-william -l-1891-1980/.

3. Harry Haywood, "For a Revolutionary Position on the Negro Question," 1958, Marx-istLeninist.com, November 18, 2009, https://marxistleninist.wordpress.com /2009/11/18/harry-haywood-for-a-revolutionary-position-on-the-negro-question-2/.

4. Verso Books, "Authors: Theodore W. Allen," www.versobooks.com/authors /934-theodore-w-allen.

5. Olive Vassell and Todd Steven Burroughs, "No Common Ground Left: *Freedom-ways*, Black Communists vs. Black Nationalism/Pan-Africanism," *Africology: The Journal of Pan-African Studies* 8, no. 10 (March 2016), http://www.jpanafrican .org/docs/vol9no1/9.1-3-daterev-Vassell.pdf.

6. Sophia Gillmer, "Jesse Gray (1923–1988)," BlackPast, December 16, 2018, https:// www.blackpast.org/african-american-history/gray-jesse-1923-1988/.

7. "James Haughton, Who Fought Racial Barriers in Building Trades, Dies at 86," *New York Times*, May 6, 2016, https://www.nytimes.com/2016/05/06/nyregion /james-haughton-who-fought-racial-barriers-in-building-trades-dies-at-86.html.

8. "Vicki Ama Garvin (1915–2007), Organizer and Pan-African Internationalist," Pan-African News Wire, Monday, October 15, 2007, http://panafricannews .blogspot.com/2007/10/vicki-ama-garvin-1915-2007-organizer.html.

9. Herb Boyd, "James Haughton, Crusader Against the Construction Industry," *Amsterdam News*, May 12, 2016, http://amsterdamnews.com/news/201 /may/12/james-haughton-crusader-against-construction-indus/.

10. Tomas Peña, "JDP archives: In Conversation with Francisco Mora Catlett," September 2, 2016, https://jazzdelapena.com/profiles/artist-profile-drummer -composer-leader-visionary-francisco-mora-catlett/.

11. Wikipedia, "Concepción Muedra Benedito," https://es.wikipedia.org/wiki/Con-cepci%C3%B3n_Muedra_Benedito; Wikipedia, "Ramón Xirau Subías," https://es.wikipedia.org/wiki/Ram%C3%B3n_Xirau.

Part Four: A Public Intellectual in the Black Freedom Struggle

1. Stanford University, Martin Luther King Jr. Institute, encyclopedia entry: "O'Dell: Hunter Pitts Jack," https://kinginstitute.stanford.edu/encyclopedia/odell-hunter -pitts-jack.

2. Robert F. Williams, *Negroes with Guns* (Martino Fine Books, 2013).

3. John H. Bracey and Muhammad Ahmad, discussion, "COINTELPRO & Revolutionary Action Movement (RAM)," recorded June 13, 2015, at the Charles H. Wright Museum of African American History, Detroit, Michigan, https://www.youtube.com/watch?v=edZpZSgyXRY.

4. Robert F. Williams Collection, Bentley Historical Library, University of Michigan, Ann Arbor; Thomas Sugrue, Sweet Land of Liberty: The Forgotten Struggle for Civil Rights in the North (Random House Publishing, 2008).

5. Jessie Kratz, "Fighting for Independence: Sixth Archivist Robert M. Warner," National Archives, June 16, 2016, https://prologue.blogs.archives.gov /2016/06/20/fighting-for-independence-sixth-archivist-robert-m-warner.

Part Five: Making a Better World with Creative History

1. Jefferson Morley, "How Mexican Presidents Became CIA Agents," *Geopolitics and Empire* podcast, April 19, 2017, http://guadalajarageopolitics.com /2017/04/19/jefferson-morley-how-mexican-presidents-became-cia-agents-046/.

2. David Amsden, "Building the First Slave Museum in America," *New York Times*, February 26, 2015, https://www.nytimes.com/2015/03/01/magazine/building -the-first-slave-museum-in-america.html.

3. David Firestone, "Identity Restored to 100,000 Louisiana Slaves," *New York Times*, July 30, 2000, https://www.nytimes.com/2000/07/30/us/identity -restored-to-100000-louisiana-slaves.html.

4. Gwendolyn Midlo Hall, "Afro-Louisiana History and Geneaology, 1719–1829" database, http://www.ibiblio.org/laslave/.

5. Michigan State University Department of History, "Slave Biographies," Atlantic Database Network, database, http://slavebiographies.org/.

6. Michigan State University, "Enslaved Conference 2019," https://www.youtube .com/playlist?list=PLZNZm8ynCL3EcBTDkgXObRFLyIDG-TXfb.

7. *Journal of Slavery and Data Preservation*, "Enslaved: Peoples of the Historical Slave Trade," database, http://www.enslaved.org/.

Index

About Haymarket Books

Haymarket Books is a radical, independent, nonprofit book publisher based in Chicago. Our mission is to publish books that contribute to struggles for social and economic justice. We strive to make our books a vibrant and organic part of social movements and the education and development of a critical, engaged, international left.

We take inspiration and courage from our namesakes, the Haymarket martyrs, who gave their lives fighting for a better world. Their 1886 struggle for the eight-hour day—which gave us May Day, the international workers' holiday—reminds workers around the world that ordinary people can organize and struggle for their own liberation. These struggles continue today across the globe—struggles against oppression, exploitation, poverty, and war.

Since our founding in 2001, Haymarket Books has published more than five hundred titles. Radically independent, we seek to drive a wedge into the risk-averse world of corporate book publishing. Our authors include Noam Chomsky, Arundhati Roy, Rebecca Solnit, Angela Y. Davis, Howard Zinn, Amy Goodman, Wallace Shawn, Mike Davis, Winona LaDuke, Ilan Pappé, Richard Wolff, Dave Zirin, Keeanga-Yamahtta Taylor, Nick Turse, Dahr Jamail, David Barsamian, Elizabeth Laird, Amira Hass, Mark Steel, Avi Lewis, Naomi Klein, and Neil Davidson. We are also the trade publishers of the acclaimed Historical Materialism Book Series and of Dispatch Books.

Also Available from Haymarket Books

The Brother You Choose: Paul Coates and Eddie Conway Talk About Life,
Politics, and The Revolution
Susie Day, afterword by Ta-Nehisi Coates

C. L. R. James and Revolutionary Marxism
Selected Writings of C.L.R. James 1939-1949
Edited by Paul Le Blanc and Scott McLemee

Detroit: I Do Mind Dying: A Study in Urban Revolution
Dan Georgakas and Marvin Surkin

Feminist Freedom Warriors: Genealogies, Justice, Politics, and Hope
Edited by Linda E. Carty and Chandra Talpade Mohanty

Floodlines: Community and Resistance from Katrina to the Jena Six
Jordan Flaherty, foreword by Amy Goodman, preface by Tracie Washington

Freedom Is a Constant Struggle
Ferguson, Palestine, and the Foundations of a Movement
Angela Y. Davis, edited by Frank Barat, preface by Cornel West

How We Get Free: Black Feminism and the Combahee River Collective
Edited by Keeanga-Yamahtta Taylor

Organized Labor and the Black Worker, 1619-1981
Philip S. Foner, Foreword by Robin D. G. Kelley

Repair: Redeeming the Promise of Abolition
Katherine Franke

The Torture Machine: Racism and Police Violence in Chicago
Flint Taylor